# NCERT SOLUTIONS

with Chapterwise **Study Notes**

## BIOLOGY 11th

Fully Updated as per
Latest NCERT Textbook

# NCERT SOLUTIONS

with Chapterwise **Study Notes**

## BIOLOGY 11th

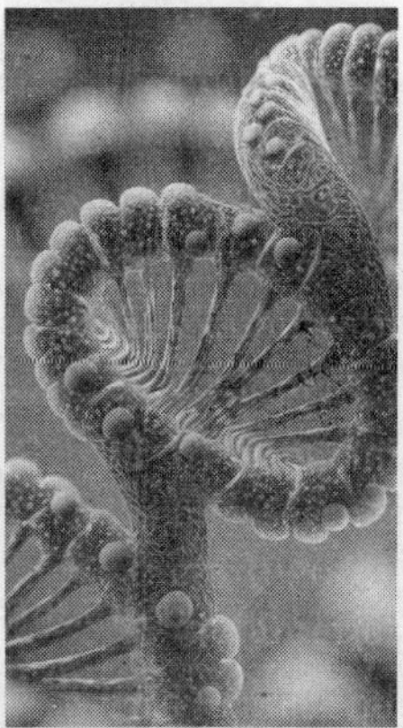


***Author***
Anubhuti Jain


Including Selected Questions of **DIKSHA**


arihant
SUCCESS AND NOTHING LESS

arihant
SUCCESS AND NOTHING LESS

**ARIHANT PRAKASHAN (Series), MEERUT**



**卐 Administrative & Production Offices**

**Regd. Office**

'Ramchhaya' 4577/15, Agarwal Road, Darya Ganj, New Delhi -110002
Tele: 011- 47630600, 43518550

**卐 Head Office**

Kalindi, TP Nagar, Meerut (UP) - 250002
Tel: 0121-7156203, 7156204

**卐 Sales & Support Offices**

Agra, Ahmedabad, Bengaluru, Bareilly, Chennai, Delhi, Guwahati, Hyderabad, Jaipur, Jhansi, Kolkata, Lucknow, Nagpur & Pune.

卐 **PRICE** ₹210.00

卐 PO No. : TXT-59-T065238-05-25

Published by Arihant Publications (India) Ltd.

For further information about the books published by Arihant, log on to www.arihantbooks.com or e-mail at info@arihantbooks.com

Follow us on

# Preface

Feeling the immense importance and value of NCERT books, we are presenting this book, having the **NCERT Exercises Solutions**. For the overall benefit of the students we have made this book unique in such a way that it presents not only solutions but also detailed explanations. Through these detailed and through explanations, students can learn the concepts which will enhance their thinking and learning abilities.

We have introduced some Additional Features with the solutions which are given below:

- **Explanatory Solutions** Along with the solutions to questions we have given all the points that tell how to approach to solve a problem. Here we have tried to cover all those loopholes which may lead to confusion. All formulae and hints are discussed in full detail.
- Simplest language ensuring a thorough understanding of each solution.
- Expertly crafted and clearly labeled illustrations.

Apart from all those who helped in the compilation of this book a special note of thanks to all. With the hope that this book will be of great help to the students, we wish great success to our readers.

**Anubhuti Jain**

# Contents

# The Living World

CHAPTER 01

## Important Points

**01** Biodiversity is the variety and variability of life on earth. It is typically a measure of variation at the genetic, species and ecosystem level.

**02** **Classification** is the process of grouping of living organisms based on their similarities and differences.

**03** **Taxonomy** is the science of classification based on the characters.

**04** **Nomenclature** standardises the naming of organisms so they are known by the same name worldwide.

**05** **Identification** is the process of correctly recognising and describing an organism to assign it a specific name.

**06** Scientists use standard procedures to assign unique scientific names, governed by the **ICBN** for plants and **ICZN** for animals. These universal names ensure clarity and avoid duplication globally.

**07** Biologists use **binomial nomenclature,** a system that assigns each organism in a two part name the genus and species. This system was introduced by Carolus Linnaeus. For example, *Mangifera indica,* where *Mangifera* is the genus and *indica* is the species.

### 08 Taxonomic Categories

| Taxonomic Category | Definition |
|---|---|
| Kingdom | The broadest category, grouping organisms based on fundamental biological similarities (*e.g.*, animals. plants). |
| Phylum | Groups of organisms based on basic body structure and organisation (*e.g.*, vertebrates. arthropods). |
| Class | Subdivision of phylum, grouping organisms with similar characteristics (*e.g.*, mammals, birds). |
| Order | A category within a class, grouping organisms that share more specific traits (*e.g*, carnivores, primates). |
| Family | Groups of related organisms within an order (*e.g.*, Felidae for cats, canidae for dogs). |
| Genus | A group of closely related species (*e.g.*, *Homo* for humans, *Panthera* for lions and tigers). |
| Species | The most specific category referring to individual organisms capable of interbreeding (*e.g.*, *Homo sapiens* for humans). |

# Exercises

**Question 1** Why are living organisms classified?

**Sol.** It is important to classify living organisms in groups to understand their origin, diversity, distribution and inter relationship. Classification is the grouping and ranking of organisms in the hierarchy of taxonomy on the basis of similarities and dissimilarities. Its purpose is to organise the vast number of known plants and animals into categories that could be named, remembered and studied systematically.

**Question 2** Why are the classification systems changing every now and then?

**Sol.** Evolution is the major factor responsible for the change in classification systems. Since, evolution still continues, so many newly discovered plant and animal species are identified, classified and then named according to the already existing classification systems. Due to evolution, animal and plant species keep on changing, so necessary changes in the already existed classification systems are necessary to place every newly discovered plant and animal species in their respective ranks.

**Question 3** What different criteria would you choose to classify people that you meet often?

**Sol.** Different criteria one might choose to classify people they meet often include behaviour, geographical location, physical appearance, gender, family members etc.

**Question 4** What do we learn from identification of individual and populations?

**Sol.** Identification of individuals and population help categorised them into species as each species has unique characteristic features. On the basis of these features, it can be distinguished from other closely related species.

*e.g.,*

| Genus Species | |
|---|---|
| *Solanum tuberosum* | Both are different species of potato / *Solanum* |
| *Solanum nigrum* | |

**Question 5** Given below is the scientific name of mango. Identify the correctly written name.

*Mangifera Indica*

*Mangifera indica*

**Sol.** The correctly written scientific name of mango is *Mangifera indica*. Where, *Mangifera* is the generic name and *indica* is the species name or specific epithet.

**Question 6** Define a taxon. Give some examples of taxa at different hierarchical levels.

**Sol.** A **Taxon** is a group of organisms classified together based on shared characteristics at a specific level in the biological classification system.

**Examples-**

| Common Name | Potato | Man |
|---|---|---|
| Botanical Name | *Solanum tuberosum* | *Homo sapiens* |
| Genus | *Solanum* | *Homo* |
| Family | Solanaceae | *Hominidae* |
| Order | Solanales | Primata |
| Class | Dicotyledonae | Mammalia |
| Phylum/Division | Division Angiospermae | Phylum choradata |
| Kingdom | Plantae | Animalia |

**Question 7** Can you identify the correct sequence of taxonomical categories?

(a) Species ⟶ Order ⟶ Phylum ⟶ Kingdom

(b) Genus ⟶ Species ⟶ Order ⟶ Kingdom

(c) Species ⟶ Genus ⟶ Order ⟶ Phylum

**Sol.** The correct sequence of taxonomical categories is as follows :

(a) Species⟶ Order ⟶ Phylum ⟶ Kingdom

(c) Species ⟶ Genus ⟶ Order ⟶ Phylum.

**Question 8** Try to collect all the currently accepted meanings for the word 'species'. Discuss with your teacher the meaning of species in case of higher plants and animals on one hand and bacteria on the other hand.

**Sol.** In biological term species is the basic taxonomic rank. It can be defined as a group of similar organisms that are capable of interbreeding under natural conditions to produce fertile offspring. Therefore, a group of similar individuals that are respectively isolated form a species.

In higher plants and animals the term 'species' refers to a group of individuals that are able to interbreed freely and produce fertile offspring.

But is case of bacteria interbreeding cannot serve as the best criteria for delimiting species because bacteria usually reproduce asexually Hence in bacteria, species are defined based on genetic similarity, shared traits and ecological roles.

**Question 9** Define and understand the following terms

(i) Phylum (ii) Class

(iii) Family (iv) Order

(v) Genus

**Sol.**

(i) **Phylum** A category, which is higher than class and consisting of one or more related classes with certain common features. Botanists use the term division for plants.

(ii) **Class** A taxonomic category higher in rank than order and consisting of one or more related orders with some common features.

(iii) **Family** A category having one or more related genera with some similar common features.

(iv) **Order** (Cohort) A category consisting of one or more related families having some common or correlated characters.

(v) **Genus** A taxonomic category higher in rank than species having one or more assemblage of related species, having a common ancestory and similar correlated characters.

**Question 10** Illustrate the taxonomical hierarchy with suitable examples of a plant and an animal.

**Sol.** **Classification of a plant (Mango)-Classification of human being**

| Kingdom | Plantae | Kingdom | Animalia |
|---|---|---|---|
| Division | Angiospermae | Phylum | Chordata |
| Class | Dicotyledonae | Class | Mammalia |
| Order | Sapindales | Order | Primata |
| Family | Anacardiaceae | Family | Hominidae |
| Genus | *Mangifera* | Genus | *Homo* |
| Species | *indica* | Species | *Sapiens* |

**Q.11** *Brassica campestris* linn

(a) Give the common name of the plant.

(b) What do the first two parts of the name denote?

(c) Why are they written in italics?

(d) What is the meaning of linn written at the end of the name?

**Sol.**

(a) The common name of *Brassica campestris linn* is mustard.

(b) The first part denotes the genus of the plant while the second part denotes the species of it.

(c) These names are written in italics to show their latin origin. Moreover, it is a strict rule to write scientific name in italics.

(d) The term 'linn' means that this species was first discovered and studied by Linnaeus.

## DIKSHA APP Questions

### ☐ Multiple Choice Questions

**Q.1** Which taxonomic aid gives comprehensive information about a taxon

(a) Taxonomic key (b) Herbarium (c) Flora (d) Monograph

**Sol.** *d*-A taxonomic aid which provides comprehensive information about a taxon is a monograph. A monograph provides a detailed description of all available information about a genus, family or higher group.

**Q.2** Which coined the term 'systematics'.

(a) John Ray (b) Corolus Linnaeus

(c) Julian Huxley (d) Charies Darwin

**Sol.** (b) Systematics is a branch of biological science that deals with study of diversity of living organisms of present and past. The term systematics was coined by Carolus Linnaeus.

# Biological Classification

CHAPTER 02

## Important Points

**01** The first attempt to classify organisms on scientific basis was done by **Aristotle.**

**02** Linnaeus gave the **two kingdom classification** and divided living organisms into kingdom plantae and animalia

**03** **RH Whittaker** (1969) proposed 'a' **five kingdom classification** **Monera**, **Protista**, **Fungi**, **Plantae** and **Animalia**.

Classification was done on the basis of cell structure body organisation, mode of nutrition, reproduction and phylogenetic relationships.

**04** **Kingdom–Monera** includes prokaryotic microorganism like bacteria.

**05** They do not have well defined nucleus and membrane bound cell organelles are absent. They live in extreme habitats like hot springs, snow, deep oceans as free living or parasites.

**06** Archaebacteria differs from other bacteria in having different cell wall structure and this feature is responsible for their survival in extreme conditions such as salty area (halophiles), hotspring (thermoacidophiles) and marshy area (Methanogens).

**07** Another class–**Eubacteria** is also known as 'true bacteria' and is characterised by the presence of rigid cell wall.

**08** They could be photosynthetic autotrophs, chemosynthetic, autotrophs and heterotrophic bacteria.

**09** Mycoplasma lacks cell wall and are the smallest cell to survive without oxygen.

**10** **Kingdom–Protista** includes unicellular eukaryotes.

**11** They include chrysophytes, dinoflagellates, euglenoid, slime mould, protozoans.

(i) Chrysophytes include diatoms and golden algae. Diatomaceous earth is formed from the accumulation of the silica-rich cell walls of diatoms over long periods of time.

(ii) Dinoflagllates appear red, yellow, green, brown and blue due to the presence of different pigments. (Very often), red dinoflagellates (*Gonyaulax*) undergo rapid multiplication and forms red tides.

(iii) Euglenoids have protein rich layer called pellicle and in presence of sunlight, they behaves an autotrophs, while in its absence they behave as heterotrophs.

(iv) Slime moulds are saprophyte and they form an aggregation called plasmodium.

(v) **Protozoans** are heterotrophs and lives as predators or parasites. These include amoeboid protozoans,flagellated protozoans, ciliated protozoans and sporozoans.

**12** **Kingdom–Fungi** consist or heterotrophic organism that rely on extracellular digestion.

**13** They resides in air, water, soil or another animals and the cell wall is made up of chitin and polysaccharides.

**14** They also exist in symbiotic relationship with algae known as **lichens** and with roots of higher plants called **mycorrhiza**.

**15** Algal component in lichen is known as **phycobiont** and fungal component as **mycobiont.** Algae prepare food for fungi and fungi provide shelter to algae.

**16** Fungi is divided into various classes on the basis of morphology of mycelium, mode of spore formation and fruiting bodies such as.

(i) Phycomycetes are obligate parasite on plant and the mycelium is aseptate. *e.g., Mucor.*

(ii) Ascomycetes are known as sac fungi usually multicellular, except **Yeast** which is unicellular. Their sexual spores are produced endogenously in sac-like structure called asci, which are found in ascocarp. *e.g., Aspergillus.*

(iii) Basidiomycetes include mushrooms bracket fungi/puffballs. Sex organs are absent but plasmogamy occurs resulting in formation of basidiospores which are produced exogenously on basidium. *e.g., Puccinia*.

(iv) Deuteromycetes are known as **imperfect fungi**, since sexual reproduction is not known *e.g., Alternaria*.

**17** **Kingdom–Plantae** includes all eukaryotic, autotrophic and chlorophyll containing organisms and few members are partially heterotrophic such as insectivorous plants like venus flytraps and pitcher plants.

**Kingdom plantae includes algae**, bryophytes, pteridophyte, **gymnosperms** and **angiosperms**.

**18** Lifecycle of plants has two distinct phases-diploid sporophytic phase and haploid gametophytic phase that alter with each other.

**19** **Kingdom–Animalia** includes heterotrophic, eukaryotic and multicellular organisms and their cells lack cell walls

**20** Mode of nutrition is **holozoic.**

**21** Viruses are non cellular organisms that are characterised by having an inert crystalline structure outside the living cells.Their genetic material can either be DNA or RNA but never both.

**22** Many scientists have conducted various experiments, such as M.W. Beijerinek named the term 'Virus' and called the fluid causing infection in healthy tobacco plant as *Contagium vivum fluidum* (infections living fluid) These viruses remain inert outside their specific host and exist in crystalline form, as demonstrated by W.M. Stanley.

**23** Viruses that infect plants are typically ssRNA, while those infect animals have either ss RNA dsRNA or ds DNA viruses that infect bacteria are referred to as **bacteriophage.**

**24** **Viroids** are the infectious agent, which have naked nucleic acid (mainly RNA). It was discovered by **TO Diener** in year **1971** and it causes **potato spindle tuber disease.**

**25** **Prions** consists of abnormal folded proteins and acts as an agent to transfer various neurological diseases and are similar is size to viruses.

**26** Bovine spongiform encephalopathy (BSE) also known as mad cow disease in cattle and its analogous variant Cr-Jacob disease (CJD) in humans are caused by prions.

## Exercises

**Question 1** Discuss how classification systems have undergone several changes over a period of time?

**Sol.**

(i) Aristotle was the first person to introduce scientific classification. He used simple morphological characters to classify plants into trees, shrubs and herbs. He also divided animals into two groups, those which had red blood and those that did not.

(ii) In Linnaeus time, Linnaeus proposed a two kingdom system of classification included all plants and animals respectively. But as this system did not distinguish between the eukaryotes and prokaryotes, unicellular and multicellular organisms and photosynthetic (green algae) and non-photosynthetic (fungi) organisms, so scientists found it an inadequate system of classification.

(iii) The two kingdom system of classification was replaced by three kingdom system, then by four and finally by five kingdom system of classification of RH Whittaker (1969).

(iv) The five kingdoms included Monera, Protista, Fungi, Plantae and Animalia. This is the most accepted system of classification of living organisms.

Thus, over a period of time, classification system have undergone several changes.

**Question 2** State two economically important uses of

(a) Heterotrophic bacteria (b) Archaebacteria

**Sol.**

(a) **Heterotrophic bacteria**

Maintain soil fertility by nitrogen fixation, The milk products such as butter, cheese, curd, etc., are obtained by the action of bacteria.

(b) **Archaebacteria**

Methanogens are responsible for the production of methane (biogas) from the dung of these animals.

Archaebacteria help in the degradation of waste materials.

**Question 3** What is the nature of cell wall in diatoms?

**Sol.** In case of diatoms, the cell wall forms two thin overlapping shells, which fit together as in a soap box. The cell wall is made up of silica and thus the walls are indestructible.

**Question 4** Find out what do the term 'algal bloom' and 'red tides' signify?

**Sol.** Algal bloom refers to the excess growth of algae especially blue green algae in polluted water. Red tide refers to the red colour imparted to the sea water by the rapid multiplication of dinoflagellates like *Gonyaulax*.

**Question 5** How are viroids different from viruses?

**Sol.** Viroids different from viruses in following ways :

| S.N. | Virus | viroids |
|---|---|---|
| 1. | These are smaller than bacteria. | These are Smaller than viruses. |
| 2. | Either RNA or DNA present. | Only RNA is present. |
| 3. | Protein coat present. | Protein coat absent. |
| 4. | Causes diseases like mumps and AIDS. | Causes plant diseases like spindle tuber diseases-potato. |

**Question 6** Describe briefly the four major groups of Protozoa?

**Sol.** Protozoans are divided into four major groups

(i) **Flagellates** These protozoans possess one to several flagella for locomotion. Zooflagellates are generally uninucleate, occasionally multinucleate. The body is covered by a firm pellicle. The member of this group are either free living or parasitic.
**Examples** *Trypanosoma,*

(ii) **Amoeboids** These protozoans possess pseudopodia for locomotion. Pseudopodia are also used for engulfing food particles. Amoeboid protozoans are mostly free living, found in freshwater, sea water and on damp soil only a few are parasitic. Examples *Amoeba*

(iii) **Sporozoans** All of them are endoparasites. Locomotory organelles (cilia, flagella, pseudopodia, etc.) are absent. Nutrition is parasitic (absorptive). Example *Plasmodium.*

(iv) **Ciliates** These are aquatic, actively moving organisms because of the presence of thousands of cilia. They have a cavity (gullet) that opens to the outside of the cell surface. The coordinated movements of rows of cilia causes the water laden with food to enter into the gullet, *e.g., Paramecium.*

**Question 7** Plants are autotrophic can you think of some plants that are partially heterotrophic?

**Sol.** Plants are autotrophs, *i.e.,* they prepare their own food through the process of photosynthesis.

But, in nature there are also some other plants which are partially heterotrophic, *i.e.,* they partially depend upon another organisms for food requirements, *e.g.,*

(i) Insectivorous plants have special leaves to trap insects. The trapped insects are killed and digested by proteolytic enzymes secreted by the epidermis of the leaves, *e.g.*, pitcher plant.

(ii) Parasitic plant, *e.g.*, *Cuscutta* develops haustoria, which penetrate, the vascular bundles of the host plant to absorb water and solutes.

**Question 8** What do the terms phycobiont and mycobiont signify?

**Sol.** In case of lichens (*i.e.*, an association of algae and fungi), the algal partner which is capable of carrying out photosynthesis is known as phycobiont, whereas the fungal partner which is heterotrophic in nature is known as **mycobiont**.

**Question 9** Give a comparative account of the classes of kingdom fungi under the following

(i) Mode of nutrition

(ii) Mode of reproduction

**Sol.** Comparison between mode of nutrition and mode of reproduction are as follows :

| Fungal Class | Mode of Nutrition | Mode of Reproduction |
|---|---|---|
| Phycomycetes | Mostly parasites | Asexually by zoospore (motile) and aplanospore (non-motile); Sexually by formation of zygopore (can be similar or dissimilar in morphology) |
| Ascomycetes | Saprophytes or parasites | Asexually by conidia and sexually by formation of ascospores. |
| Basidiomycetes | Saprophytes or parasites | Asexually by vegetative reproduction (fragmentation) and sexually by formation of basidiospores only. |
| Deuteromycetes | Saprophytes or parasites | Asexually by conidia. |

**Question 10** What are the characteristic features of euglenoids?

**Sol.** The characteristic features of euglenoids are as follows:

(i) They occur in freshwater habitats and damp soils.

(ii) They have two flagella, a short and a long one.

(iii) Mode of nutrition is holophytic, saprophytic and holozoic.

(iv) Instead of a cell wall, they have a protein rich layer called pellicle.

(v) In presence of sunlight they behave as autotrophs while in its absence they behave as heterotrops.

**Question 11** Give a brief account of viruses with respect to their structure and nature of genetic material. Also name four common viral diseases.

**Sol.** The viruses are non-cellular, organisms that are characterised by having an inert crystalline structure outside the living cell. Genetic material could be either DNA or RNA which is present inside the protein coat. The virus that infects plants have single stranded RNA whereas viruses that infect animals have either single or double stranded RNA or double stranded DNA. The capsid is the protein coat which is made of small subunits called capsomeres, protecting the nucleic acid.

Common viral diseases are, AIDS, mumps, herpes and influenza.

Four common viral diseases are

(i) Polio, (ii) AIDS, (iii) Hepatitis-B, (iv) Rabies.

**Question 12** Organise a discussion in your class on the topic are viruses living or non-living?

**Sol.** Viruses are considered as intermediate between non-living and living organisms. On the basis of characters, such as non-cellular organisation, inactivity outside the host organism, lack of respiration and cellular metabolism, they are called non-living. Moreover, similar to non-living objects viruses can be crystallised and precipitated.

**Living Feature** Similar to living beings, they possess genetic material (DNA or RNA), property of mutation, irritability, can grow and multiply inside the host cell. They are intracellular obligate parasites and attack specific hosts. Thus, keeping these points in mind, it is quite difficult to ascertain whether viruses are living or non-living.

# DIKSHA APP Questions

## ☐ Very Short Answer Type

**Q.1** Expand MLO and PPLO

**Sol.** MLO-Mycoplasma like organisms
PPLO-Pleuropneumonia like organisms

**Q.2** Why we keep food in refrigerator ?

**Sol.** Refrigerator slows bacterial growth or fungal infections.

## ☐ Short Answer Type

**Q.1** What observable features in *Trypanosoma* would make you classify it under kingdom Protista?

**Sol.** There are some characters of *Trypanosoma* make us classify it under kingdom Protista: It is unicellular eukaryotic organism.

*Trypanosoma* in its parasitic form causes disease such as sleeping sickness.

Method of reproduction is asexual.

Reserve food material is in the form of cukaryotic granules.

## ☐ Long Answer Type

**Q.1** Differentiate between the kingdom plantae and animalia in detail

**Sol.** Kingdom plantae

1. It includes all eukaryotic chlorophyll-containing organisms commonly called plants.
2. A few members are partially heterotrophic such as the insectivorous plants or parasites. Bladderwort and venus fly trap are examples of insectivorous plants and *Cuscuta* is a parasite.
3. The plant cells have eukaryotic structure with prominent chloroplasts and cell wall mainly made of cellulose.
4. Plantae includes algae, bryophytes, pteridophytes, gymnosperms and angiosperms.
5. Life cycle of plants has two distinct phases-the diploid sporophytic and the haploid gametophytic-that alternate with each other. The lengths of the haploid and diploid phases, and whether these phases are free-living or dependent on others, vary among different groups in plants. This phenomenon is called alternation of generation.

**Kingdom Animalia**

1. This kingdom is characterised by heterotrophic eukaryotic organisms that are multicellular and their cells lack cell walls.
2. They directly or indirectly depends on plants for food. They digest their food in an internal cavity and store food as glycogen or fat.
3. Their mode of nutrition is holozoic-by ingestion of food.
4. They follow a definite growth pattern and grow into adults that have a definite shape and size.
5. Higher forms show elaborate sensory and neuromotor mechanism. Most of them are capable of locomotion.
6. The sexual reproduction is by copulation of male and female followed by embryological development.

**Q.1** What is meant by the term symbiosis? Explain its importance. Describe the characteristics of symbionts with example.

**Sol.** Whenever two organisms of different species exist in close physical contact for the benefit of both organisms, this phenomenon is called symbiosis.

Importance of symbiosis is it can occur between animals, plants, fungi or any combination.

Each organism contributes something that benefits the survival of the other, and in turn receives a survival benefit of its own.

Fungi can live as symbiont in association with algae as lichens and with roots of higher plants as mycorrhiza.

# Plant Kingdom

CHAPTER 03

## Important Points

**01** Plants were classified on the basis of different characters. There are three main types of classification **Artificial**, **Natural** and **Phylogenetic system**.

**02** Classification can be done on basis of cytological information (cytotaxonomy), chemical constituents of plant (chemotaxonomy) and on number and codes (numerical taxonomy)

**03** Kingdom–Plantae includes **algae**, **bryophytes**, **pteridophytes**, **gymnosperms** and **angiosperms**.

**04** Algae are autotrophic chlorophyll bearing thalloid and mostly aquatic organisms. They include unicellular forms like *Chlamydomonas*, filamentous like *Ulothrix*, *Spirogyra* and colonial form like *Volvox*.

**05** They plays an important role in carbon dioxide fixation on earth through photosynthesis and increase the level of $O_2$.

**06** Algae is divided into three main classes–**Chlorophyceae**, **Phaeophyceae** and **Rhodophyceae**. Their main characteristics are given in the table below.

They reproduce by vegetative (fragmentation), asexual (zoospores) and sexual (fusion of gametes) methods.

Divisions of Algae and their main characteristics

| Classes & common name | Major Pigments | Stored Food | Cell Wall | Habitat |
|---|---|---|---|---|
| Chlorophyceae Green algae | Chlorophyll $a, b$ | Starch | Cellulose | Fresh water, brackish water, salt water |
| Phaeophyceae Brown algae | Chlorophyll $a, c$, fucoxanthin | Mannitol, laminarin | Cellulose and algin | Fresh water (rare) brackish water, salt water |
| Rhodophyceae Red algae | Chlorophyll $a, d$, phycoerythrin | Floridean starch | Cellulose, pectin and poly sulphate esters | Fresh water (some), brackish water, salt water (most) |

**07** **Bryophytes** are known as **amphibians of plant kingdom**. They grow in soil but are dependent on water for fusion of gametes or sexual reproduction. They are thallus like, prostrate or erect and attached to substratum by unicellular or multicellular rhizoids.

**08** Bryophytes are divided into **liverworts** and **mosses**.

(i) **Liver worts** are thallus like structures closely attached to substratum. Leafy members have tiny appendages usually grow in moist, damp, shady habitats. *e.g., Marchantia.*

(ii) They reproduce asexually by the formation of gemmae or the fragmentation of thalli and sexually by the fusion of antherozoids and archegonium.

(iii) **Mosses** are green, leafy, upright and radial in symmetry. They are highly developed of all the bryophytes.

(iv) Asexual reproduction occurs through fragmentation or through bud in secondary protonema while sexual reproduction occurs in a similar way as in case of liverworts.

**09** **Pteridophytes** are called **vascular cryptogams**, also known as **seedless vascular plants**. They produce spores rather than seeds. They include **horsetails** and **ferns** and are found near the marshy cool and damp places.

**10** Dominant phase in pteridophytes is sporophyte, which is differentiated into true root, stem and leaf. Majority of pteridophytes produces single type of spore called homosporous, while some species produces two different types of spores, known as heterosporous *e.g., Selaginella.* and *salvinia* heterosporous Pteridophytes are also considered as precursor to the **seed habit.**

**11** Pteridophytes are divided into four classes.
(i) **Psilopsida** (*Psilotum*) (ii) **Lycopsida** (*Lycopodium*)
(iii) **Sphenopsida** (*Equisetum*) **(iv) Pteropsida** (*Pteris*)

**12** **Gymnosperms** are **naked seeded plants**, which were evolved earlier than the flowering plants.

**13** Dominant phase is sporophyte. They are heterosporous produce haploid megaspores and microspores, which are produced within sporangia borne on sporophyll, which are arranged spirally along an axis to form compact cones.

**14** **Angiosperms** are distinct group of seed plants. They are also called **flowering plants**. Seeds are enclosed by fruit.

**15** They are divided into two classes **dicotyledons** and **monocotyledons**.

**16** Dicotyledon have two cotyledon in their seed and monocotyledon have one.

## Exercises

**Question 1** What is the basis of classification of algae?

**Sol.** Algae are classified on the basis of type of pigments they possess, chemical nature of reserve food material, number of flagella and composition of cell wall.

**Question 2** When and where does reduction division take place in the life cycle of a liverwort, a moss, a fern, a gymnosperm and an angiosperm?

**Sol.** Reduction divisions in the life cycle of a liverwort, a moss, a fern and a gymnosperm take place during the production of spores from spore mother cells.

In case of an angiosperm, the reduction division occurs during pollen grain formation in anther and during formation of embryo sac in ovule.

**Question 3** Name three groups of plants that bear archegonia. Briefly describe the life cycle of any one of them.

**Sol.** The group of plants that bear archegonia are :

1. Bryophyta 2. Pteridophyta 3. Gymnosperms

**Life cycle of a bryophyte**

The plant body of a bryophyte is a gametophyte. At maturity the gametophytic body develops sex organs which are archegonia (female) and antheridia (male). Archegonia develop egg (*n*) through mitosis and antheridia develop antherozoids (male gametes) which are biflagellate.

The antherozoids swim in a thin film of water, reach to archegonia. One of the antherozoids enter into archegonia and fuse with the egg resulting into zygote. The zygote is the first cell of sporophyte. It undergoes embryogeny to develop the sporophytic body which is differentiable into foot, seta and capsule. Capsule behaves as sporangium and produces haploid spores through meiotic division. The spores germinate to develop into the gametophytic plant body. This type of life cycle is haplo-diplontic.

**Question 4** Mention the ploidy of the following protonemal cell of a moss; primary endosperm nucleus in dicot, leaf cell of a moss; prothallus cell of a fern; gemma cell in *Marchantia*; **meristem cell of monocot**, ovum of a liverwort and zygote of a fern.

**Sol.** Ploidy for the following are as follows :

(i) Protonemal cell of moss-haploid.
(ii) Primary endosperm nucleus of a dicot-triploid.
(iii) Leaf cell of a moss-haploid.
(iv) Prothallus cell of a fern-haploid.
(v) Gemma cell in *Marchantia*-haploid.
(vi) Meristem cell of monocot-diploid.
(vii) Ovum of a liverwort-haploid.
(viii) Zygote of a fern-diploid.

**Question 5** Write a note on economic importance of algae and gymnosperms.

**Sol.** **Economic importance of algae** Various species of algae have great economic importance

1. Altogether 70 species of marine algae including *Porphyra, Laminaria, Sargassum* are used as food.
2. Some of the marine brown and red algae produce large amount of hydrocolloids which are used as solidifying agents. Algin obtained from brown algae and 'Agar' obtained from red algae *Gelidium* and *Gracilaria* are used in preparation of variety of creams including ice creams and jellies.
3. Agar is used to prepare tissue culture media for growing microbes.

4. *Chlorella,* an unicellular green alga has been the source of single cell protein (SCP). It is used as a source of $O_2$, for disposal of $CO_2$ and as food supplements by space travellers.
5. Iodine is extracted from brown algae.

**Economic importance of gymnosperms**

1. Gymnosperms, especially conifers, are the source of very good quality timbers as they provide soft wood and include tallest trees.
2. Taxol, an anticancer drug, is obtained from *Taxus*.
3. Various species of *Cycas* have been good source of starch-sago is obtained from *Cycas circinalis.*
4. Chilgoza, s type of dry fruit is obtained from *Pinus gerardiana.*

**Question 6** Both gymnosperms and angiosperms bear seeds, then why are they classified separately?

**Sol.** Both gymnosperms and angiosperms bear seeds, but they are yet classified separately, because, in case of gymnosperms the seeds are naked, *i.e.,* the seeds are not produced inside the fruit but in case of angiosperms the seeds are enclosed inside the fruit.

**Question 7** What is heterospory? Briefly comment on its significance. Give two examples.

**Sol.** Heterospory is the phenomenon of formation of two types of spores, *i.e.,* smaller microspore and larger megaspore.

Occurence of heterosporous condition has been the precursor of seed habit. Evolution of heterospory in pteridophytes marked a significant evolutionary step towards development of seed plants, *i.e.,* gymnosperms and angiosperms. Formation of megaspores and its retention within megasporangium and parent sporophyte plant body has led to the evolution of seed habit. The phenomenon of heterospory leads to the reduction of gametophyte, *in situ* germination of spores, retention of female gametophyte on the parent sporophyte and finally to the seed development. Examples of heterospory are *Selaginella,* and *Salvinia,* etc.

**Question 8** Explain briefly the following terms with suitable examples. (i) Protonema (ii) Antheridium (iii) Archegonium (iv) Diplontic (v) Sporophyll (vi) Isogamy.

**Sol.**

(i) **Protonema** It is the juvenile stage of a moss, which develops directly from the germinating spore. When fully grown, it consists of a slender, green, branching system of filaments called protonema.

(ii) **Antheridium** It is male sex organ developed by member of algae, bryophyte and pteridophyte. It has a single-layered sterile jacket absent in algae enclosing a large number of androcytes. The androcytes metamorphosed into flagellated motile antherozoids.

(iii) **Archegonium** The female sex organ of bryophytes, which is multicellular and differentiated into neck and venter. The neck consists of neck canal cells and venter contains the venter canal cells and egg.

(iv) **Diplontic** A kind of life cycle in which the sporophyte is dominant, photosynthetic, independent phase of the plant and alternate with haploid gametophytic phase which is reduced and dependent is known as diplontic life cycle.

(v) **Sporophyll** They are specialised leaves which bears sporangia on its abaxial or adaxial surface. These may be microsporophylls bearing microspongia and megasporophylls bearing megasporangia.

(vi) **Isogamy** It is the process of fusion between two similar gametes, *i.e., Spirogyra.*

**Question 9** Differentiate between the following

(i) red algae and brown algae.

(ii) liverworts and moss.

(iii) homosporous and heterosporous pteridophyte.

**Sol.**

(i) **Differences between red Algae and brown Algae** are as follows :

| S.N. | Red Algae | Brown Algae |
|---|---|---|
| 1. | It belongs to the class–Rhodophyceae. | It belongs to the class–Phaeophyceae. |
| 2. | It is red in colour due to the presence of pigments chlorophyll-*a*, *d* and phycoerythrin. | It is brown in colour due to the presence of pigments like carotenoids fucoxanthin, chlorophyll *a* and *c* |
| | **Example** *Polysiphonia, Gracilaria* | **Example** *Sargassum, Fucus* |

(ii) **Differences between liverworts and moss are as follows :**

| S.N. | Liverwort | Moss |
|---|---|---|
| 1. | Thallus is dorsiventrally flattened and closely appressed to the substrate | Mosses exhibit leafy gametophyte. |
| 2. | Rhizoids unicellular | Rhizoids are multicellular. and branched |
| 3. | Elaters are present in capsule to assist dispersal of spores. | Elaters are absent, but peristome teeth are present in the capsule to assist dispersal of spores. |

(iii) **Differences between homosporous and heterosporous Pteridophytes** are as follows :

| Homosporous Pteridophyte | Heterosporous Pteridophyte |
|---|---|
| Pteridophyters, which produce only one kind of spores. | These produce two kinds of spores, *i.e.*, large megaspore and smallar microspore. |
| **Example** *Lycopodium* | **Example** *Selaginella* |

**Question 10** Match the following column I and Column II.

| Column I | Column II |
|---|---|
| A. *Chlamydomonas* | 1. Moss |
| B. *Cycas* | 2. Pteridophyte |
| C. *Selaginella* | 3. Algae |
| D. *Sphagnum* | 4. Gymnosperm |

**Sol.**

| Column I | Column II |
|---|---|
| A. *Chlamydomonas* | 3. Aglae |
| B. *Cycas* | 4. Gymnosperm |
| C. *Selaginella* | 2. Pteridophyte |
| D. *Sphagnum* | 1. Moss |

**Question 11** Describe the important characteristics of gymnosperms.

**Sol.** Gymnosperms are vascular plants with naked seeds. The important characters of gymnosperms are as follows:

(i) The plants are perennial forming a dominant flora in colder areas.

(ii) Leaves are generally dimorphic, foliage and scaled leaves.

(iii) Root is tap root.

(iv) All gymnosperms are heterosporous producing both the spores within sporangia borne on sporophylls produce strobili or cones.

(v) Microsporophylls do not show distinction of filament and anther. Megasporophylls are also not rolled-like carpels.

(vi) Ovules are unitegmic (sometimes bitegmic in gnetales). Each ovule has a mass of tissue called nucellus. It is equivalent to megasporangium. A megaspore mother cell develops on it which after meiosis forms haploid megaspores.

(vii) Female gametophyte develops archegonia.

(viii) Pollination wind brings pollen grains over the micropylar end of ovules (direct pollination), siphonogamy occurs.

(ix) The lifecycle of gymnosperm is diplontic as the gametophyte has no free existence.

(x) Secondary growth is present in some gymnosperms.

# DIKSHA APP Questions

## ☐ Multiple Choice Questions

**Q.1** Phylogenetic classification seeks :

(a) the similarity in sexual mode of reproduction.
(b) the similarity in the asexual mode of reproduction.
(c) evolutionary relationship among organisms.
(d) None

**Sol.** (c) Phylogenetic classification seeks to determine the evolutionary relationships among organisms based on common ancestry and evolutionary history.

**Q.2** "Artificial classification" by Linnaeus was not accurate because

(a) it gave equal weightage to vegetative as well as the sexual mode of reproduction.
(b) it was primarily based upon superficial morphological character like color, shape, and number of leaves.
(c) it did not consider internal structure like anatomy, embryology, phytochemistry.
(d) All

**Sol.** (d) Linnaeus article classification was inaccurate because it relied on superficial morphological traits like colour and shape, without considering internal structures, anatomy, embryology, or phytochemistry.

**Q.3** The cytological classification relies on cytological information like

(a) chromosome number (b) chromosome structure
(c) chromosome behavior (d) All

**Sol.** (d) Cytological classification relies on cytological information such a chromosome number, structure and behaviour to classify organisms.

**Q.4** Why vegetative mode of reproduction does not weight equally to the sexual mode of reproduction?

(a) Vegetative propagation is common in the plant kingdom.
(b) Vegetative reproduction is not so complicated, like sexual reproduction.
(c) Environmental factors easily alter vegetative characters.
(d) None

**Sol.** (c) Vegetative reproduction results in genetically identical offspring, making them more susceptible to environmental changes that can alter vegetative traits. In contrasts, sexual reproduction introduces genetic diversity, enhancing adaptability.

**Q.5** Plant kingdom comprises

(a) algae
(b) bryophytes and pteridophytes
(c) angiosperms and gymnosperms
(d) All

**Sol.** (d) The plant kingdom comprises algae, bryophytes, pteridophytes, angiosperms, and gymnosperms, representing the various groups of plants.

**Q.6** Blue-green alga belongs to the group

(a) plantae (b) animalia
(c) algae (d) cyanobacteria

**Sol.** (d) Blue-green algae belong to the group cyanobacteria, which are photosynthetic bacteria that are often mistaken for algae.

**Q.7** Fusion of two gametes which are dissimilar in size is termed as

(a) oogamy (b) isogamy (c) anisogamy (d) zoogamy

**Sol.** (c) Fusion of two gametes which are similar in size is called isogamy while the fussion of gametes which are dissimilar only in size is called anisogamy. Oogamy is the fusion of gametes which are dissimilar in size and physiology.

**Q.8** Which of the following red algae are suitable for human consumption.

(a) *Laminaria* and *Fucus* (b) *Gracilaria* and *Chondrus*
(c) *Porphyra* and *Spirogyra* (d) *Rhodymenia* and *Porphyra*

**Sol.** (d) *Laminaria* and *Fucus* are brown algae, while *Spirogyra* is a green alga. The red alga *Porphyra* is rich in dietary fibers while *Rhodymenia* contains vitamins and fibers. These qualities make both suitabe for human consumption.

**Q.9** Protonema is

(a) haploid and is found in mosses
(b) diploid and is found in liverworts
(c) diploid and is found in pteridophytes
(d) haploid and is found in pteridophytes

**Sol.** (a) The protonema represents first gametophytic stage of the life cycle of moss which is developed directly from a spore. It develops into adult form of gametophytic plant body.

**Q.10** A plant producing seeds but lacking flowers is

(a) gymnosperm
(b) pteridophyta
(c) angiosperm
(d) bryophyte

**Sol.** (a) Gymnosperms is a group of plants which produce seeds but lack flowers although the male reproductive part is represented by micro sporophyll while female reproductive part by megasporophyll. These plants have naked ovary.

**Q.11** The embryo sac of an angiosperm is made up of

(a) 8 Nuclei
(b) 7 cells
(c) 7 cells and 8 nuclei
(d) 7 cells and 7 nuclei

**Sol.** (c) The polygonum type (most common) of embryo sac in angiosperms is 7-celled, 8-nucleate. It is composed of egg apparatus (one egg cell and two synergids), 3-antipodal cells and one central cell of two polar nuclei. The polar nuclei fuse with male gamete to form primary endosperm nuclues ($3n$), while zygote is formed by fusion of egg cell and another male gamete.

**Q.12** Conifers are adapted to tolerate extreme environmental conditions because of

(a) thick cuticle
(b) presence of vessels
(c) broad hard leaves
(d) superficial stomata

**Sol.** (a) Conifers are gymnospermic plants, which are adapted to tolerate extreme environmental conditions because of

(i) Sunken Stomata which minimize water loss
(ii) Needle-like leaves which reduces their surface areas
(iii) Thick cuticle that is protective waxy layer covering epidermal cells of leaves

## ☐ Short Answer Type

**Q.1** "Bryophytes are amphibians of the plant kingdom", Explain.

**Sol.** Bryophytes are also called amphibians of the plant kingdom because these plants can live in soil but are dependent on water for sexual reproduction. They usually occur in damp, humid and shaded localities. They play an important role in plant succession on bare rocks/soil. The bryophyte sperm, antherozoid is biflagellate and requires water for fertilisation.

# Animal Kingdom

CHAPTER 04

## Important Points

**01** Animals are classified on the basis of level of organisation, body symmetry, body cavity or coelom and pattern of arrangement of cells.

**02** Animals exhibit different levels of organisation, like cellular level, and organ level of organisation.

**03** Animals are also categorised on the basis of symmetry. There are three types of symmetry, *i.e.*,

(i) Asymmetrical, (ii) Radial symmetry and (iii) Bilateral symmetry.

**04** Embryonic cells in animals are arranged into different embryonic layers. On the basis of it animals are classified as diploblastic and triploblastic.

**05** **Coelom** is the body cavity, which is lined by mesoderm. Classification of animals is also based on presence and absence of coelom as in acoelomate, pseudocoelomate and coelomate.

**06** In some animals, the body is externally and internally divided into segments with a serial repetition of at least some organs *e.g.*, earthworm. This phenomenon of segmentation is known as **metamerism**.

**07** During embryonic development, mesodermal cells forms a rod-like structure on the dorsal surface called **notochord**. Animals with notochord are known as **chordates** and animals without notochord are known as **non-chordates.**

(i) **Phylum–Porifera** includes **sponges** which are generally marine and mostly asymmetrical animals. These are primitive, multicellular animals with a water transport system for food gathering, respiration and waste removal, and they reproduce both sexually and asexually *e.g., Sycon*

(ii) **Phylum–Cnidaria** (Coelenterata) consist of aquatic, marine, free-swimming or sessile, radially symmetrical animals. They are diploblastic and have central gastrovascular cavity. They have cnidoblasts present on tentacles and the body and have two morphological forms polyp and medusa *e.g., Adamsia* (sea anemone)

(iii) **The members of Phylum-Ctenophora** are known as **sea walnuts** or **comb jellies** are exclusively marine, radially symmetrical, diploblastic organisms and show property of bioluminescence. *e.g., Pleurobrachia* and *Ctenoplana.*

(iv) The members of **Phylum–Platyhelminthes** are with dorso-ventrally flattened body hence, called **flatworms.**
   (a) They have specialised cells called **flame cells**
   (b) Some members like *Planaria* possess high regeneration capacity.
   *e.g., Taenia* (Tapeworm) and *Fasciola* (Liver fluke).

(v) The members of **Phylum–Aschelminthes** are known as **round worms** because they possess cylindrical body tapering at both ends.
   (a) They may be free living, aquatic, terrestial or parasitic in plants and animals
   (b) They are bilaterally symmetrical, triploblastic and pseudocoelomate animal.
   *e.g., Ascaris* (Roundworm), *Wuchereria* (Filaria worm) and *Ancylostoma* (Hookworm).

(vi) Members of **Phylum–Annelida** are also known as (segmented worms).
   (a) They exhibit organ system level of organisation, triploblastic as well as shows bilateral symmetry.
   (b) They are metamerically segmented and nephridia is present for osmoregulation and excretion.
   e.g. *Nereis, Pheretima* (Earthworm), *Hirudinaria* (Leech).

(vii) **Phylum–Arthropoda** is the largest phylum of Animalia, which includes **insects**. (Arthro = Jointed, Podos = Legs)

(a) They are triploblastic, segmented, bilaterally, symmetrical coelomate animals. Body is covered by chitinous exoskeleton. *e.g., Apis* (Honey bee), *Bombyx* (Silkworm) and *Laccifer* (Lac insect).

(viii) **Phylum–Mollusca** is the second largest phylum.

(a) They are terrestial or aquatic and are bilaterally symmetrical, triploblastic and coelomate animals.

(b) Body is covered by a calcareous shell. *e.g., Pila (Apple snail), Octopus, (Devilfish) Pinctada* (Pearl oyster) and *Sepia*. (Cuttle fish)

(ix) Members of **Phylum–Echinodermata** have an endoskeleton of **calcareous ossicles** and named as Echinodermata.

(a) They are radially symmetrical at adult stage but bilaterally symmetrical at larval stage.

(b) Water vascular system is present, which helps in locomotion, capture and transport of food and respiration. *e.g., Asterias* (Star fish), *Echinus* (Sea urchin), *Cucumaria* (Sea cucumber) and *Ophiura* (Brittle star).

(x) **Phylum–Hemichordata** was earlier considered as a sub-phylum under the phylum Chordata.

(a) It consist of worm-like marine animals and are triploblastic, coelomate and bilaterally symmetrical animals.

(b) Their body is cylindrical and composed of an anterior proboscis a collar and a long trunk and excretion occur through proboscis gland. *e.g., Balanoglossus* and *Saccoglossus*.

(xi) **Phylum–Chordata** These are characterised by following distinguishing features

(a) Presence of notochord.

(b) Pharynx is perforated by gill slits.

(c) Central nervous system is dorsal, hollow and single.

(d) Phylum–Chordata is divided into three sub-phylum—

- Urochordata or Tunicata, Cephalochordata and Vertebrata

(e) In case of vertebrates notochord is replaced by **vertebral column** in adults.

(f) Vertebrates are divided into two divisions—

- Agnatha (lacks jaw)
- Gnathostomata (bears jaw)

(g) Agnatha have one class **cyclostomata**.

(h) Gnathostomata is divided into two super-class.

- **Pisces** (bear fins)
- **Tetrapoda** (bear limbs).

(i) Pisces are divided into two sub-class—

- Chondrichthyes and Osteichthyes

(j) Tetrapoda are divided into four class—
(i) Amphibia, (ii) Reptilia, (iii) Aves and (iv) Mammals.

**08** Members of **class–Cyclostomata** are ectoparasites on some fishes.

(i) Possess 6-15 pair of gill slits for respiration.

*e.g., Petromyzon* (Lamprey) and *Myxine* (Hagfish).

**09** Member of **class–Chondrichthyes** are **cartilaginous fishes,** always marine, with streamlined body. Skin is covered with placoid scales.

(i) Notochord is persistant throughout life.

(ii) Gill slits are separate and without operculum

(iii) Some of them have electric organs (*e.g., Torpedo)* and some posses poison sting (*e.g., Trygon)*

**10** Member of **class–Osteichthyes** includes both marine and fresh water bony fishes.

(i) Four pairs of gills are covered by an operculum on each side.

(ii) Presence of air bladder which regulate buoyancy.
*e.g.*, **Marine** *Exocoetus* (Flying fish).

**Freshwater** *Labeo* (Rohu),
**Aquarium** *Betta* (Fighting fish).

**11** Members of **class–Amphibia** can live in aquatic or moist land. They are the first terrestrial organism observed.

(i) They are **poikilothermic,** (cold-blooded animals).

(ii) Body is divisible into **head** and **trunk**.

(iii) Respiration is through moist skin, gills and lungs.

**Tympanum** represents the ear.

Sexes are separate and fertilisation is external.
Alimentary canal, urinary and reproductive tract opens into a common chamber called **cloaca**.

*e.g., Bufo* (Toad), *Rana* (Frog), *Hyla* (Tree frog), *Salamandra* (Salamander) and *Ichthyophis* (Limbless amphibia).

**12** Members of **class–Reptilia** are the first true terrestrial vertebrates.

(i) They exhibit creeping or crawling mode of locomotion.

(ii) They are **poikilotherms.**

*e.g., Chelone* (Turtle), *Chameleon* (Tree lizard),

**Poisonous snakes** *Naja* (Cobra),

**13** Members of **class–Aves** are characterised by the presence of **feathers**. Most of them can fly except flightless bird, (*e.g.,* Ostrich).

(i) They possess beak. Forelimbs are modified into wings.

(ii) They are **homoiothermous, or warm–blooded animals**.

*e.g., Pavo* (Peacock), *Aptenodytes* (Penguin) and *Neophron* (Vulture).

**14** Members of **class–Mammalia** are characterised by the presence of milk producing glands called **mammary glands** and are homoiothermous.

(i) Skin is glandular with sweat gland and is unique in possessing hair.

*e.g.,* Oviparous *Ornithorhynehus (platypus)* viviparous *Felis (Cat), Rattus* (Rat).

## Exercises

**Question 1** What are the difficulties that you would face in classification of animals, if common fundamental features are not taken into account?

**Sol.** Following difficulties we will face-

1. Common fundamental features are essential characteristics shared among groups of animals as they help in organising and classifying the vast diversity of animals life. If fundamental characters are not taken into account it will be impossible to deal with every animal form separately at individual level.
2. The inter-relationship among different animals will not be established.
3. Examples of convergent evolution, adaptive radiation, animals with vestigeal organs, e.t.c. will provide hinderance in classification.

**Question 2** If you are given a specimen, what are the steps that you would follow to classify it?

**Sol.** For classifying a given specimen following steps has to be taken

(i) Characterisation-Study various characters of the specimen both morphological and anatomical.

(ii) Identification-Based upon various characters the given specimen is identified for (a) Level of organisation (b) Symmetry, (c) Body cavity or coelom, (d) Mode of segmentation.

(iii) Classification-Finally on the basis of identification, the given specimen can be placed on specific phylum, class order, etc. Further classification will be done based on the criteria.

**Question 3.** How useful is the study of the nature of body cavity and coelom in the classification of animals?

**Sol.** Presence or absence of a cavity between the body wall and the gut wall is very important in classification. The body cavity which is lined by mesoderm is called coelom.

(i) Animals possessing coelom are called coelomates, *e.g.*, annelids, molluscs, arthropods, echinoderms, hemichordates and chordates.

(ii) In some animals, the body cavity is not lined by mesoderm, instead the mesoderm is present as scattered pouches in between the ectoderm and endoderm. Such a body cavity is called pseudocoelom and the animals possessing them are called pseudocoelomates, *e.g.*, Aschelminthes.

(iii) The animals in which the body cavity is absent are known as Acoelomates, *e.g.*, Platyhelminthes.

**Question 4** Distinguish between intracellular and extracellular digestion?

**Sol.** Differences between intracellular and extracellular are as follows :

| Intracellular Digestion | Extracellular Digestion |
|---|---|
| Digestion occur inside the cell. | Digestion occur in the cavity of alimentary canal, *i.e.*, outside the cell |
| It involve the use of lysosomes | It involve the secretion of enzyme secreted by digestive glands. |
| Digestive products are diffused into the cytoplasm | Digestive products are diffused across the intestinal wall into various parts of body. |
| It occur is unicellular organisms | It occurs in multicellular organisms. |

**Question 5** What is the differences between direct and indirect development?

**Sol.** Differences between direct and indirect development are as follows :

(i) **Direct development** · In case of direct development, the life cycle of an adult individual lacks any larval stage in its life cycle. The young ones resemble the aduct in all respect. e.g., mammals.

(ii) **Indirect development** It is present mostly in case of lower animals the adult individual gives rise to eggs mostly which develop into adult after being passing through several larval stages *e.g.*, echinoderms, *Ascaris*, cockroach.

**Question 6** What are the peculiar features that you find in parasitic platyhelminthes?

**Sol.** The characteristic features of parasitic platyhelminthes are as follows.

(i) Body wall is three-layered. Outermost covering is epidermis which is often cilliated and covered by cuticle.

(ii) Digestive tract is incomplete or absent.

(iii) Presence of hooks and suckers for attachment to host surface.

(iv) They perform anaerobic respiration.

(v) Reproductive system of parasitic forms is highly developed with enormous power to reproduce.

**Question 7** What are the reasons that you can think of for the arthropods to constitute the largest group of the animal kingdom?

**Sol.** Arthropods constitute the largest group of the animal kingdom. The chief characteristics of arthopods is their chitinous exoskeleton. Arthropods are equipped with jointed appendages, which are variously adapted for walking, swimming, feeding, sensory reception and defence. The appendages of abdomen are associated with locomotion, reproduction and in some cases with defence as well. The appendages of head are related to defence, whereas those of thorax are mainly associated with locomotion. These features are responsible for its large diversity.

**Question 8.** Water vascular system is the characteristic of which group of the following?

(i) Porifera (ii) Ctenophora

(iii) Echinodermata (iv) Chordata

**Sol.** Echinodermata have the water vascular system.

**Question 9** 'All vertebrates are chordates but all chordates are not vertebrates'. Justify the statement.

**Sol.** Notochord is a characteristic feature of all chordates. The members of sub-phylum—Vertebrata possess notochord during the embryonic stage. But in adults the notochord is replaced by a cartilaginous or bony vertebral column.

whereas in member of other sub-phyla of Chordata the notochord remain as such. Cephalochordata retain the notochord during their entire life cycle. Thus, the absence of notochord in adult vertebrates suggest that all vertebrates are chordates but all chordates are not vertebrates.

**Question 10** How important is the presence of air bladder in pisces?

**Sol.** Presence of air bladder in pisces is very important as it helps in maintaining buoyancy. Thus, it helps fishes to ascend or descend and stay in the water current. It helps in conserve energy also.

**Question 11** What are the modifications that are observed in birds that help them fly?

**Sol.** Flight adaptations in birds are

(i) Streamlined body helps to propel through the air easily.

(ii) Feathery covering for insulation.

(iii) Forelimbs modified into wings and hind limbs used for walking perching and swimming.

(iv) Extremely powerful muscles that enables the wings to work during flight.

(v) Bones are light, hollow and provide more space for muscle attachment. Presence of pneumatic bones which reduces the weight of body and help in flight.

(vi) Presence of air sacs to supplement respiration.

**Question 12** Could the number of eggs or young ones produced by an oviparous and viviparous mother be equal? Why?

**Sol.** The number of eggs or young ones produced by an oviparous or viviparous mother cannot be equal. An oviparous mother gives rise to more number of eggs as some of them die during hatching and as they also have to pass through a large number of developmental stages before becoming an adult. On the other hand, a viviparous mother gives rise to fewer number of young ones because there are less chances of their death.

Moreover, they did not have to pass through any larval stage. Therefore to compensate the loss during development in oviparous animals, the number of eggs are much more.

**Question 13.** Segmentation in the body is first observed in which of the following

(i) Platyhelminthes (ii) Annelida

(iii) Aschelminthes (iv) Arthropoda

**Sol.** (ii) Segmentation in the body is first observed in annelida. This phenomenon is known as metamerism.

# DIKSHA APP Questions

## Multiple Choice Questions

**Q.1** Animals are classified on the basis of

(a) locomotory organs
(b) cellular organisation
(c) the habitats they live in
(d) Way of reproduction

**Sol.** (b) Animals are primarily classified based on their cellular organisation, which includes levels like cellular (*e.g.*, sponges), tissue (*e.g.* cnidarians), organ (*e.g.* flatworms) and organ system (*e.g.* mammals).

**Q.2** The organisms of following group have only two body layers

(a) platyhelminthes (b) cnidarians
(c) annelida (d) molluscans

**Sol.** (b) Animals of phylum coelenterate (also called cnidaria) have two germ layers hence called diploblastic. The inner layer is called endoderm while outer layer is called ectoderm.

**Q.3** An example for bilaterally symmetrical organism is

(a) start fish (b) human beings
(c) *Amoeba* (d) earth worm

**Sol.** (b) Humans are bilaterally symmetrical, which means their body can be divided into two identical halves along a single plane.

**Q.4** Water transportation through canal system is found in

(a) porifera
(b) coelenterate
(c) echinodermata
(d) chordata

**Sol.** (a) Water transportation through a canal system is a characteristic feature of porifera. This system helps in the circulation of water for feeding, respiration or excretion.

**Q.5** Having body annuli is the feature of this phylum

(a) arthropoda
(b) chordata
(c) annelida
(d) platyhelminths

**Sol.** (c) Animals of phylum annelida have a cylindrical body, which is divided into ring-like segments called annulus (annuli).

**Q.6** Organisms having monoecious bodies are

(a) earthworm, tapeworm (b) earthworm, crab
(c) cockroach, mosquito (d) cow, hen

**Sol.** (a) Organisms with monoecious bodies have both male and female reproductive organs in the same individual. Earthworm and tapeworm are examples of monoecious organisms. In contrast, dioecious organisms, like cockroaches, cows and hens, have separate sexes.

**Q.7** The name Echinodermata is given to the group of organisms because

(a) They have spiny skin
(b) Due to water vascular system
(c) Having tube feet
(d) Dorsoventarally compressed body

**Sol.** (a) The name Echinodermata is given to this group of organisms because they possess spiny skin, derived from calcareous plates or spines.

**Q.8** The Primitive fishes, having circulatory jawless mouth belong to

(a) cyclostomes (b) hemi chordata
(c) vertebrates (d) semi chordates

**Sol.** (a) Cyclostomes are primitive jawless fishes, which include organisms like lampreys and higfishes. They have circular mouth and are considered the most primitive living vertebrates.

**Q.9** Fresh water fishes have

(a) airbladder, opercula
(b) no Scales on the body
(c) viviparous
(d) lungs

**Sol.** (a) The fresh water fishes typically have an air bladder to regulate buoyancy and an operculum, which is a bony covering that protect gills.

**Q.10** Honeybee, house fly, butterfly, prawn and crabs belong to following phylum

(a) chordata (b) hemichordate
(c) arthropoda (d) mollusca

**Sol.** (c) Honeybee, house fly, butterfly, prawn and crabs all belong to the phylum arthropoda, which is characterised by jointed legs, an exoskeleton made of chitin and segmented bodies.

## ☐ Short Answer Types

**Q.1** *Taenia solium* is an endoparasite of man. Write any four characters by which we can identify the organism?

**Sol.** Four characters by which one can identify. *Taenia solium are as follows :*

1. No digestive system is present.
2. They are hermaphrodites
3. No eyes are present.
4. Hooks and suckers are present in parasitic form.

**Q.2** Write four important characteristics of phylum arthropoda.

**Sol.** Four important characteristics of phylum arthropoda are

1. The body of arthropods is covered by chitinous exoskeleton.
2. They have jointed legs;
3. Sensory organs like antennae compound eyes are present.
4. Open circulatory system is present.

**Q.3** Write three important differences between invertebrates and vertebrates/chordates?

**Sol.** Three important differences between invertebrates and vertebrates are as follows :

1. Presence of vertebral column at dorsal side in vertebrates where as vertebral column are not present in invertebrates.
2. Presence of endoskeleton in vertebrates and exoskeleton in invertebrate.
3. Presence of two pairs of locomotory organs, in vertebrates, and in invertebrates either no locomotory organs or many appendages are found.

**Q.4** Identify the important characters *a*, *b*, *c*, *d*, *e*, and *f* of the organisms mentioned in the following gird.

Cyclostomes $\leftarrow a$ $b \rightarrow$ Chondrichthyes

$c \rightarrow$ Osteichthyes Amphibian $\leftarrow d$

$e \rightarrow$ Cephalochordate Vertebrate $\leftarrow f$

**Sol.** (a) Cyclostomes have circular mouth.

(b) Condrichthyes have cartilaginous endoskeleton.

(c) Osteichthyes have bony endoskeleton,

(d) Having no neck/cutaneous respiration/metamorphic life cycle/three chambered heart are important characters of amphibiSol.

(e) Having notochord at anterior region is an important character of cephalochordates.

(f) Invertebrates, notochord is replaced by vertebral column.

**Q.5** (i) How are amphibians, aves and reptiles different from one another, with respect to their processes considering *a* and *b*

(a) reproduction

(b) respiration

(ii) Write any four important characters of mammals?

**Sol.** (i) (a) External, in amphibians and internal; in aves and reptiles

(b) By cutaneous, lungs and gills in amphibians; by lungs in aves and reptiles.

(ii) Four important character of mammals are as follows :

Having-a. mammary glands, external body hair, b. defined head, thorax, abdomen region c. viviparous d. having five fingered limbs.

# Morphology of Flowering Plants

CHAPTER 05

## Important Points

**01** Morphology (Morpho = form, Logos = Study) deals with the study of form and features of different plant organs like roots, stems, leaves, flowers, seeds fruits, etc.

**02** The main axis of plant is divided into the root system and shoot system.

**03** Root

(i) The root is normally non-green, cylindirical and descending part that normally grows downwards into the soil.

(ii) In case of dicotyledonous plant, primary root elongates and bears lateral root of several orders referred to as secondary and tertiary roots. This system is called as **tap root system**.

(iii) In monocot plants, like wheat, primary root is short lived and are replaced by numbers of roots that arise from base of stem and constitute **fibrous root system.**

(iv) Adventitious roots are present is some plants in which root arises from parts of the plants other than radicle.

**04** Regions of the roots

(i) The roots is covered at the apex by a thimble like structure called root cap.

(ii) A few millimeter above the root cap is the region of meristematic and the region of elongation followed by region of maturation.

**05** **Stem** is the ascending part of the axis forming shoot system of the plant body. In develops from plumule of the embryo of a germinating seed and bears nodes and internodes.

**06** Leaves are flattered , green structure which manufactures the food by photosynthesis and are most important vegetative organs of the plant. A typical leaf consists of three parts, *i.e.*, (a) leaf base (b) petiole (c) Lamina

**07** Venation is the arrangement of veins and veinlets in the lamina of the leaf. Two type of venation are present, *i.e.*, reticulate and parallel venation.

**08** Leaves are of two types

**Leaves**

- **Simple**
  When insicision of lamina do not touch the midrip
- **Compound**
  When the incision of lamina reaches to midrib breaking it into a number of leaflets
  - **Pinnately Compound Leaves**
    Number of leaflets present on a common axis called rachis, *e.g.*, in neem
  - **Palmately Compound Leaves**
    Leaflets are attached at a common point *e.g.*, in silk cotton

**09** Pattern of arrangement of leaves on the stem or branch is called phyllotaxy. It is of three types, *i.e.*, alternate, opposite and whorled.

**10** Inflorescence is the arrangement of flowers on the floral axis. The two major type of inflorescence are

(a) Racemose (b) Cymose

**11** Flower is the reproductive unit of a plant and is meant for sexual reproduction

(i) A typical flower has four different kinds of whorls namely calyx, corolla as non essential whorls whereas androecium and gynoecium as essential whole.

(ii) In symmetry, the flower may be actinomorphic radial symmetry) or zygomorphic (bilateral symmetry)

(iii) On the basis of position of gynoecium in respect of calyx, corolla and androecium, flower are described as hypogynous (superior ovary), perigynous (half-inferior ovary) and epigynous (inferior ovary)

**12** Various parts of the flower are

(i) Calyx-It is outermost whorl of flower and members are called sepals.

(ii) Corolla-It is composed of petals and are usually bright coloured.

(iii) Arrangement of sepals and petals in flower with respect to other members of the same whorl is called **aestivation**. Main type of aestivation are valvate, twisted, imbricate and vexillary.

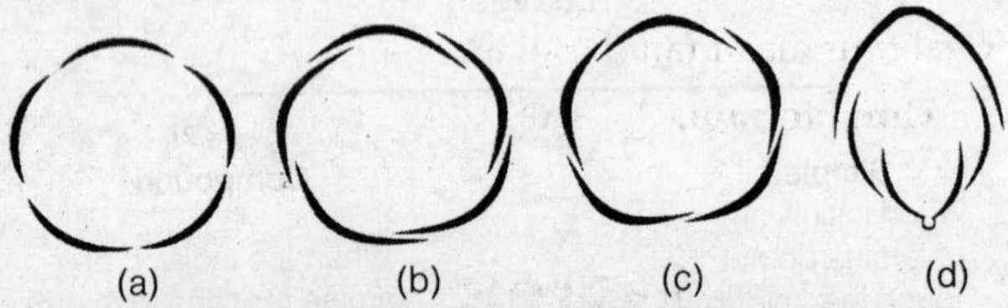

▲ Types of aestivation in corolla : (a) Valvate (b) Twisted (c) Imbricate (d) Vexillary

**13** **Androecium** is composed of stamens which represents the male reproductive organ consist of a stalk/ filament and an anther.

(i) Each **Anther** is usually bilobed having two chambers in each lobe the pollen sac which produces pollen grains.

(ii) A sterile stamen is called staminode.

**14** Gynoecium is female reproductive part of flower which consist of three part, namely (a) Ovary (b) Style and (c) Stigma.
The arrangement of ovules within the ovary is known as placentation. It may be marginal (in pea), axile (in tomato), parietal (mustard), basal (sun flower) and free central (in *Dianthus*)

**15** After fertilisation, ovary matures and ripens to form fruit.
If fruit is formed without fertilisation, it is known as parthenocarpic fruit.

**16** **Seed** After fertilisation ovules develops into seed, which is made up of seed coat and an embryo.
On the basis of number of cotyledons present they are divided into

(i) monocotyledonous seed. (ii) dicotyledonous seed.

| Monocotyledonous seed | Dicotyledonous seed |
|---|---|
| Embryo with one cotyledons | Embryo with two cotyledons |
| The reserve food material is stored inside the endosperm. | The reserve food material is stored either in cotyledon or inside the endosperm |
| The radicle and plumule are protected by protective sheath | The radicle and plumule are not covered by protective sheath |
| Aleurone layer is present | Aleurone layer is absent. |

**17** Floral formula and floral diagram represent the floral characters, inflorescence and flower parts.

**18** Floral formula of family solanaceae

**Floral formula** $- \oplus, ⚥\ K_{(5)}\ \overparen{C_{(5)}\ A_5}\ \underline{G}_{(2)}$

# Exercises

**Question 1** How is a pinnately compound leaf different from a palmately compound leaf?

**Sol.** In pinnately compound leaf, the number of leaflets are present on a common axis, the rachis, which represents the midrib of the leaf as in neem where as in case of a palmately compound leaf, the leaflets are attached at a common point, *i.e.*, at the tip of petiole, as in silk cotton.

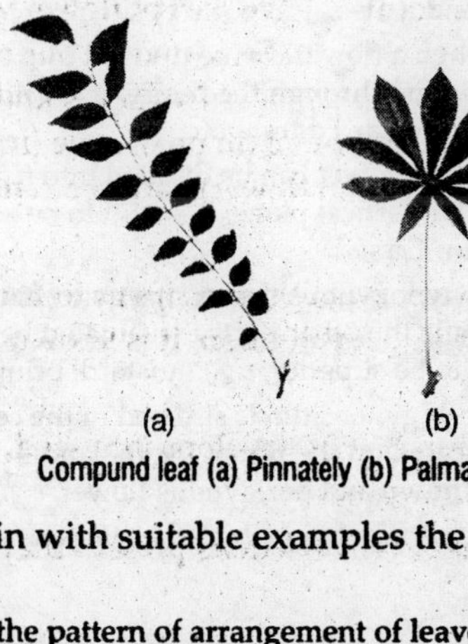

(a) (b)

Compund leaf (a) Pinnately (b) Palmately

**Question 2** Explain with suitable examples the different types of phyllotaxy.

**Sol.** Phyllotaxy is the pattern of arrangement of leaves on the stem or branch. This is usually of three types – alternate, opposite and whorled.

(i) In **alternate** phyllotaxy, a single leaf arises at each node in alternate manner, as in china rose, mustard and sunflower plants.

(ii) In **opposite** type of phyllotaxy, a pair of leaves arise at each node and lie opposite to each other as in *Calotropis* and guava plants.

(iii) In whorled phyllotaxy more than two leaves arise at each node and form a whorl as in *Alstonia*.

Different types of phyllotaxy (a) Alternate (b) Opposite (c) Whorled

**Question 3** Define the following terms

(a) Aestivation (b) Placentation (c) Actinomorphic
(d) Zygomorphic (e) Superior Ovary (f) Perigynous Flower
(g) Epipetalous

**Sol.**

(a) **Aestivation** The mode of arrangement of sepals or petals in floral bud with respect to the other members of the same whorl is known as aestivation. The main types of aestivations are twisted, valvate, imbricate, and vexillary.

(b) **Placentation** The arrangement of ovules within the ovary is known as placentation. The main types of placentations are marginal, parietal, basal, free central and axile.

(c) **Actinomorphic** When a flower can be divided into two equal halves in any radial plane passing through the centre, it is said to be actinomorphic, *e.g.*, mustard datura etc.

(d) **Zygomorphic** When a flower can be divided into two similar halves only in one particular vertical plane, it is said to be zygomorphic, e.g., pea, gulmohar, bean, *Cassia*.

(e) **Superior ovary** In hypogynous flower, the gynoecium occupies the highest position while the other parts are situated below it. The ovary in such flower is said to be superior, *e.g.*, mustard, brinjal

(f) **Perigynous flower** If gynoecium is situated in the centre and other parts of the flower are located on the rim of the thalamus almost at the same level. Then this is known as a perigynous flower, *e.g.*, plum, peach.

(g) **Epipetalous flower** A flower in which the stamens are attached to the petals as in brinjal.

**Question 4** Differentiate between

(a) Racemose and cymose inflorescence

(b) Apocarpous and syncarpous ovary

**Sol.** (a) Difference between racemose and cymose inflorescence are as follows

| Recemose inflorescence | Cymose inflorescence |
|---|---|
| It is indeterminate or indefinite inflorescence in which peduncle can produce indefinite number of flower. | In this inflorescence, the main axis terminates in a flower, hence is limited in growth. |

(b) Difference between apocarpous and syncarpous ovary are as follows:

| Apocarpous ovary | Syncarpous ovary |
|---|---|
| If there are two or more carpels and they are free, then this condifion, is called apocarpous, e.g., in lotus and rose | If the carpels are two or more, and are fused. The fused condition carpel is known as syncarpous, e.g., in mustard |

**Question 5** Draw the labelled diagrams of the following

(a) Gram seed (b) V.S. of maize

**Sol.**

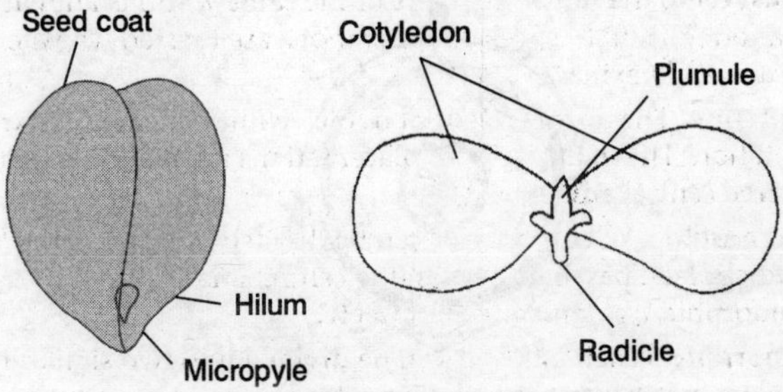


(a) Gram seed

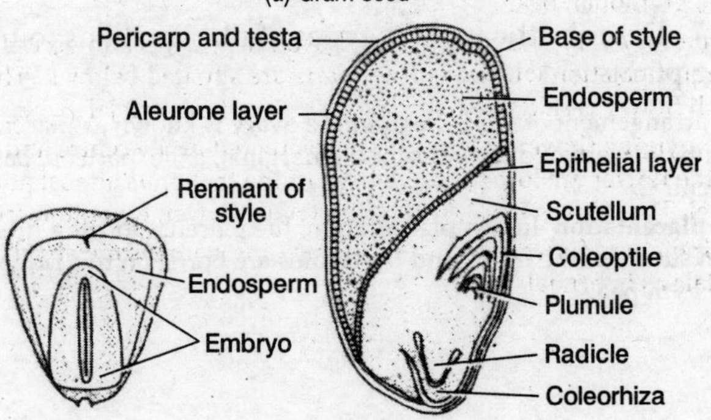


(b) V.S. of maize seed

**Question 6** Take one flower of the family Solanaceae and write its semi-techni description. Also draw their floral diagram.

*Solanum tuberosum* (potato) flower of family–Solanaceae.

**Sol.** Vegetative characters

Plants mostly herbs, shrubs, and rarely small trees

**Stem :** Herbaceous rarely wood, aerial, erect, cylindrical, branched, solid or hollow, hairy or glabrous, underground stem.

**Leaves :** Alternate, simple, rarely, pinnately compound, exstipulate, reticulate venation.

**Floral characters**

**Inflorescence :** Solitary, cymose or axillary as in *Solanum*

**Flower :** Bisexual, actinomorphic, complete, hypogynous

**Calyx :** 5 sepal, united, valvate aestivation

**Coralla :** 5 petals, united, valvate aestivation

**Androeciun :** Stamen 5, epipetalous.

**Gynoecium :** bicarpellary, syncarpous, superior ovary axile.

**Fruit :** berry or capsule.

**Seed :** endospermous, many

**Floral Formula** $\oplus\ \text{⚥}\ K_{(5)}\ \overset{\frown}{C_{(5)}\ A_5}\ \underline{G}_{(2)}$

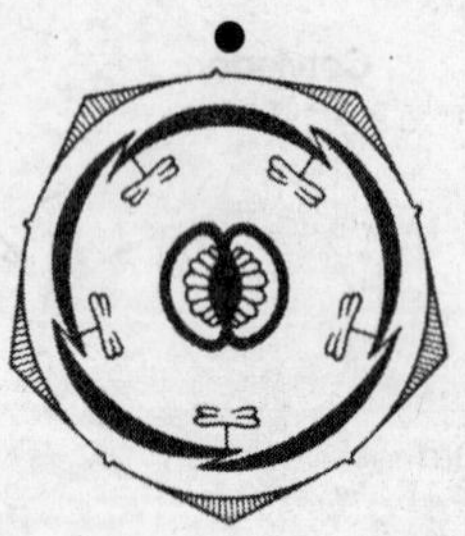

Floral formula of *Solanum*

**Question 7** Describe the various types of placentations found in flowering plants.

**Sol.** The arrangement of ovules within the ovary is known as placentation. The placentations are of different types – marginal, axile, parietal, basal, central and free central.

**Marginal placentation** In this placentation, the placenta forms a ridge along the ventral suture of the ovary and the ovules are borne on this ridge forming two rows, as in pea.

**Axile placentation** In this placentation, the placenta is axial and the ovules are attached to it in a multilocular ovary, as in china rose, tomato, etc.

**Parietal placentation** In this placentation, the ovules develop on the inner wall of the ovary or on peripheral part. Ovary is one chambered but it becomes two chambered due to the formation of a false septum *e.g.*, mustard and *Argemone*

**Free central placentation** In this type of placentation, the ovules are present on the central axis of ovary and septa are absent as in *Dianthus* and *Primrose*.

**Basal placentation** In this placentation, the placenta develops at the base of ovary and a single ovule is attached to it, as in sunflower.

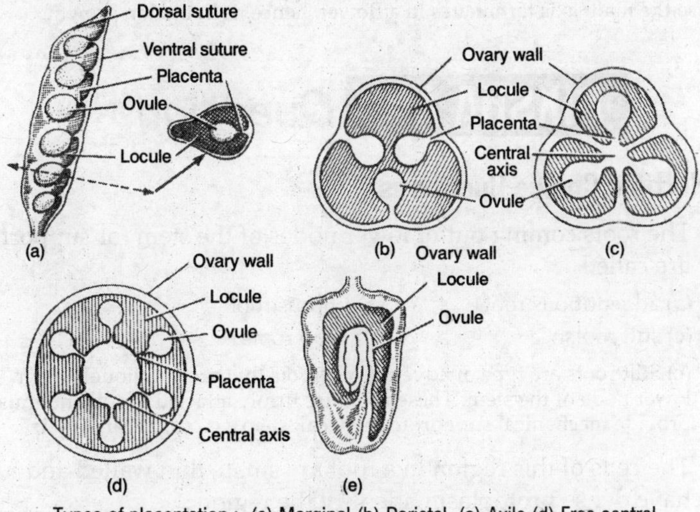


Types of placentation : (a) Marginal (b) Parietal (c) Axile (d) Free central (e) Basal

**Question 8** What is a flower? Describe the parts of a typical angiospermic flower.

**Sol.** Flower is a condensed modified reproductive shoot found in angiosperms. It often develops in the axile of a small leaf-like structure called **bract**. The stalk of the flower is called pedicel. The tip of the pedicel or the base of flower has a broad highly condensed multinodal region called **thalamus**.

A flower has four floral structures:

(i) **Calyx** It is made up of sepals. They are green in colour.

(ii) **Corolla** It is the brightly coloured part containing petals.

(iii) **Androecium** It represents the male reproductive organ which consists of stamens. A stamen has a long filament and terminal anther. The anther produces pollen grains.

(iv) **Gynoecium** It is the female reproductive part which consists of carpels. A carpel has three parts, *i.e.*, style, stigma and ovary. The ovary bears the ovules.

**Question 9** Define the term inflorescence. Explain the basis for the different types of inflorescence in flowering plants.

**Sol.** **Inflorescence** is the mode of arrangement of flowers on a floral axis (peduncles). Depending upon whether the apex gets converted into a flower or continues to grow, there are two major types of inflorescences racemose and cymose.

**Racemose inflorescence** In this type of inflorescences, the main axis continues to grow, the flowers are borne laterally in an acropetal succession.

**Cymose inflorescence** It is also called definite or determinate inflore scence because the main axis terminates in a flower, hence, is limited in growth.

# DIKSHA APP *Questions*

## ☐ Multiple Choice Questions

**Q.1** The roots coming out of lower nodes of the stem for support are called

(a) adventitious root (b) fibrous root
(c) stilt roots (d) prop roots

**Sol.** (c) Stilt roots are type of adventitious roots that grow obliquely from lower node of the stem. These roots are firmly attacted to soil and thus provide mechanical support to the weak stem *e.g.*, sugar cane. maize.

**Q.2** The cells of this region in a root are small, thin walled and have dense protoplasm, identify the region :

(a) region of maturation
(b) region of root hair
(c) region of elongation
(d) region of meristematic activity

**Sol.** (d) Region of meristematic activity is the small region in root having thin walled cells with dense cytoplasm cells of this region are undifferentiated and highly active for cell division and other parts of the root *i.e.* region of elongation, maturation have differentiated cells.

**Q.3** The two examples of offset stem modification are

(a) banana and jasmine (b) mint and jasmine
(c) *Pistia* and mint (d) *Pistia* and *Eichhornia*

**Sol.** (d) A thick short, horizontal branch which grows from the leaf axil of a plant by producing a rosette of leaves above while adventitious roots below is offset stem modification. This is commonly found in aquatic plants like *Eichhornia* and *Pistia*.

**Q.4** The stem modification that develops from axillary bud, slender and spirally coiled

(a) runner (b) tendril
(c) sucker (d) rhizome

**Sol.** (b) Tendril is the modification of stem that develops from an axillary bud, slender and spirally coiled. This helps the plants in climbing *e.g.*, pumpkin, watermelon.

**Q.5** The swollen leaf base in leguminous plants is called

(a) stipules (b) pulvinus
(c) petiole (d) lamina

**Sol.** (b) In certain leguminous plants the leaf base is swollen and called as pulvinus. Leaf base is the lower most part of leaf helping in joining of leaf to the node.

**Q.6** Choose the correct example for alternate phyllotaxy

(a) guava
(b) sunflower
(c) *Calotropis*
(d) marigold

**Sol.** (b) The arrangement of leaves on the stem is called phyllotaxy. Alternate phyllotaxy deals with the manner that single leaf arises at each node in alternate manner *e.g.*, peepal, china rose, mustard, sunflower

**Q.7** The flowers are arranged in which order in cymose inflorescence

(a) acropetal
(b) axipetal
(c) basipetal
(d) tapetal

**Sol.** (c) Inflorescence is the arrangement of flowers. In cymose type of inflorescence the flowers are arranged in basipetal manner *i.e.* younger flowers are at the base while older flowers are at the top. Here the main axis ends in a flower thus has limited growth.

**Q.8** The arrangement of the flowers on the floral axis is called

(a) phyllotaxy
(b) inflorescence
(c) placentation
(d) corymb

**Sol.** (b) Inflorescence is the arrangement of flowers on the floral axis. Based on the growth of limited or unlimited the inflorescence is of two type is *i.e.*, cymose and racemose.

**Q.9** Stamens attached to the petals are called

(a) epipetalous
(b) epiphyllous
(c) staminode
(d) perianth

**Sol.** (a) Stamen is the male reproductive part of the plant. When stamens are united or attached with petals, they are called epipetalous *e.g.*, solanaceae.

Term epiphyllous is used for attachment of stamens to perianth.

**Q.10** The ovules in ovary are attached to which part

(a) placenta
(b) hilum
(c) funicle
(d) Locule

**Sol.** (a) Ovary is the female reproductive part. In ovary, the ovules are attached to placenta through stalk-like structure called funicle. The pattern of ovule attachment is called placentation.

## ☐ Very Short Answer Type

**Q.1** State the difference between gamosepalous and polysepalous.

**Sol.** Difference between gamosepalous and polysepalous are as follows :

| Gamosepalous | Polysepalous |
|---|---|
| It refers to a condition of flowers in which sepals are united or fused. | Polysepalous refers to a condition in flowers that possesses a calyx, consisting of separate sepals. |

**Q.2** Name the type of root present in *Rhizopus* and the function they serve.

**Sol.** The root present in *Rhizopus* is pneumatophores and its function is to help get oxygen for respiration.

## ☐ Short Answer Type

**Q.1 Petals and sepals in a flower can be arranged in different ways. Identify the term used for their arrangement and explain the various arrangements with diagram.**

**Sol.** **Term aestivation is used for the arrangement of petals and sepals in flower.**

**Four types of arrangement are as follows :**

**1. Twisted petals overlap in particular pattern**

**2. Imbricate petals overlap but not in particular direction**

3. Valvate margins of sepals or petals don't overlap

4. Vexillary five petals, two inner most fused (keel), two lateral petals (wings), largest overlapping all (standard).

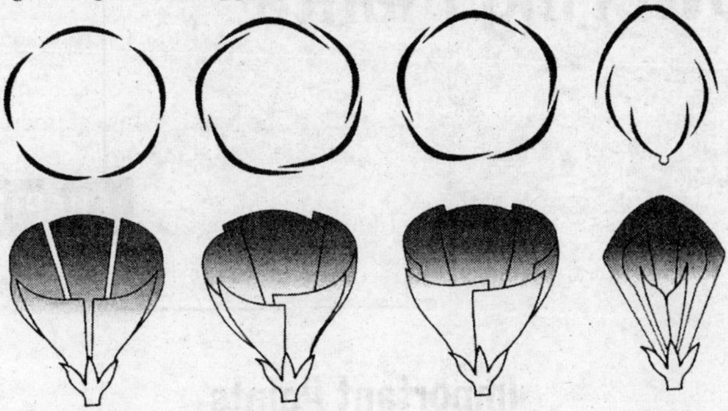

(a) (b) (c) (d)

Type of avestivation (a) valvate (b) Twisted (c) Imbricate (d) vexillary.

# Anatomy of Flowering Plants

CHAPTER 06

## Important Points

**01** Anatomy includes the study of internal structure and functional organisation of plants.

**02** On the basis of structure and location, the tissue system in plants is of three types.

(i) **Epidermal tissue system** forms outermost covering of whole plant body. It comprises of

(a) Epidermal cell (b) Stomata

(c) Epidermal appendages

(ii) **Ground tissue system** includes all tissues except epidermis and vascular bundles. It consists of simple tissue such as **parenchyma, collenchyma** and **sclerenchyma**.

(iii) **Vascular tissue system** consists of complex tissues the **phloem** and the **xylem**.

- Depending upon the relative position of xylem and phloem, vascular bundles are classified as **radial** and **conjoint**.

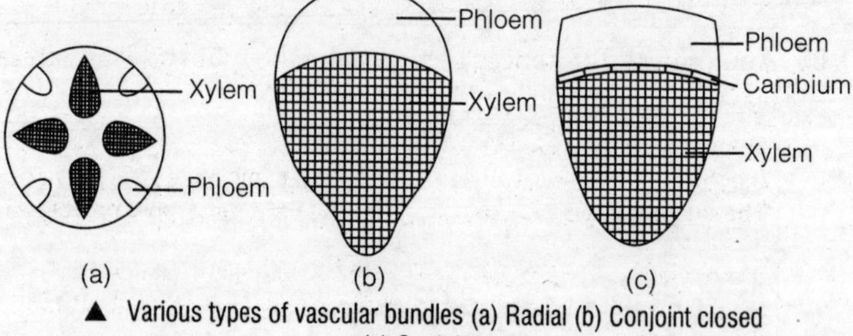


▲ Various types of vascular bundles (a) Radial (b) Conjoint closed (c) Conjoint open

(iv) Cambium is present in between xylem and phloem called vascular cambium which produces secondary xylem and phloem, and hence are called open vascular bundle. When cambium is absent, it is called closed vascular bundle.

**03** Anatomical difference between dicotyledonous and monocotyledonous root are as follows :

| Feature | Dicotyledonous root | Monocotyledonous root |
|---|---|---|
| Number of Xylem and phloem | limited cusually 2-4 vascular bundles | Numerous vascular bundles (more than 6) |
| Pith | Small or absent | Large and well developed |
| Pericycle | Give rise to lateral roots, cork cambium and part of vascular cambium | Give rise only to lateral roots |
| Secondary growth | Present due to activity of vascular cambium | Absent |

**04** Anatomical differences between monocot and dicot stem are as follows :

| | Monocot Stem | Dicot Stem |
|---|---|---|
| 1. | Dumb-bell-shaped guard cell present in stomata. | Kidney-shaped guard cell present in stomata. |
| 2. | Ground tissue is uniform and there is no differentiation. | Ground tissue differentiated into cortex, endodermis, pericycle and pith. |
| 3. | The vascular bundles are scattered in ground tissue and are many in numbers and vary in size. | The vascular bundles are arranged in a ring. |
| 4. | Normally, no secondary growth takes place. | Secondary growth takes place |
| 5. | The primary vascular tissues remains functional throughout the life of the plant. | The older vascular tissues cease functioning after sometimes and are replaced by new ones. |
| 6. | There is little increase in size. | The stem also increase in diameter with age due to secondary growth. |

**05** Anatomical differences between dorsivental and isobilateral leaves are as follows :

| Dorsiventral leaf | Isobilateral leaf |
|---|---|
| It occurs in dicot | It occurs in monocot |
| The sunlight can expose on dorsal surface | The sunlight can expose on both surfaces. |
| It show reticulate venation | It shows parallel venation |
| Stomata are distributed in the ventral surface | Stomata are found in both surfaces |
| Guard cells present in stomata are kidney in shape. | Guard cells present in stomata are dumbbell in shape |

# Exercises

**Question 1** Draw illustrations to bring out the anatomical differences between

(a) Monocot root and dicot root

(b) Monocot stem and dicot stem

**Sol.** (a) Differences between monocot and dicot root are as follows :

| S.N. | Monocot Root | Dicot Root |
|---|---|---|
| 1. | Cortex is very wide. | Cortex is comparatively narrow. |
| 2. | Endodermis contains prominant casparian strips only in young roots. | Endodermis contains prominant casparian strips. |
| 3. | Xylem and phloem bundles are numerous typically or more. | Xylem and phloem bundles are less, generally from 2-6. |
| 4. | Metaxylem vessels are oval or rounded. | Metaxylem vessels generally angular. |
| 5. | No secondary growth takes place. | Secondary growth takes place. |
| 6. | Pith is large and well-developed. | Pith is small or absent. |

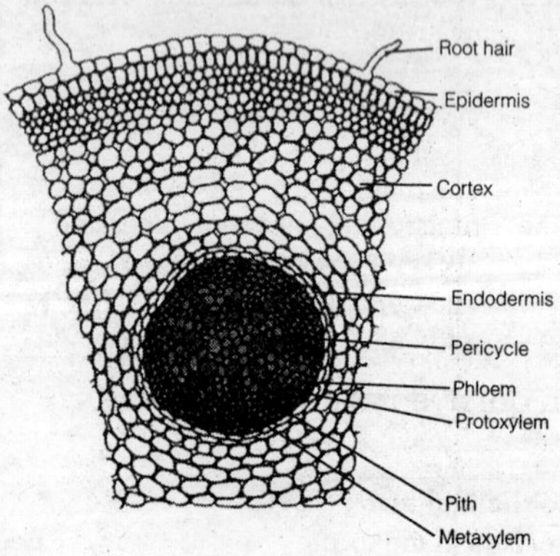


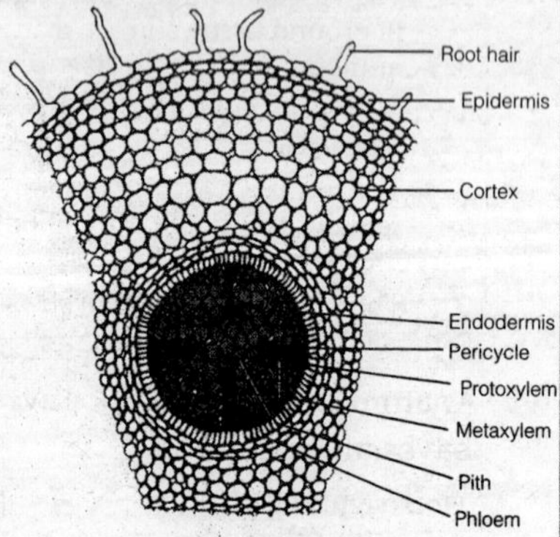

(b) Differences between monocot and dicot stem are as follows :

| S.N. | Monocot Stem | Dicot Stem |
|---|---|---|
| 1. | Dumb bell-shaped guard cells present in stomata. | Kidney-shaped guard cells present in stomata. |
| 2. | Ground tissue is uniform and there is no differentiation. | Ground tissue differentiated into cortex, endodermis, pericycle and pith. |
| 3. | The vascular bundles are scattered in ground tissue and are many in numbers and vary in size. | The vascular bundles are arranged in a ring. |
| 4. | Normally, no secondary growth takes place. | Secondary growth takes place. |
| 5. | The primary vascular tissues remains functional throughout the life of the plant. | The older vascular tissues cease functioning after sometimes and are replaced by new ones. |
| 6. | There is little increase in size. | The stem also increase in diameter with age due to secondary growth. |

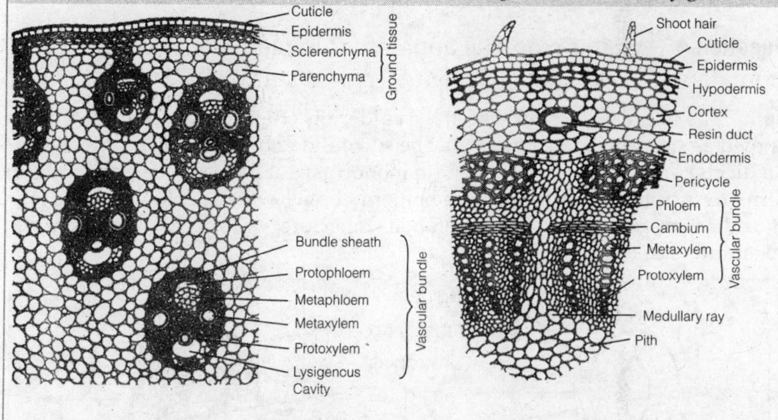


**Question 2** Cut a transverse section of young stem of a plant from your school garden and observe it under the microscope. How would you ascertain whether it is a monocot stem or a dicot stem? Give reasons.

**Sol.** One can ascertain wheather the transverse section of young stem is of monocot or dicot by observing the vascular bundles.

Transverse section of a monocot stem possess following characters

(i) Vascular bundles are conjoint and closed.

(ii) Uniform ground tissue showing no tissue differentiation.

(iii) More than 8 scattered vascular bundles are present.

(iv) Bundle sheaths are present.

(v) Water containing cavities are present within the vascular bundles.

**Transverse section of a dicot stem has following characters**

(i) Differentiation of ground tissue into cortex, endodermis, pericycle and pith.
(ii) The vascular bundles are arranged in a ring around the centrally located pith.
(iii) The vascular bundles are conjoint collateral and open.
(iv) Bundle sheaths are absent.
(v) Medullary rays are present between the vascular bundles.

**Question 3** The transverse section of a plant material shows the following anatomical features

(a) The vascular bundles are conjoint, scattered and surrounded by a sclerenchymatous bundle sheaths.
(b) Phloem parenchyma is absent. What will you identify it as?

**Sol.** It is a transverse section of monocotyledons stem.

**Question 4** What is stomatal apparatus? Explain the structure of stomata with a labelled diagram.

**Sol.** The minute pores present in the epidermis of leaves and green stem are known as stomata. The stomata may be surrounded by either kidney-shaped (in dicots) or by dumb-bell shaped (in monocots) guard cells. The guard cells in turn are surrounded by specialised epidermal cells, which are known as subsidiary or accessory cells. The stomatal aperture, guard cells, accessory cells constitute the stomatal apparatus.

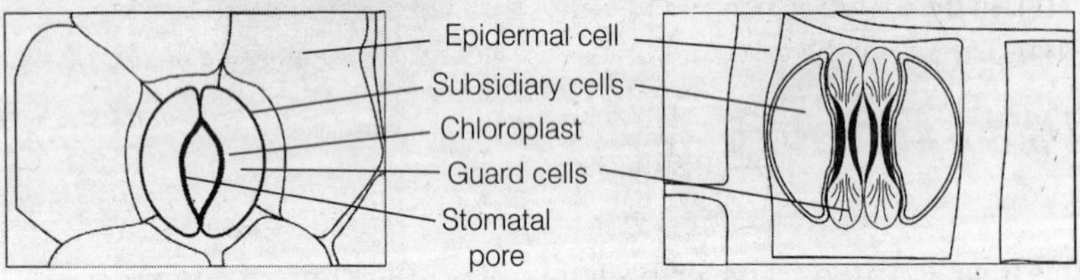


Diagrammatic representation of stomatal apparatus (a) stomata with bean-shaped guards cells (b) stomata with dumb-bell shaped guard cells

**Question 5** Name the three basic tissue systems in the flowering plants. Give the tissue names under each system.

**Sol.** On the basis of structure and location, the three basic tissue systems in the flowering plants are

(i) **Epidermal tissue system** It comprises epidermal cells, stomata and the epidermal appendages which constitute trichome and hairs.
(ii) **Ground tissue system** It consists of simple tissues such as parenchyma, collenchyma and sclerenchyma.
(iii) **Vascular tissue system** It constitutes complex tissues like xylem and phloem.

**Question 6** How is the study of plant anatomy useful to us?

**Sol.** Plant anatomy is the study of internal structure of plants. It is useful to us in the following ways.

(i) It heps us to differentiate between monocots, dicots and gymnosperms. This study is linked to plant physiology and plays important role in improving food crops.

(ii) Study of internal structure of plants helps to understand their adaptations to diverse environments.

(iii) The study of plant anatomy also help in understanding the functional organisation of higher plants.

**Question 7** Describe the internal structure of a dorsiventral leaf with the help of labelled diagrams?

**Sol.** **Internal Structure of a Dorsiventral (dicotyledonous) leaf**

(i) It shows three main parts namely epidermis, mesophyll and vascular system.

(ii) The epidermis which covers both the upper surface (adaxial epidermis) and lower epidermis (abaxial surface) and are covered with thick layer of cuticle.

(iii) The tissue between the upper and lower epidermis is known as mesophyll which is made up of parenchyma and possess chloroplasts which carryout photosynthesis, .

(iv) The mesophyll parenchyma has two types of cells, *i.e.*, palisade parenchyma and spongy parenchyma.

(v) In the midrib region and in veins vascular bundles can be seen.

(vi) The size of the vascular bundles are dependent on the size of veins. The veins vary in thickness in the reticulate venation of dicot leaves.

(vii) The vascular bundles are surrounded by bundle sheath cells.

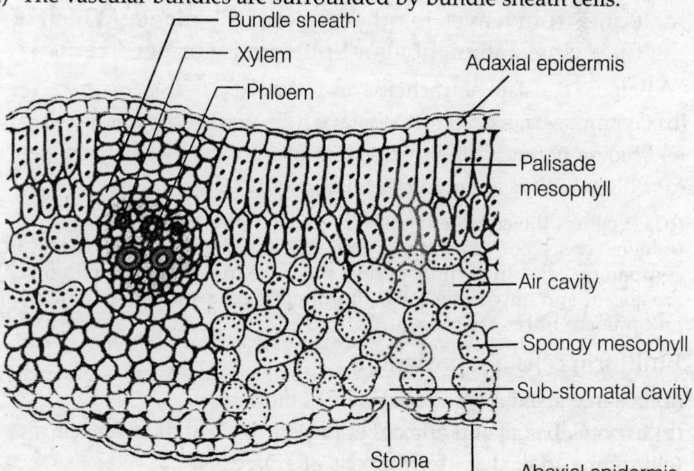


T.S of dicot leaf

## DIKSHA APP Questions

### ☐ Multiple Choice Questions

**Q.1** Which of the following statements is correct for parenchyma tissues ?

(a) Cells have thickened corners due to deposition of lignin
(b) Generally, occurs below epidermis in dicot plants
(c) They are oval, spherical or polygonal shaped cells and often contain chloroplasts
(d) Cells are isodiametric, with thin cellulosic walled and loosely packed having intercellular space.

**Sol.** (d) Parenchyma tissue is characterised by presence of isodiametric ells, having thin cellulose wall and loosely packed due to intercellular space. This is responsible for storage and air exchange (gas exchange.)

**Q.2** Read the given statements about epidermal tissue system and identify the incorrect statement.

(a) Epidermal tissues are made up of elongated, compactly arranged cells, which form a continuous layer
(b) Epidermal hairs on the stem are a called trichomes
(c) Stomata are present in the epidermis of leaves
(d) Epidermal tissue system consists of xylem and phloem

**Sol.** (d) The epidermal tissue system in plants consists of epidermis, stomata cuticle and appendages like trichomes whereas complex tissue is composed of xylem and phloem, which is absent in epidermis

**Q.3** Phloem is a conducting tissue which transports food materials from leaves to other parts of the plants. Which of the following statement about phloem is correct ?

(a) Phloem consists of tracheids and vessels
(b) Gymnosperms do not have sieve tubes and companion cells
(c) Phloem parenchyma is present in most of the monocotyledons
(d) Phloem fibres are made of collenchyma cells

**Sol.** (b) Phloem is the complex tissue in vascular plants. In angiosperms, phloem consists of sieve tubes, phloem parenchyma, phloem fibre and companion cells. In gymnosperms, the sieve tubes and companion cells are absent and only sieve cells, albuminous cells, phloem parenchyma and phloem fibres are present.

**Q.4** Bulliform cells are present in

(a) in some abaxial epidermal cells of monocots
(b) in both abaxial and adaxial epidermal cells of dicot leaves
(c) in some adaxial epidermal cells of grasses
(d) in adaxial epidermal cells of dicot leaves

**Sol.** (c) Bulliform cells (also called motor cells) are large, bubble-shaped cells found in abaxial (upper) epidermis of monocots. Usually, they are found at the mid view part of the leaf.

**Q.5** Secondary growth is shown by

(a) monocot stem (b) monocot root

(c) both monocot and dicot stem (d) dicot stem

**Sol.** (d) Secondary growth is characterised by increase in thickness of root and stem due to formation of secondary vasular tissue. This activity is due to presence of cambium. The cambium is absent in monocots thus they lack secondary growth.

**Q.6** Annual rings seen in a cut stem give an estimate of the age of the plant. What is the age of the tree if its section shows 50 dark and 50 light rings ?

(a) 100 (b) 50 (c) 25 (d) 75

**Sol.** (b) An annual ring is a layer of wood that is formed during a single growing season. One dark and one light ring represent one years of trees life so if the section has 50 dark and 50 light rings, the age of the plant will be 50 years.

**Q.7** Observe the given diagram and select the correct option for arrangement of vascular bundles

**Sol.** (c) In dicot stem, each vascular bundle is conjoint, opend and with endarch protoxylem.

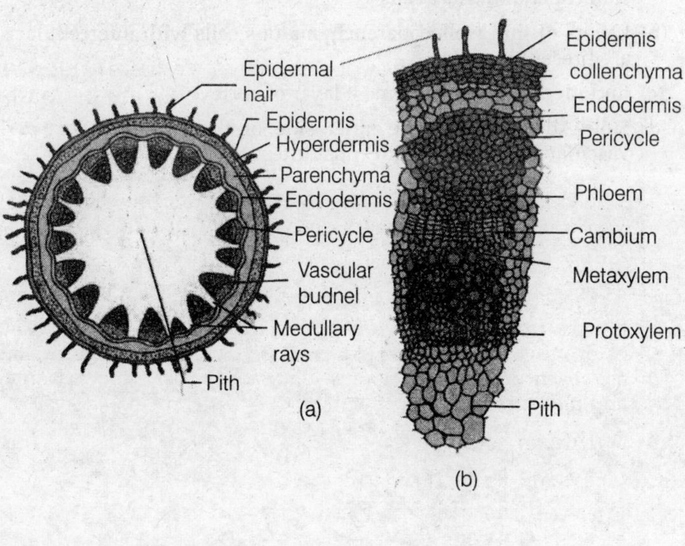

## ☐ Very Short Answer Type

**Q.2** Write the scientific terms for the following

(a) Epidermal hairs on the stems

(b) Specialised cells in the vicinity of guard cells

(c) Specialised parenchymatous cells, closely associated with sieve tube elements.

(c) Few layered thick walled parenchymatous cells, next to endodermis

**Sol.** (a) Trichomes (b) Subsidiary cells (c) companion cells (d) pericycle

## ☐ Short Answer Type

**Q.1** Answer the following questions with reference to anatomy of dicot root:

(a) What are casparian strips and where are they present?

(b) Type of cells present in cortex.

(c) Name the innermost layer of the cortex

(d) What is meant by stele?

**Sol.**

(a) Casparian strips are the depositions of the waxy material-suberin which is impermeable to water, present on the tangential and radial walls of endodermal cells

(b) Layers of thin walled parenchymatous cells with intercellular spaces are present in cortex.

(c) Endodermis is the innermost layer of cortex.

(d) Stele-All tissues on the inner side of the epidermis *i.e.*, pericycle, vascular bundles and pith constitutes stele.

## ☐ Long Answer Type

**Q.1** (a) Draw a neat and well labelled diagram of transverse section of monocot root.

(b) Mention the characteristics of stele of monocot root which differentiates it from dicot root.

**Sol.** (a) Diagram of transverse section of monocot root

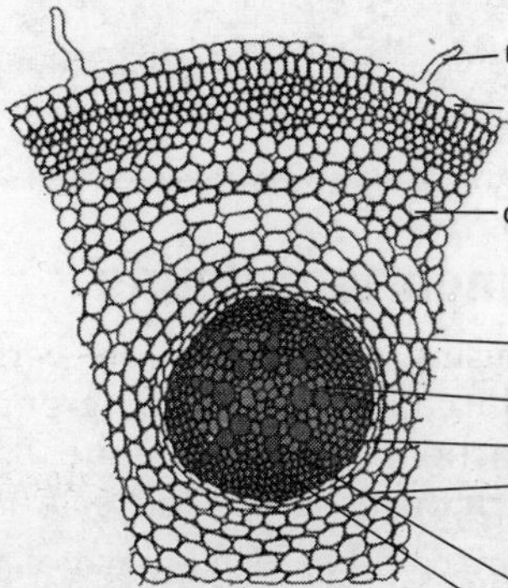


T-S of Monocot root

(b) Difference between the stele of monocot and dicot root are as follows :

| Stele of Monocot root | Stele of dicot coot |
|---|---|
| More than 6 vascular bundles are present | Two to four xylem and phloem patches are present |
| Pith is large and well developed | Pith is very small |
| Secondary growth is absent | Secondary growth is present |
| Cambium is absent | Cambium is present |

# Structural Organisation in Animals

CHAPTER 07

## Important Points

**01** In unicellular organisms, all functions are performed by a single cell, while in multicellular organism, group of similar cells, perform specific functions known as **tissue**. Basic tissue organise to form organs, which then combine to create an organ system.

**02** Frog (*Rana tigrina)* are cold-blooded animals classified under the class amphibia and exhibit key characteristics such as camouflage, hibernation and aestivation.

**03** The body of a frog is divided into a head, which includes the anterior mouth, and a trunk consisting of the thorax and abdomen.

**04** Frogs have smooth, moist and scaless skin.

(i) Digestive system consists of alimentary canal and digestive glands. The alimentary canal consists of buccal cavity, pharynx, oesophagus, stomach, intestine rectum, and finally opens outside by the cloaca.

(ii) Circulatory system of frog consists of blood vascular system and lymphatic system. Heart of the frog is situated in the thoracic region within pericardial cavity and is three-chambered (two atria and one ventricle).

(iii) Excretory system consist of a pair of kidneys, a pair of ureters, the urinary bladder and cloaca and it is ureotelic animal.

(iv) Both neural and endocrine systems are well developed, and chemical co-ordination achieved through hormones secreted by endocrine glands.

(v) Sensory organs includes organ of touch (sensory papillae), taste (taste buds), smell (nasal epithelium), vision (eyes) and hearing (tympanum with internal ears).

(vi) The male reproductive organs include a pair of yellowish, ovoid testes attached to upper part of kidney by a double fold of peritoneum called mesorchium. They also consists of vasa efferentia, a urinogenital duct, and a cloaca.

(vii) Female reproductive organs includes a pair of ovaries, which are not connected with kidneys. A pair of oviduct arises from ovary and opens into cloaca. On an average, a mature female can lay 2500 to 3000 ova at a time.

(viii) Fertilisation is external and requires water. Development involves larval stage called tadpole, which undergo metamorphosis to form the adult.

# Exercises

**Question 1** Draw a neat diagram of digestive system of frog.

**Sol.** A neat diagram of digestive system of frog given below.

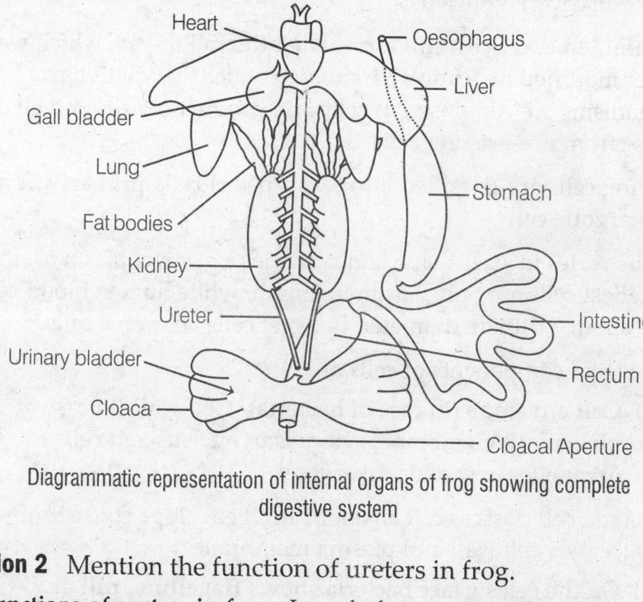


Diagrammatic representation of internal organs of frog showing complete digestive system

**Question 2** Mention the function of ureters in frog.

**Sol. Functions of ureters in frog** In male frog, two ureters emerge from the kidneys. The ureters act as urinogenital duct which opens into cloaca. Thus, the ureters carry both sperms and excretory wastes to the cloaca. In female frog, the ureters and oviduct opens separately in the cloaca. Thus the ureter in frog have a dual role in the excretory and reproductive systems.

# Cell :
# The Unit of Life

CHAPTER 08

## Important Points

**01** **Cell** is the basic functional and structural unit of all living organisms.

**02** **Antony von Leeuwenhoek** firstly saw living cell Robert Brown later discovered nucleus.

**03** **Schleiden** and **Schwann** formulated the cell theory, which was later modified by **Rudolf virchow**. It states that all living organisms are composed of cells and product of cells and all cells arise from pre-existing cells.

**04** Living cells are classified into two types of cells-**prokaryotic** and **eukaryotic cell**.

**05** Cells varies in size, shape and activities *e.g.*, mycoplasm as, the smallest cells are only 0.3 μm in length, while human blood cells are about 7.0 μm in diameter. Longest cells are nerve cells.

**06** The chief components of cells are

(i) **Cell envelope** (in case of bacteria)/ **Cell wall** (in case of plants),cell membrane, cytoplasm, nucleus and cell organelles in case of eukaryotes

**07** Bacteria cell possess cell envelope. Cell envelope consists of glycocalyx, cell wall and plasma membrane

(i) On the cell surface bacteria shows **flagellum, pili** or **fimbriae**.

(ii) Some inclusion bodies are also present like starch grains, glycogen granules, fat droplets, alurone grains and crystals.

08 **Plant cells** are covered by rigid structure called cell wall, which plays an important role in protection, help in cell to cell interaction.

(i) In plants cell wall consists of cellulose, hemicellulose, pectin and lignin.

09 Components of the cells are enclosed in a membrane called **plasma membrane.** It is composed of lipids and protein. It is a **selectively permeable** membrane *i.e.,* it allows only certain component to go in and out. The cell membrane is mainly made up of lipids (especially phospholipids) and proteins (peripheral and integral proteins)

In 1972, **Singer** and **Nicolson** had proposed widely accepted model of membrane called **fluid mosaic model.**

10 In cytoplasm non-membranous RNA-protein complexes are present known as **ribosomes.** These are the site of protein synthesis. They are of two basic types *i.e.,* **70 S** present in prokaryotes and **80 S** present in eukaryotes.

11 **Endoplasmic reticulum, Golgi complex, lysosomes** and **vacuoles** forms endomembrane system because their functions are coordinated.

12 **Endoplasmic reticulum** is a network or reticulum of tiny tubular structure, which are extensions of nuclear membrane.
There are two types of endoplasmic reticulum smooth endoplasmic reticulum and rough endoplasmic reticulum

13 **Golgi apparatus** is the group of cisternae first time observed by Camillo Golgi (1898). They consist of many flat, disc-shaped sacs or cisternae of 0.5-1.0 μm diameter.

14 **Lysosomes** are membrane bound vesicular structures formed by the process of packaging in the golgi apparatus. These structures mainly contain hydrolytic enzymes and aids in cellular digestion.

15 **Vacuoles** are the membrane bound space found in cytoplasm. It contain water, sap, excretory product and other materials not useful for the cell.

16 **Mitochondria** is sausage-shaped or cylindrical having a diameter of 0.2 – 1.0 μm and length of 1.0 – 4.1 μm

(i) Mitochondria is known as **power house of cell**. as, it is associated with cellular respiration and energy generation.

**17** **Plastids** are exclusively found in plant cell and in euglenoids. They have specific type of pigments, thus imparting specific colour to the plants.

(i) They are classified into **chloroplasts, chromoplasts** and **leucoplasts**.

**18** **Chloroplast** are involved in photosynthesis. It contain chlorophyll and carotenoids, which trap light energy for photosynthesis.

(i) Chloroplast is two membranous structure. It is bounded by an outer and an inner membrane with an intermembrane space.

(ii) The matrix inside chloroplast is known as **stroma**. Stroma contains disc-shaped membranous sacs called **thylakoids**. The group of thylakoids forms grana, (sing.-granum).

**19** Shaps maintenance, mechanical support and motility in the cell are maintained by **cytoskeleton**. It includes micro filaments microtubules and intermediate filaments.

**20** **Centrosome** and **centrioles** are the cylindrical structures, which are involved in the spindle formation during cell division.

**21** **Nucleus** was first time described by **Robert Brown** in 1831. It contain chromatin, nucleoplasm and nucleoli, with a nuclear envelope that separates the nucleus from the cytoplasm. Nuclear pores allow the movement of RNA and proteins between the nucleus and cytoplasm, and nucleoli are involved in ribosomal RNA synthesis.

(i) Chromosome contains two sister chromatids, which are joined together at **centromere**. These forms a disc-like structure called **kinetochore,** where mitotic spindles attach during cell division. On the basis of position of centromere the chromosomes are classified into four types

(a) Metacentric chromosome
(b) Sub-metacentric chromosome
(c) Acrocentric chromosome
(d) Telocentric chromosome

# Exercises

**Question 1** Which of the following is not correct?

(a) Robert Brown discovered the cell.

(b) Schleiden and Schwann formulated the cell theory.

(c) Virchow explained that cells are formed from pre-existing cells.

(d) A unicellular organism carries out its life activities within a single cell.

**Sol.** (a) Robert Brown discovered the cell.

**Question 2** New cells generate from

(a) bacterial fermentation

(b) regeneration of old cells

(c) pre-existing cells

(d) abiotic materials

**Sol.** (c) New cell generate from pre-existing cells.

**Question 3** Match the following columns.

| | Column I | | Column II |
|---|---|---|---|
| A. | Cristae | 1. | Flat membranous sacs in stroma. |
| B. | Cisternae | 2. | Infoldings in mitochondria. |
| C. | Thylakoids | 3. | Disc-shaped sacs in golgi apparatus. |

**Sol.**

| | Column I | | Column II |
|---|---|---|---|
| A. | Cristae | 2. | Infoldings in mitochondria. |
| B. | Cisternae | 3. | Disc-shaped sacs in golgi apparatus. |
| C. | Thylakoids | 1. | Flat membranous sacs in stroma. |

**Question 4** Which of the following is correct?

(a) Cells of all living organism have a nucleus.

(b) Both animal and plant cells have a well defined cell wall.

(c) In prokaryotes, there are no membrane bound organelles.

(d) Cells are formed *de novo* from abiotic materials.

**Sol.** (c) In prokaryotes, there are no membrane bound organelles.

**Question 5** What is a mesosome in a prokaryotic cell? Mention the functions that it performs.

**Sol.** Mesosome is a special membranous structure, which is formed by the extension of the plasma membrane in a prokaryotic cell. They helps in cell wall formation, DNA replication and its distribution to daughter cells. They also helps in respiration, secretion processes, increase the surface area of the plasma membrane and enzymatic content.

**Question 6** How do neutral solutes move across the plasma membrane? Can the polar molecules also move across it in the same way? If not, then how are these transported across the membrane?

**Sol.** Neutral solutes can move across the membrane by the process of simple diffusion along the concentration gradient.

No. polar molecules cannot pass through the non-polar lipid bilayer, they require a carrier protein to facilitate their transport across the membrane.

A few ions or molecules are transported across the membrane against their concentration gradient, i.e.,from lower to the higher concentration. Such transport is energy dependent process, in which ATP is utilised and is called active transport, e.g., $Na^+/K^+$ pump.

**Question 7.** Name two cell organelles that are double membrane bound. What are the characteristics of these two organelles. State their functions and draw labelled diagrams of both

**Sol.** Chloroplasts and mitochondria are double membrane bound organelles.

**Characteristics of Mitochondria**

(i) The mitochondria is a sausage-shaped or cylindrical having a diameter of 0.2-1.0 µm and (average 0.5 µm) and length 1.0-4.1 µm.

(ii) Each mitochondrion is a double membrane bound structure.

(iii) The inner compartment is filled with a dense homogenous substance called the matrix.

The outer membrane of mitochondria forms the continuous limiting boundary of the organelle.

(iv) The inner membrane forms a number of infoldings called the cristae (single crista) towards the matrix. The cristae increases the surface area.

(v) The two membranes have their own specific enzymes associated with the mitochondrial function.

(vi) The matrix of mitochonrdria also possess single circular DNA molecule, a few RNA molecules, ribosomes (70 S) and the components required for the synthesis of proteins.

**Functions of mitochondria** Mitochondria are the sites of aerobic respiration. They produce cellular energy in the form of ATP, hence they are known as, 'power houses of the cell.'

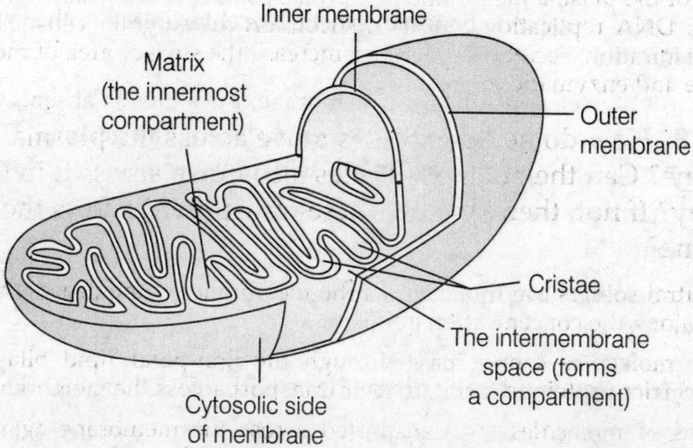


Structure of mitochondria

## Characteristics of Chloroplasts

(i) The chloroplasts are double membrane bound organelles.

(ii) The space limited by the inner membrane of the chloroplast is called stroma.

(iii) A number of organised flattened membranous sacs called the thylakoids are present in the stroma.

(iv) Thylakoids are arranged in stacks-like the piles of coins called grana.

(v) In addition, there are flat membranous tubules called the stroma lamellae connecting the thylakoids of the different grana.

(vi) The membrane of the thylakoids enclose a space called a lumen.

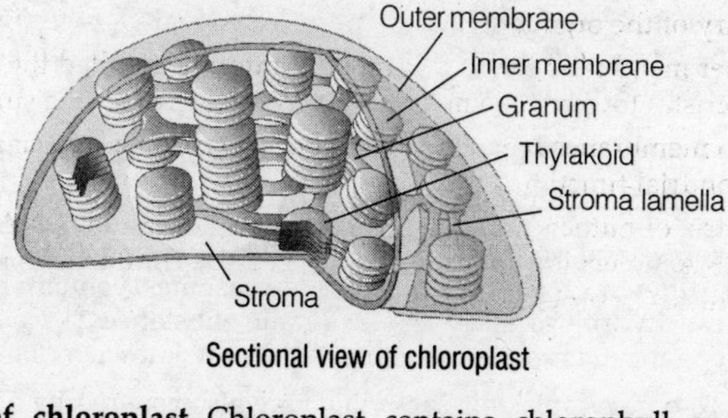


Sectional view of chloroplast

**Functions of chloroplast** Chloroplast contains chlorophyll and car..e.oid **pigments which are responsible for trapping light energy esse.... for photosynthesis.**

**Question 8** What are the characteristics of prokaryotic cells?

**Sol.** Characteristics of prokaryotic cells are as follows :

(i) A prokaryotic cell, *i.e.,* bacteria is surrounded by a cell membrane.

(ii) Absence of membrane bound organelle like chloroplast, mitochondria, nucleus, etc.

(iii) The true nucleus with nuclear membrane, nucleolus is absent. Genetric material is basically naked, known as nucleoid. The genomic DNA of a prokaryotic cell is either circular or single chromosome.

(iv) The cytoplasm is filled with dense granules. Most of these granules are ribosomes.

(v) Many bacteria have small extrachromosomal/extra genomic DNA called plasmid.

**Question 9** Multicellular organisms have division of labour. Explain.

**Sol.** The body of a multicellular organism has cell as a basic structural unit. The cells organised to form tissues such as blood, bone, etc. The tissues organised to form organs such as heart, kidney, etc. The organs then organised to form organ systems such as digestive system, reproductive system and respiratory system, etc. The various organ systems of an organism get arranged to form a complete individual.

**Question 10** Cell is the basic unit of life. Discuss in brief.

**Sol.** Cells are the basic units of life capable of doing all the required biochemical processes that a normal cell has to do in order to live. The basic needs for the survival of all living organisms are same. These processes include respiration, digestion and excretion Cells are capable of performing all processes of body. Hence, cells are called as functional unit of life.

**Question 11** What are nuclear pores? State their function.

**Sol.** Nuclear pores are minute pores in the nuclear membrane formed by the fusion of its two membranes.

**Functions of nuclear pores** Nuclear pores are highly selective in their permeation. They only allow the movements of RNA and proteins in both directions between the nucleus and the cytoplasm.

**Question 12** Both lysosomes and vacuoles are endomembrane structures, yet they differ in terms of their functions. Comment.

**Sol.** Both lysosomes and vacuoles are covered by a single membrane. Both of them perform different types of functions. Lysosomes contain hydrolysing enzymes and can hydrolyse all types of organic substances, except cellulose. They perform phagocytic function. Therefore, they are known as suicidal bags.

The vacuoles are non-cytoplasmic sacs which are also covered by a membrane. The sap vacuoles store sap or water with dissolved organic and inorganic substances. They maintain osmotic pressure or turgidity. Some freshwater invertebrates such as *Amoeba, Paramecium* have contractile vacuoles, which perform osmoregulation and excretion. There are another type of vacuoles such as food vacuole which store food.

Thus, both lysosomes and vacuoles differ from each other in the type of functions they perform.

**Question 13** Describe the structure of the following with the help of labelled diagrams.

(i) Nucleus (ii) Centrosome

**Sol.**

(i) **Nucleus** It is a double membrane bounded protoplasmic body that carries hereditary information. Chemically it contains DNA, basic proteins, non-basic proteins, RNA, lipids and minerals, etc. It is composed of following parts :

(a) **Nuclear envelope** It is made up of two nuclear membranes separated by perinuclear space. The outer membrane is rough due to the presence of ribosomes. Nuclear envelope has many pores which are formed by fusion of two membranes.

(b) **Nucleoplasm or nuclear matrix** It is a colloidal complex that fills the nucleus. Nucleoplasm contains nucleolus and chromatin.

(c) **Chromatin** It is a fibrous hereditary material formed by DNA-histone complex, some non-histone proteins and also RNA.

(d) **Nucleolus** It is naked roughly rounded darkly stained structure which is a site for synthesis of ribosomal RNA. More nucleoli are present in cell, actively carrying out protein synthesis.

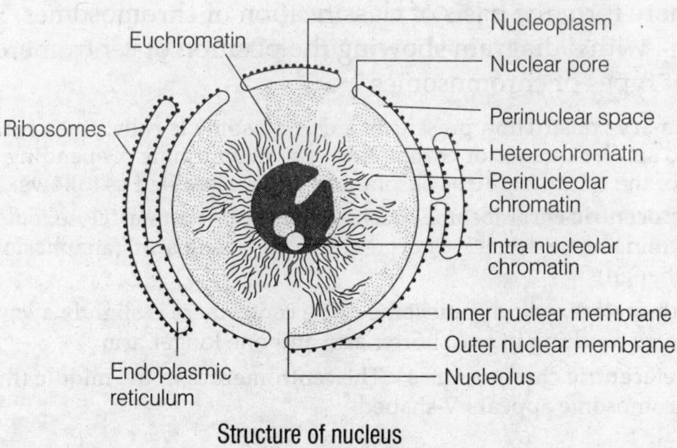


Structure of nucleus

(ii) **Centrosome** It is an organelle usually containing two cylindrical structure called **centrioles**. They are surrounded by amorphous pericentriolar materials. Both the centrioles in a centrosome lie perpendicular to each other.

They are made up of nine evenly spaced, triplet peripheral fibrils of tubulin protein. The central part of the proximal region of centriole is called **hub**, which is connected with tubules of the peripheral triplet by radial **spokes** made of protein.

The centriole form the basal bodies of cilia or flagella and spindle fibres that give rise to spindle apparatus during cell division in animal life.

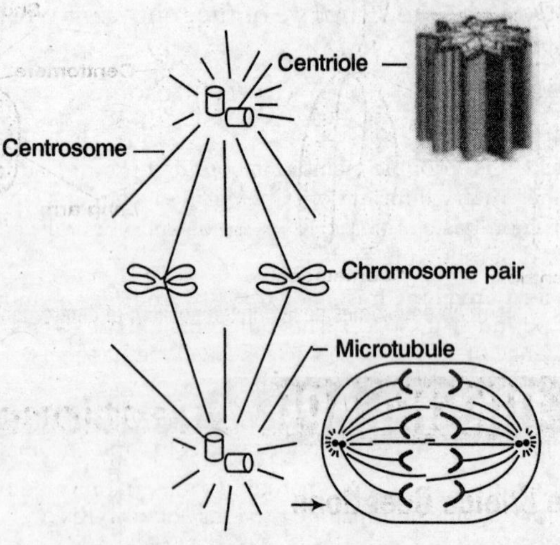


Structure of centrosome

**Question 14.** What is a centromere? How does the position of the centromere form the basis of classification of chromosomes. Support your ans. with a diagram showing the position of centromere on different types of chromosomes.

**Sol.** Primary constriction present in a chromosome is called the centromere It holds two similar threads or chromatids of a chromosome. Depending upon the position of the centromere, the chromosomes are classified as follows

(i) **Acrocentric chromosome** Centromere sub-terminal, close to its end, forming one extremely short and one very long arm. (anaphasic stage J-shaped).

(ii) **Sub-metacentric chromosome** The centromere is slightly away from centre resulting in one shorter arm and one longer arm.

(iii) **Metacentric chromosomes** The centromere is in the middle (the chromosome appears V-shaped.)

(iv) **Telocentric chromosome** Centromere is terminal, (anaphasic stage is I-shaped).

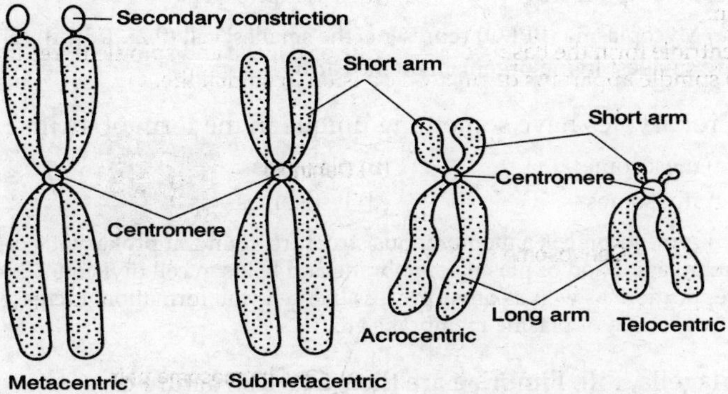


Types of chromosomes based on the position of centromere

## DIKSHA APP Questions

### ☐ Multiple Choice Questions

**Q.1** Who reported that cells had a thin outer layer which is today known as the plasma membrane ?

(a) Robert Hooke (b) Robert Brown
(c) Schleiden (d) T. Schwann

**Sol.** (d) Cell theory was proposed by Schleiden and Schwann. Theodore Schwann British (zoologist) reported that cells had a thin outer layer, presently known as plasma membrane. Robert Hooke for the first time discovered cells (actually cell wall). Robert Brown discovered nucleus of the cell.

**Q.2** Cell organelle which is present in cell-cytoplasm, mitochondria, r-ER and plastids

(a) lysosome (b) ribosome
(c) centriole (d) golgi body

**Sol.** (b) Ribosomes are cell organelles found in cytoplasm, mitochondria plastids and on the surface of rough Endoplasmic reticulum. The ribosomes of mitochondria and plastids are much similar to prokaryotic ribosomes. Ribosomes are responsible for protein synthesis

Lysosome and centriole are found mostly in cytoplasm of cells and not plastids (plant cells).

**Q.3** The smallest cells, only 0.3 μm in length

(a) Mycoplasma (b) RBC's

(c) B. lymphocytes (d) T. lymphocytes

**Sol.** (a) Mycoplasma (PPLO) represents the smallest cell (0.2 – 0.3 μm). These are smallest living organism on the earth.

**Q.4** Prokaryotes have something unique in the form of inclusions

(a) mesosome (b) plasmids

(c) ribosomes (d) lysosomes

**Sol.** (a) A mesosome is a membranous structure found in prokaryotic cell. It is an invagination of plasma membrane and helps in cell division, DNA replication as well as other process like cell wall formation, increase surface area of plasma membrane etc.

**Q.5** Flagella, Pili, Fimbriae are the surface structure of

(a) fungal cell (b) viruses

(c) viroids (d) bacterial cells

**Sol.** (d) Flagella, pili, fimbriae are surface structure of bacterial cells. The main function of flagella is to assist the bacteria in movement. Pili are elongated tubular structure that help in bacterial attachment, movement and DNA uptake. Fimbriae are small bristle like protein appendages that help the bacteria to attach to other bacteria and surface.

**Q.6** Reserve material in prokaryotic cells are stored in the cytoplasm in the form of

(a) m RNA (b) centrioles

(c) inclusion bodies (d) lysosomes

**Sol.** (c) In prokaryotic cells, the reserve material is stored in form of inclusion bodies in cytoplasm, *e.g.*, glycogen granules, cyanophyceas granules and phosphate granules.

**Q.7** Fluid mosaic model was proposed by

(a) Matthias Schleiden (b) Leeuwenhoek

(c) Theodore Schwann (d) Singer and Nicolson

**Sol.** (d) Fluid mosaic model of the cell membrane was proposed by Singer and Nicolson. It discribes how the components of cell membrane such as proteins, phospholipids and carbohydrate set together to develope a dynamic system for separating inner and outer environment of the cell.

**Q.8** Non-living rigid structure of cell is called

(a) plasma wall (b) cell wall

(c) nuclear membrane (d) vacuole

**Sol.** (b) Cell wall is the non-living rigid structure of plant cells. It provides structural support and protection It also develops cementing layer between adjacent plant cells.

**Q.9** Which of them is not include in Endomembrane system?

(a) ER (b) golgi body
(c) mitochondria (d) vacuoles

**Sol.** (c) Endomembrane system in eukaryotic cells is a group of organelles and membranes that works together to modify, package and transport proteins and lipids. The endomembrane system includes and endoplasmic reticulum, golgi body, lysosomes, vacuoles. Since, the functions of mitochondria, chloroplast and peroxisomes are not coordinated so they are not considered as a part of endomembrane system.

**Q.10** Membrane bound vesicular structure of cell are

(a) lysosomes (b) vacuoles
(c) golgi apparatus (d) mitochondria

**Sol.** (a) Lysosomoes are membrane bound vesicular strucuture of the cell. These organelles contain digestive enzymes which functions at acidic pH. Lysosomes are formed by packing of enzymes into vesicles by budding from golgi apparatus.

**Q.11** Granum and stroma are the internal structure of

(a) chloroplast (b) vacuole
(c) nucleus (d) ER

**Sol.** (a) Chloroplast is found in plant and euglenoids. This is double membrane bound organelles. The internal space is filled with stroma. Granum is formed by thylakoids, which are Hatlened membranous sac like structure. These are site of photosynthesis.

**Q.12** Eukaryotic ribosomes are

(a) 80S (b) 505S
(c) 70S (d) 60S

**Sol.** (a) Ribosomes are ribonucleoprotein particles. In eukaryotic cell, 80 S ribosomes are found having subunit of 60 S and 40 S. Where as in prokaryotic cells, 70 S ribosomes are found having 50 S and 30 S subunit. Ribosomes are also found in chloroplast and mitochondria but their size is smaller than cytoplasmic ribosomoes. (80s)

**Q.13** Centrioles are the cylindrical structures of

(a) nucleus
(b) centrosome
(c) chromosomes
(d) cytoskeleton

**Sol.** (b) Centrosome is made up of two centrioles surrounded by pericentriolar material. Centrosome is involved in cell division, cell mobility, signaling, adhesive and protein trafficking.

**Q.14** Material of nucleus was given the name chromatin by

(a) Fleming (b) Robert Hooke
(c) Schwann (d) Robert brown

**Sol.** (a) Walther Flemming used the term chromatin to describe the material of nucleus which was stained by basic dyes.

**Q.15** Chromosome has middle centromere forming two equal arms of the chromosomes is called

(a) metacentric (b) sub metacentric
(c) telo centric (d) acrocentric

**Sol.** (a) In metacentric chromosome, the centromere is located in the middle *i.e.* *V* shaped chromosome.

In submeta, centric chromosomes, the centromere is located slightly away from the centre *i.e.* *L* shaped

In telocentric chromosomes, the centromere is terminal so rod shaped chromosomes.

The chromosome having centromere close to its end is called acrocentric.

## ☐ Short Answer Type

**Q.1** What do you understand about the endomembrane system of cells? Explain any two cell organelles which are not considered as part of the endomembrane system.

**Sol.** The endomembrane system of cells is a group of membrane bound and organelles in eukaryotic cells that works together to modify, package, and transport lipids and proteins.

Mitochondria and chloroplast are not considered as part of endomembrane system.

### Mitochondria

The mitochondria is a double membrane bound structure with the outer membrane and the inner membrane dividing its lumen distinctly into two aqueous compartments, *i.e.*, the outer compartment and the inner compartment.

Mitochondria is essential for aerobic respiration.

### Chloroplast

They are green coloured plastids which are disc shaped. The space limited by inner membrane of chloroplast is called stroma and it has organised flattened membranous sac called the thylakoids.

Photosynthesis is performed in chloroplast.

**Q.2** Draw a well labelled diagram of chromosome which shows satellite and secondary constriction. Write the type of chromosome.

**Sol.** The type of chromosome present in above diagram showing satellite and secondary constriction is metacentric chromosome.

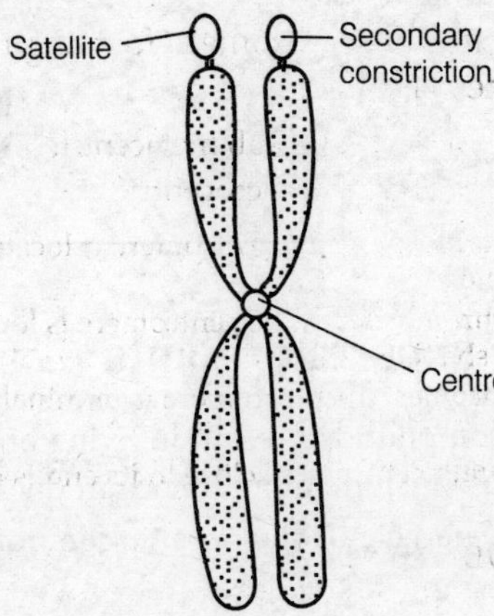


**Q.3** Write the name of four prokaryotic cells. Write the name of two types of bacterial cells on the basis of its cell envelope.

**Sol.** Bacteria, blue green algae, mycoplasma (the smallest cell), PPLO (Pleuropneumonia like organisms) are prokaryotic cells.

Gram positive and Gram Negative are two types of bacterial cells on the basis of it cell envelope.

# Biomolecules

CHAPTER 09

## Important Points

**01** All the chemical compounds present in living organisms is called **biomolecules**.These include inorganic components such as $Na^+$, $K^+$, $Ca^{++}$, $Mg^{++}$, water, etc, while organic components are discussed below.

**02** **Amino Acids**

(i) Organic compounds containing an amino group and an acidic group as substituents on the same carbon, *i.e.*, the α-carbon. Hence, they are called α-amino acids.

(ii) There are four substituent groups occupying the four valency positions → hydrogen, carboxyl group, amino group and a variable group designated as *R* group.

(iii) Chemical and physical properties.
Based on number of amino and carboxyl groups they can be acidic (glutamic acid), basic (lysine), neutral (valine) and aromatic amino acid (tyrosine)

**04** **Lipids** are generally water insoluble; could be simple fatty acids and glycerol

A fatty acid consists of a carboxyl group attached to an *R* group (1-19 carbon atom) and can be either saturated or unsaturated. Many lipids contain both glycerol and fatty acids, forming glycerides which are collectively referred to as fats and oils.

**05** **Nucleosides** Nitrogen base + sugar, *e.g.*, adenosine, guanosine, thymidine, uridine, cytidine.

**06 Nucleotides** Nitrogen base + sugar + phosphate group, *e.g.*, adenylic acid, thymidylic acid, guanylic acid, uridylic acid, cytidylic acid.

**07 Primary Metabolites** These are the organic compounds such as amino acids, sugars, etc.

**08 Secondary Metabolites** They are found in plant, fungal and microbial cells. *e.g.*, Alkaloids, flavonoids, rubber, essential oils, antibiotics, coloured pigments, scents, gums, spices, etc.

**09 Biomacromolecules** They are found in the acid insoluble fraction (molecular weights more than one thousand daltons).

**10 Proteins** They are polypeptides with linear chains of amino acids linked by peptide bonds.

**11 Polysaccharides**

(i) They are long chains of sugars, containing different monosaccharides as building blocks.

(ii) In a polysaccharide chain, right end is reducing end, left end is non-reducing end.

**12 Nucleic Acid** Nucleic acids are polynucleotides, with DNA containing deoxyribose and RNA containing ribose.

**13 Structure of Proteins**

(i) **Primary structure** Sequence of a chain of amino acids.

(ii) **Secondary structure** Hydrogen bonding of the peptide backbone causes the amino acids to fold into a repeating pattern.

(iii) **Tertiary structure** Three dimensional folding pattern of a protein due to side chain interactions.

(iv) **Quaternary structure** Some proteins consisting of more than one polypeptide or sub-units.

**14 Enzymes**

(i) Almost all enzymes are proteins, except ribozyme (nucleic acid behave like enzymes).

(ii) Enzymes have active sites, through which they catalyse the reaction at a high rate.

**15 Chemical Reactions** When bonds are broken and new bonds are formed during transformation, is called **chemical reactions** :

**Organic chemical reaction**-Hydrolysis of starch into glucose.

Rate of a physical or chemical process = Amount of product formed per unit time.

$$\text{Rate} = \frac{\delta P}{\delta t}$$

**16 Working of Enzymes**

Enzyme bind to substrates at their active sites, forming an enzyme-substrate complex that undergo a transition state. This lowers the activation energy, allowing reactions to proceed faster and more efficiently.

**17 Activation Energy**

The minimum energy required for a reaction to occur. It represents the energy barrier that reactants must overcome to be converted into products.

**18 Nature of Enzyme Action**

When the substrate binds tightly to the enzyme's active site, it forms a new enzyme-product complex. After the product is released, the enzyme becomes free to bind with another substrate molecule.

**19 Factors Affecting Enzyme Activity**

(i) Temperature and pH.

(ii) Concentration of substrate

**20 Classification and Nomenclature of Enzymes**

Oxidoreductase-oxidation-reduction reaction

Transferases Transfer group from one substrate to another

Hydrolases Add water across bond to effect hydrolysis of bond

Lyases Addition of group across double bond or loss of group to leave double bond.

Isomerases Interconversion of isomers

Ligases Formation of new bond between two substrates with participation of ATP.

**21 Co-factors**

(i) In some cases, non-protein constituents called co-factors are bound to the enzyme to make enzyme catalytically active.

(ii) Protein portion is called apoenzyme.

**Types of co-factors**

(a) **Prosthetic group** Organic compound.

(b) **Co-enzymes** Organic compound, but their association with the apoenzyme is only transient usually occurring during the course of catalysis.

(c) **Metal ions**, is a co-factor.

# Exercises

**Question 1** What are macromolecules? Give examples.

**Sol.** Chemical compounds which are found in the acid insoluble fraction are called macromolecules or biomacromolecules. For example, proteins, lipids starch and glycogen etc.

**Question 2** What is meant by tertiary structure of proteins?

**Sol.** Tertiary structure of proteins is generally stabilised by non-local interactions, most commonly the formation of a hydrophobic core, along with salt bridges, hydrogen bonds, and disulphide bonds.

The term 'tertiary structure' is often used as synonymous with the term fold. The tertiary structure is what controls the basic function of the protein.

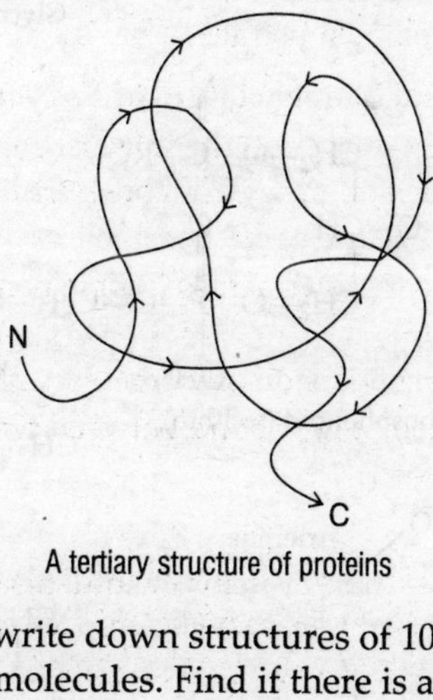


A tertiary structure of proteins

**Question 3** Find and write down structures of 10 interesting small molecular weight biomolecules. Find if there is any industry which manufactures the compounds by isolation. Find out who are the buyers.

**Sol.**

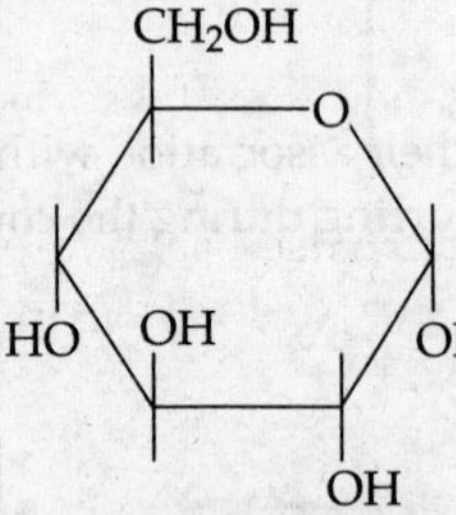

$C_6H_{12}O_6$ (Glucose)

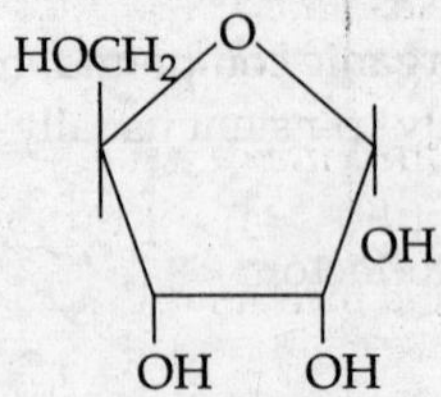

$C_5H_{10}O_5$ (Ribose)

Sugars (carbohydrates)

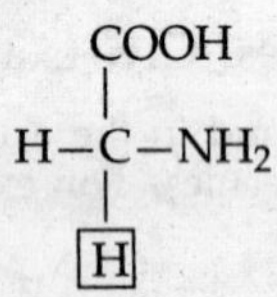

Glycine

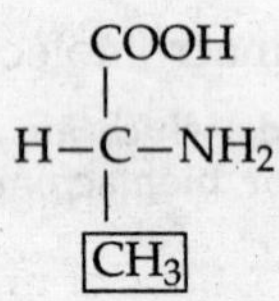

Alanine

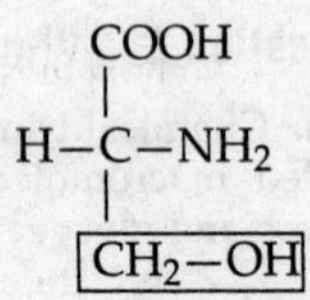

Serine

$CH_3-(CH_2)_{14}-COOH$

Fatty acid
(Palmitic acid)

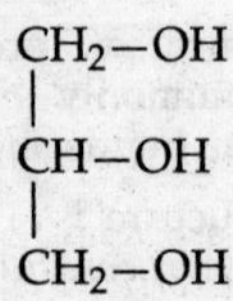

Glycerol

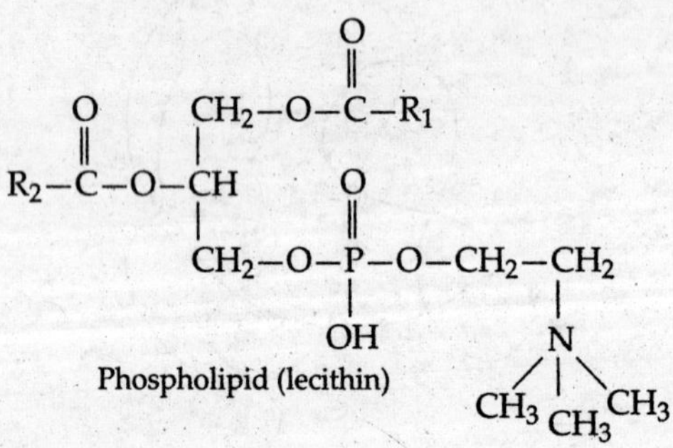

Phospholipid (lecithin)

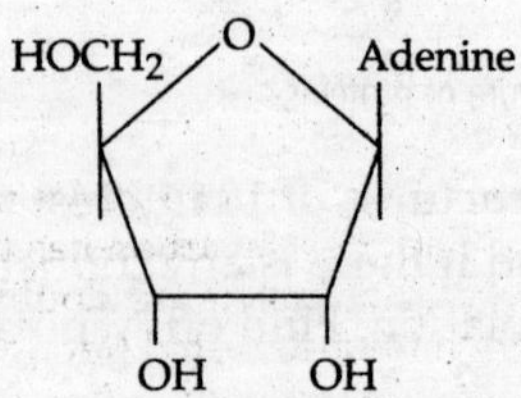


Adenosine

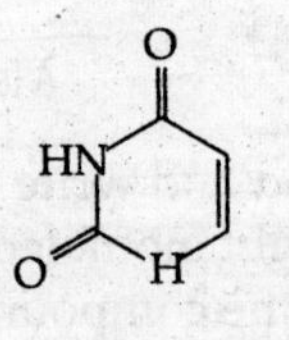

Uracil (pyrimidine)

**Diagrammatic representation of small molecular weight**

Kosha impex (*P*) etd, marudhar apparels and map ltd. e.t.c. are the industry which manufactures the compound by isolation.

Research laboratories, educational institutes and other industries which uses biomolecules as a precursor are the buyers.

**Question 4** Find out and make a list of proteins used as therapeutic agents. Find other applications of proteins (*e.g.*, cosmetics, etc.)

**Sol.** (i) Some proteins and their functions

| Protein | Functions |
|---|---|
| Insulin (Hormone) | used to treat diabetes |
| Streptokinase (enzyme) | used for dissolving clots |
| Immunoglobulin (antibodies) | Treatment of various diseases. |
| Oxytocin (Hormone) | used for inducing uterine contractions to induce labour during pregnancy |

(ii) Other applications of proteins are in manufacture of biological buffers, research methods, the dairy and textile industries, and cosmetics.

**Question 5** Explain the composition of triglyceride.

**Sol.** Triglycerides are composed of two types of molecules, *i.e.*, glycerol (3 carbon molecules) esterified with three fatty acids. The following is a structural representation of a triglyceride at the molecular level

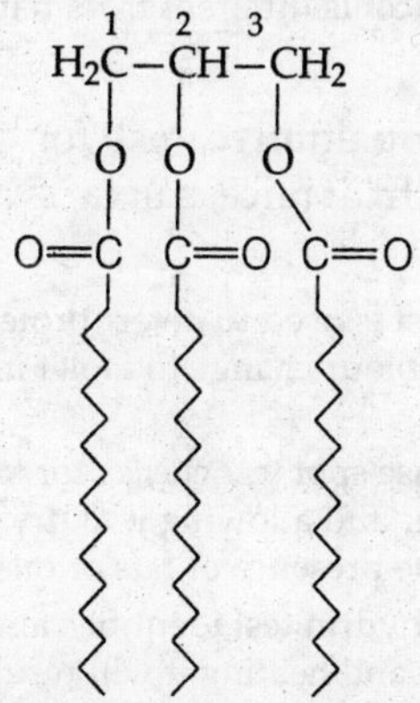

Fatty acids are long chains of hydrocarbons ranges from 4-22 (or more) carbons atoms along with a carboxyl group at one end. If each carbon has two hydrogen atoms, the fatty acid is saturated. If two carbon atoms are double-bonded, so that there is less hydrogen in the fatty acid, it is unsaturated (monounsaturated). If more than two carbon atoms are unsaturated, the fatty acid is polyunsaturated.

**Question 6** Can you attempt building models of biomolecules using commercially available atomic models (Ball and stick models).

**Sol.** Yes, we can make models of biomolecules using commercially available atomic models.

**Question 7** Draw the structure of the amino acid, alanine.

**Sol.**

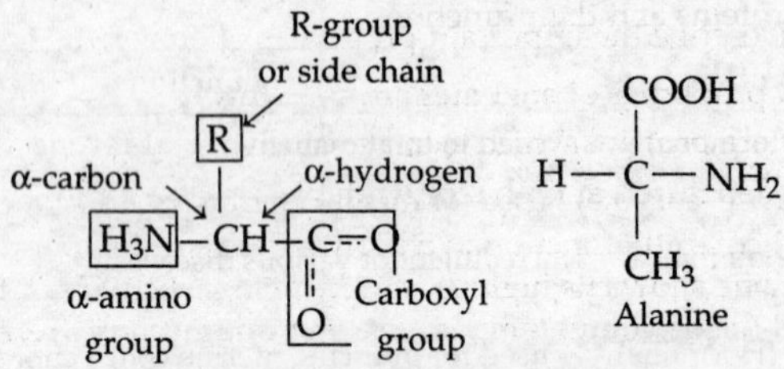


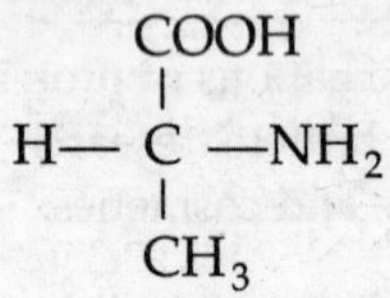

Alanine

**Question 8** What are gums made of? Is fevicol different?

**Sol.** Gums are made of carbohydrates, *i.e.,* L-rhamnose, D-galactose and D-galacturonic acid, etc. Fevicol is different from natural gums. It is a synthetic product.

**Question 9.** Find out a qualitative test for proteins, fats and oils, amino acids and test any fruit juice, saliva, sweat and urine for them.

**Sol.**

1. **Proteins** The Biuret test is used to detect proteins; when Biuret reagent is added to a sample, a colour change to violet indicates the presence of proteins.
2. Fats and Oils The grease spot test checks for fats and oils; by applying a sample to brown paper and allowing it to dry, a translucent spot remaining indicates the presence of fats or oils.
3. **Amino Acids** The ninhydrin test identifies amino acids; adding ninhydrin to a sample and heating it will result in a colour change (usually purple or blue) if amino acids are present.

   **Testing Samples**

   The fruits juice can be for proteins and amino acids, saliva for proteins, fats and amino acids, sweat for proteins and amino acids, and urine for proteins and amino acids.

**Question 10** Find out how much cellulose is made by all the plants in the biosphere and compare it with how much of paper is manufactured by man and hence, what is the consumption of plant material by man annually. What a loss of vegetation

**Sol.** Approximately, 100 billion tonnes of cellulose are made per year by all the plants in the biosphere and it takes 17 full grown trees to make one ton of paper. Hence, it is difficult to calculate the annual consumption of plant material by man.

**Question 11** Describe the important properties of enzymes.

**Sol.** Important properties of enzymes are as follows :

(i) Enzymes are proteins which catalyse biochemical reactions in the cells.

(ii) They are denatured at high temperatures.

(iii) Enzymes generally function in a narrow range of temperature and pH. Each enzyme shows its highest activity at a particular temperature and pH called the optimum temperature and optimum pH respectively.

(iv) With the increase in substrate concentration, the velocity of the enzymatic reaction rises at first, the reaction ultimately reaches a maximum velocity ($v_{max}$) which is not exceeded by any further rise in concentration of the substrate.

(v) The activity of an enzyme is also sensitive to the presence of specific chemicals that bind to the enzyme.

(vi) Enzymes are substrate specific in their action.

# DIKSHA APP Questions

## ☐ Multiple Choice Questions

**Q.1** Any chemical substance affecting enzyme catalysed reaction can be described as competitive inhibitor if

(a) its effect is decreased by raising substrate concentration

(b) it is the final product released during that reaction

(c) it switches off the gene synthesising the enzyme

(d) it permanently changes the shape of active site

**Sol.** (a) Any chemical substance affecting enzyme catalysed reaction can be described as competitive inhibitor if its effect is decreased by raising substrate concentration. This is because substrate and competitive inhibitor both complete for same active site. So, by raising substrate concentration the effect of competitive inhibitor can be controlled.

**Q.2** The living state is best described as

(a) state of perfect equilibrium

(b) condition in which cells do not exchange substances

(c) a non equilibrium steady state

(d) a state with no metabolic activity

**Sol.** (c) The living state is best described as a non equilibrium steady state where organisms maintain dynamic processes that allow them to stay active and functional.

**Q.3** The term cellular pool means

(a) some total of different types of biomolecules and other compounds that are present in a cell

(b) different chemical compounds and metabolites

(c) inorganic molecules and elements present int he cell

(d) minerals and organic materials present in the cell.

**Sol.** (a) Cellular pool is a collection of organic and inorganic molecules present in a cell. The organic molecules are in term of carbohydrates lipids, proteins and nucleic acids. The inorganic molecules include water and minerals.

**Q.4** The ash obtained after burning the dry tissue mainly contains

(a) minerals (b) organic elements

(c) inorganic elements (d) biomolecules

**Sol.** (c) If a dry tissue is burnt fully, the obtained ash will contain inorganic elements. All the carbon compounds will be oxidised to gaseous form.

**Q.5** Large sized complex chemicals that have higher molecular weight (usually 10,000 Daltons and above except lipids) with low solubility and complex conformation are called.

(a) monomers

(b) biomacromolecules

(c) bio micro molecules

(d) polymers

**Sol.** (b) Large sized complex chemicals having molecular weight higher than 10,000 Dalton are called biomacromolecules. They have low solubility and complex conformation. On the other hand, monomers have high solubility and simple conformation.

**Q.6** The R-group on an amino acid contains

(a) water

(b) carbon dioxide

(c) an organic molecule

(d) fatty acid

**Sol.** (c) The *R*-group of an amino acid is typically an organic molecule, and it can vary greatly depending on the amino acid. It can be simple atom like hydrogen, or a more complex structure like carboxyl group.

**Q.7** Secondary metabolites are chemicals produced inside the plants in small quantities. Their extraction from the plant is difficult and expensive, out of the following techniques which can be used for producing secondary metabolities on a larger scale for human welfare.

(a) By cultivation of plant cells in culture medium
(b) By finding out better techniques of extraction
(c) By stopping the sue of secondary metabolities inside the plants
(d) By hybridisation in different mediums

**Sol.** (a) Production and extraction of secondary metabolities from the plant is dificult and expensive, therefore, tissues culture techniques like callus culture, protoplast culture, micropagation are used for production of secondary metabolites at large scale.

**Q.8** What kind of advantage do organisms get from secondary metabolites.

(a) Behavioral (b) Ecological
(c) Structural (d) Physiological

**Sol.** (b) Secondary metabolites provide ecological advantages by helping organisms with defense, competition and attraction of pollinators

**Q.9** The carbon containing chemicals and molecules involved in metabolic processes of living organisms are called

(a) mineral elements (b) inorganic molecules
(c) biomolecules (d) organic molecules

**Sol.** (c) Carbon containing chemicals and molecules involved in metabolic processes of living organisms are called biomolecules. Inorganic molecules and mineral elements do not contain carbon.

**Q.10** Keratin, myosin, alpha and beta tubulins and Myoglobin, all these biomolecules are

(a) lipids (b) carbohydrates
(c) nucleic acids (d) proteins

**Sol.** (d) Keratin, myosin, alpha and beta tubulins and myoglobin are protein molecules. Proteins are polymers of amino acids linked by peptide bond.

**Q.11** The amide bond or NHCO is formed during the formation of

(a) proteins from amino acids
(b) nucleic acids from nucleotides
(c) polysaccharides from monosaccharides
(d) lipids from fatty acids

**Sol.** (a) The amide bond —NHCO is formed during formation of proteins from amino acids. This includes peptide synthesis. Phosphodiester bond is formed between nucleotide in nucleic acids. Glycosidic bond is formed between monomers in carbohydrate.

**Q.12** Which structure of the protein molecule will be most affected, when a hydrophilic amino acid is replaced by a hydrophobic amino acid.

(a) Primary only (b) Secondary only
(c) Primary and Tertiary (d) Primary and Secondary

**Sol.** (c) The replacement of hydrophilic amino acid by hydrophobic amino acid disrupt the interaction between amino acid and surrounding water molecules which leads to change in pattern of protein folding. By this replacement tertiary structure of protein is most affected.

**Q.13** A polysaccharide has glucose monomers with (1-4) beta linkages. There is no branching. It is

(a) cellulose (b) chitin
(c) alpha amylase (d) amylopectin

**Sol.** (a) Cellulose is a polysaccharide made up of β-glucose subunits formed by 1-4 glycosidic linkage. It is unbranched and most abundant organic compound. Chitin is an amino polysaccharide which is polymer of N-acetyl glycosamine.

**Q.14** 1-4 glcosidic linkage between glucose and galactose inside the memory glands results information of

(a) fructose (b) cellulose
(c) lactose (d) maltose

**Sol.** (c) Lactose also called milk sugar is a disaccharide made from 1-4 glycosidic linkage between glucose and galactose inside the mammary glands.

**Q.15** In nucleic acid 3 carbon of sugar of one nucleotide binds to the 5′ carbon of sugar of next nucleotide, releasing 2 water molecules. Name the bond formed during this reaction.

(a) Hydrogen bond (b) Glycosidic bond
(c) Peptide bond (d) Phosphodiester bond

**Sol.** (d) In nucleic acid 3′ carbon of sugar of one nucleotide binds to 5′ carbon of sugar of next nucleotide, releasing water molecules leads to phosphodiester bond formation. This is a covalent bond between phosphate group and hydroxyl group.

**Q.16** Upon hydrolysis of nucleic acids which of the following will not be obtained

(a) phosphoric acid (b) pentose sugar
(c) nitrogenous base (d) Alpha d-glucose

**Sol.** (d) Nucleic acid is a polymer of nucleotides. Each nucleotide is composed of pentose sugar, phosphoric acid and nitrogenous base. Alpha d-glucose is a hexose sugar.

**Q.17** The area rich in A-T base pairs can undergo easy denaturation whereas area rich in G-C base pairs is comparatively more stable, because.

(a) A-T base pairs has only two hydrogen bonds and G-C base pair has three hydrogen bonds
(b) A-T base pair has weak hydrogen bonds where as G-C base pair has strong hydrogen bond
(c) It is difficult to break bond between G-C base pairs as compared to break bonds between A-T base pairs.
(d) A-T base pairs has four hydrogen bonds and G-C base pair has three hydrogen bonds.

**Sol.** (a) DNA is double helical structure where A of one strand joined to T of complementary strand by two hydrogen bonds while G of one strand formed with C of other strand by three hydrogen bonds. Therefore, on denaturation, A-T base pairing can be easily broken as compared to G-C base pairing.

**Q.18** A multi-step interlinked series of enzyme catalysed biochemical reactions in which product of 1 reaction generally becomes substrate for the next, is known as

(a) enzyme catalysed reaction (b) metabolic pathway
(c) catabolic pathway (d) anabolic pathway

**Sol.** (b) The interlinked series of enzyme catalysed biochemical reactions where product of one reaction becomes substrate for the next reaction is called metabolic pathway.

**Q.19** The small heat stable, dialysable, nonprotein part of conjugate enzyme is known as

(a) Co-factor (b) coenzyme
(c) prosthetic group (d) apoenzyme

**Sol.** (a) A co-factor is a small, non-protein molecule or ion that binds to an enzyme and is essential for its activity.

## ☐ Short Answer Type

**Q.1** Both starch and cellulose are polymers of glucose, but starch gives blue black color with Iodine whereas no such color is obtained cellulose.

**Sol.** 1. Starch forms helical secondary structure and holds iodine molecules in the helical portion which imparts blue black color.

2. Cellulose is made up of unbranched chains of glucose molecular which are arranged parallel to each other and can not hold iodine molecules. Hence no color is imparted to cellulose by iodine.

## ☐ Long Answer Type

**Q.1** (a) Why enzyme activity gets affected by changing conditions in the medium in which they act.

(b) List various conditions that affect the activity of an enzyme.

(c) Depict graphically the effect of changing substrate concentration on the activity of enzyme.

**Sol.** (a) The activity of an Enzyme can be affected by a change in the conditions which can alter tertiary structure of proteins and all enzymes are made up of proteins, so their activity is affected by such conditions.

(b) Conditions that affect the activity of enzyme are

(i) temperature

(ii) pH

(iii) substrate concentration

(iv) any chemical that binds to the enzyme and affect the conformation of active site.

(c) $S$ = substrate, $V$ = velocity of reaction

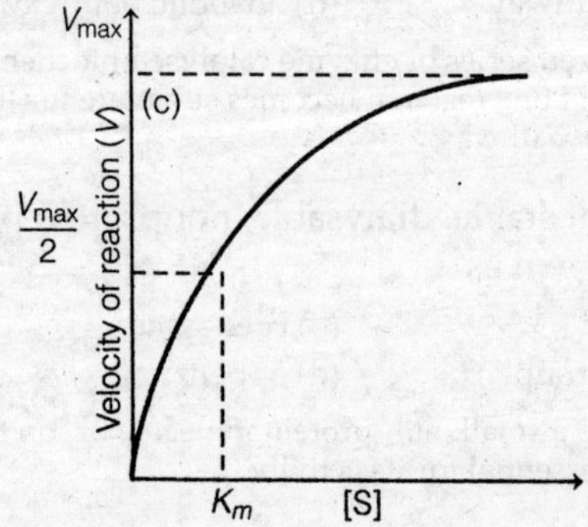


**Concentration of substrate on enzyme activity.**

# Cell Cycle and Cell Division

CHAPTER 10

## Important Points

**01** The sequence of events by which a cell duplicates its genome, synthesises the other constituents of the cell and eventually divides into two daughter cells is called **cell cycle**.

**02** **Phases of cell cycle** Cell cycle is divided into two basic phases

(i) **Interphase** It represents the phases between two successive *M* phase. It is divided into $G_1$ phase, *S*-phase and $G_2$ phase

(ii) **M-phase** (mitosis phase) represent the phase where actual cell division or mitosis occurs.
It starts with nuclear division, corresponding to the separation of daughter chromosomes (karyokinesis) and usually ends with division of cytoplasm (cytokinesis).

**03** **Quiescent Stage** ($G_0$)

Some cells that do not divide further exit $G_1$-phase to enter an inactive stage called quiescent stage ($G_0$).

**04** Mitosis has been divided into four stages of nuclear division (karyokinesis)

(i) Prophase

(ii) Metaphase

(iii) Anaphase

(iv) Telophase

(i) **Prophase**

It is first stage of mitosis. During this phase, the chromosome condense along with this nuclear membrane, nucleoles, ER, golgi apparatus starts to disappear. Centriole duplicate and more to opposite pole of the cell.

(ii) **Metaphase**

Starts with complete disintegration of the nuclear envelope and metapharic chromosome is made of two sister chromatids, which are held together by the centromere.

(iii) **Anaphase**

The centromere splits, and chromatids separate, moving to opposite poles. They are now called daughter chromosomes of the future nuclei.

(iv) **Telophase**

Chromosome cluster at opposite poles and lose their distinct identity. A nuclear envelope forms around them and the nucleolus, Golgi complex and ER are reformed.

**05 Cytokinesis**

(i) Division of cell into two daughter cells takes place by cytokinesis.

(ii) In an animal cell, cytokinesis is achieved by the appearance of a furrow in the plasma membrane.

(iii) In plant cell, wall formation starts in the centre of the cell and grows outward to meet the existing lateral walls.

**06 Significance of Mitosis**

(i) Results in the production of diploid daughter cells with identical genetic complement.

(ii) Growth of multicellular organisms is due to mitosis.

(iii) It helps cell to divide to restore the nucleocytoplasmic ratio because cell growth results in disturbing the ratio between the nucleus and cytoplasm.

(iv) It leads to cell repair. The cells of upper layer of the epidermis, cells of the lining of the gut and blood cells are being constantly replaced.

(v) Mitotic divisions in the meristematic tissues–the apical and the lateral cambium, result in a continuous growth of plants.

**07 Meiosis**

**Key Features**

(i) Involves two sequential cycles of nuclear and cell division called **meiosis**-I and **meiosis-II** but only a single cycle of DNA replication.

(ii) Four haploid cells are formed at the end of meiosis-II.

**08 Prophase-I**

Sub-divided into five phases based on chromosome behaviour.

(i) **Leptotene**–Chromosome gradually becomes visible and continues to compact throughout leptotene.

(ii) **Zygotene**–Chromosome starts pairing together (process is called synapsis).

Chromosome synapsis is accompanied by formation of complex structure called **synaptonemal complex**.

(iii) **Pachytene**

During this phase recombination nodules appear the sites at which crossing over occurs between non-sister chromatids of the homologous chromosomes.

(iv) **Diplotene**

Synaptonemal complex dissolve and chiasmata formation occur

(v) **Diakinesis**

Marks the dissapearance of the nuclear envelope around the cell

**09 Metaphase-I**

(i) Bivalent chromosomes align on the equatorial plate.

(ii) Microtubules from the opposite poles of the spindle attach to the kinetochore of homologous chromosomes.

**10 Anaphase-I** Homologous chromosomes separate, while sister chromatids remain associated at their centromeres.

**11 Telophase-I**

Nuclear membrane and nucleolus reappear, cytokinesis occurs.

**12 Interkinesis** The stage between the two meiotic divisions is called **interkinesis**. It is generally short lived.

**13 Prophase-II**

Nuclear membrane disappears by the end of prophase-II and chromosomes again becomes compact.

**14 Metaphase-II**

Chromosomes align at equator and microtubules from opposite poles of the spindle get attached to the kinetochores of sister chromatids.

**15 Anaphase-II**

Begins with simultaneous splitting of the centromere of each chromosome (which was holding the sister chromatids together) allowing them to move toward opposite poles of the cell.

**16 Telophase-II**

(i) Two groups of chromosomes once again get enclosed by a nuclear envelope.

(ii) Cytokinesis follows resulting in the formation of tetrad of cells, *i.e.*, four haploid daughter cells.

**17 Significance of Meiosis**

(i) Mechanism by which conservation of specific chromosome number of each species is achieved across generations in sexually reproducing organisms.

(ii) Increases genetic variability in the population of organisms from one generation to the next.

## Exercises

**Question 1** What is the average cell cycle span for a mammalian cell?

**Sol.** The average cell cycle span for a mammalian cell is 24 hours.

**Question 2** Distinguish cytokinesis from karyokinesis.

**Sol.** Cytokinesis is the division of cytoplasm, whereas karyokinesis is the division of nucleus of the cell.

**Question 3** Describe the events taking place during interphase.

**Sol.** The interphase, though called the resting phase, is the time during which the cell is preparing for division by undergoing cell growth and DNA replication.

The interphase is divided into three further phases:

(i) $G_1$-phase (Gap 1) (ii) S-phase (Synthesis)
(iii) $G_2$-phase (Gap 2)

$G_1$-phase corresponds to the interval between mitosis and initiation of DNA replication. During $G_1$-phase the cell is metabolically active and continuously grows but does not replicate its DNA. S or synthesis phase marks the period during which DNA synthesis or replication takes place. During this time, the amount of DNA per cell doubles.

During the $G_2$-phase, proteins are synthesised in preparation for mitosis, while cell growth continues.

**Question 4** What is $G_0$ (quiescent phase) of cell cycle?

**Sol.** $G_0$ is the quiescent stage of the cell cycle. It is also known as inactive stage of the cell cycle. Cells in this stage remain metabolically active, but no longer proliferate unless called on to do so depending on the requirement of the organisms.

**Question 5** Why is mitosis called equational cell division?

**Sol.** Mitosis is the kind of cell division in which daughter cells have the same number and kind of chromosomes as that of parent cell that's why, also known as equational cell division.

**Question 6** Name the stage of cell cycle at which one of the following events occur?

(i) Chromosomes are moved to spindle equator.
(ii) Centromere splits and chromatids separate.
(iii) Pairing between homologous chromosomes take place.
(iv) Crossing over between homologous chromosomes takes place.

**Sol.** (i) Metaphase (ii) Anaphase
(iii) Zygotene stage of meiosis-I (iv) Pachytene stage of meiosis-I

**Question 7** Describe the following words.

(i) Synapsis (ii) Bivalent (iii) Chiasmata

Draw a diagram to illustrate your answer.

**Sol.**

(i) **Synapsis** (i) During zygotene of prophase-I stage homologous chromosomes starts pairing together and this process of association is called synapsis. Electron micrographs of this stage indicate that chromosome synapsis is accompanied by the formation of complex structure called synaptonemal complex.

(ii) **Bivalent** The complex formed by a pair of synapsed homologous chromosomes is called a bivalent or a tetrad. It consists of four chromatids..

(iii) **Chiasmata** The chiasma formation is the indication of completion of crossing over and beginning of separation of chromosomes. The chiasmata is formed when the chromosomal parts begin to repel each other except in the region of crossing over Chiasmata formation is necessary for the separation of homologous chromosomes.

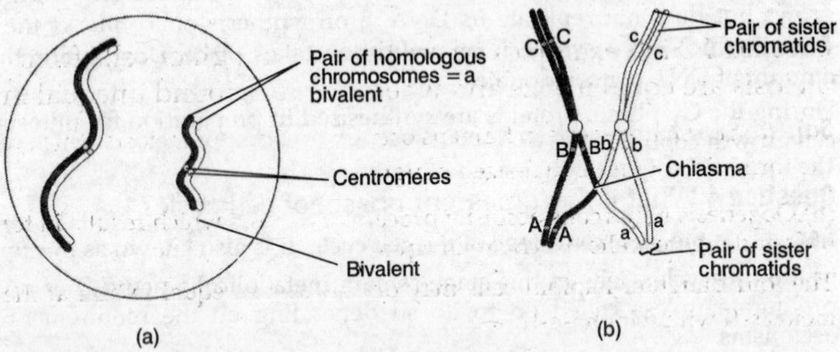


Chiasmata Formation

**Question 8** How does cytokinesis in plant cells differ from that in animal cells?

**Sol.** Cytokinesis in plant cells differs from that in animal cells are as follows

| S. No. | Plant cytokinesis | Animal cytokinesis |
|---|---|---|
| (i) | It usually occurs by cell plate method. | It takes place by cleavage. |
| (ii) | The spindle usually persists during cytokinesis. | The spindle begins to degenerate soon after anaphase. |
| (iii) | Central part of spindle grows in size and forms an interdigited complex called phragmoplast. | Non-muscle myosin and -actin filament assembled equatiorially to form a contractile ring that pull the cleavage furrows towards the centre. |
| (iv) | Vesicles derived from Golgi apparatus reach the equator of the phargmoplast and fuse to form cell plate and new cell membranes. | The event is absent in animal cytokinesis. |
| (v) | Cell plate grows centrifugally | Cleavage progresses centripetally. |
| (vi) | The cell membrane does not pinch | The cell membrane is pinched off into two daughter cells. |

**Cytokinesis in an animal cell** occurs by a process called cleavage. Which appears in plasma membrane, The cytoplasm has a ring of microfilaments made of actin associated with molecules of the protein myosin. This ring of proteins will contract causing the furrow to deepen, which will then in turn pinch the cell into two separate cells.

Cytokinesis in plant cell, In a plant, cells, wall formation starts in the middle of the parent cell.

This plate will grow outward and it accumulates more cell wall material. Eventually, the plate will fuse with the plasma membrane and the cell plate contents will join the parental cell wall. This results in two different daughter cells.

**Question 9** Find examples where the four daughter cells from meiosis are equal in size and where they are found unequal in size.

**Sol.** (a) Spermatogenesis in humans occur by process of meiosis which results in the formation of four equal-sized daughter cells.

(b) Oogenesis in humans occur by process of meiosis which results in formation of four daughter cells which are unequal in size.

The four daughter haploid cells may or may not be equal in size at the end of meiosis-II with telophase-II.

**Question 10** Distinguish anaphase of mitosis from anaphase-I of meiosis.

**Sol.** Differences between anaphase of mitosis from anaphase-I of meiosis are as follows :

| S.N. | Anaphase of mitosis | Anaphase-I of meiosis |
|---|---|---|
| 1. | Each chromosome arranged at the metaphase plate splits simultaneously and the two daughter chromatids begin to migrate towards the two opposite poles. | The spindle fibres contract and pull the centromeres of homologous chromosomes towards the opposite poles. |
| 2. | The centromere of each chromosome is towards the pole with arms of chromosome trailing behind. | The centromere is not divided, so half of the chromosomes of parent nucleus go to one pole and the remaining half to the opposite pole. |
| 3. | This stage has following key events<br>(a) Centromeres split and chromatids separate.<br>(b) Chromatids move to opposite poles. | In this stage<br>(a) Homologous chromosomes separate.<br>(b) Sister chromatids remain associated at their centromere. |

**Question 11** List the main differences between mitosis and meiosis.

**Sol.** The Main differences between mitosis and meiosis are as follows :

| S.N. | Mitosis | Meiosis |
|---|---|---|
| 1. | The division occurs in somatic cells. | It occurs in reproductive cells. |
| 2. | It is a single division. | It is a double division. |
| 3. | The daughter cells resembles each other as well as their mother cell. | The daughter cells neither resemble one another nor their mother cell. |
| 4. | Replication of chromosomes occurs before every mitotic division. | Replication of chromosomes occurs only once before meiosis-I |
| 5. | Mitosis does not introduce variations. | Meiosis introduces variations. |
| 6. | Mitosis is required for growth, repair and healing. | Meiosis is involved in sexual reproduction. |

**Question 12** What is the significance of meiosis?
The significance of meiosis are as follows

**Sol.** Meiosis is the mechanism by which conservation of specific chromosome number of each species is achieved across generations in sexually reproducing organisms.

It also increases the genetic variability in the population of organisms from one generation to the next. Variations are very important for the process of evolution.

**Question 13** Discuss with your teacher about

(i) Haploid insects and lower plants where cell division occurs.

(ii) Some haploid cells in higher plants where cell division does not occur.

**Sol.**

(i) In case of lower plants such as *Chlamydomonas*, *Spirogyra*, etc. the mitotic cell divisions occurs during the formation of gametophyte from haploid spores and meiotic divisions occur in the zygote during the formation of haploid spores. The male honey bees, wasps and ants are examples of some of the haploid insects where mitosis occurs during gametes formation .

(ii) In case of angiosperms, the synergids and antipodal cells of the embryo sac are haploid in which no cell division occurs and they get degenerated.

**Question 14** Can there be mitosis without DNA replication in S-phase?

**Sol.** No, DNA replication is required for doubling the DNA content in chromosomes during S-phase.

**Question 15** Can there be DNA replication without cell division?

**Sol.** Yes, there can be DNA replication without involvement of cell division in a cell, e.g., salivary glands of *Drosophilla.*

**Question 16** Analyse the events during every stage of cell cycle and notice how the following two parameters change?

(i) Number of chromosomes ($n$) per cell

(ii) Amount of DNA content (C) per cell.

**Sol.** During meiosis, the number of chromosomes ($n$) and the amount of DNA per cell change

(i) In S-phase, number of chromosomes remain same but each chromosome replicates so that it comes to have two chromatids. Due to this the DNA content doubles from 1C to 2 C or 2 C to 4C depending upon haploid diploid nature of cell.

(ii) In Anaphase (mitotic) number of chromosome remains the same, it is only sister chromatid which moves towards the respective poles. DNA content reduced to half (from 4C to 2C.)

In Anaphase-I of meiosis, number of chromosomes are reduced to half i.e., from 2n to n. DNA content in Anaphase-I is reduced to half from 4C to 2C and in Anphase-II, further number of chromosomes is not reduced from $n$, but the DNA content again reduced to half i.e., from 2 C to 1C.

# Photosynthesis in Higher Plants

CHAPTER 11

## Important Points

**01** Green plants carry out 'photosynthesis' a physico-chemical process by which they use light energy to drive the synthesis of organic compounds.

**02** Various experiments have been conducted by scientists such as **Joseph priestley**, Jan Ingenhousz, Julius von sachs to understand photosynthesis.

**03** Photosynthesis reaction can be expressed as:

$$6CO_2 + 12H_2O \xrightarrow[\text{Chlorophyll}]{\text{Light}} \underset{\text{Glucose}}{C_6H_{12}O_6} + 6H_2O + 6O_2$$

**04** The mesophyll cells of leaves contain a large number of chloroplasts.

**05** Within the chloroplast there is a membranous system consisting of grana, the stroma lamella and the fluid stroma.

**06** The membrane system of chloroplast traps light energy and synthesises ATP and NADPH.

**07** The colour of leaves varies due to four pigments

Chlorophyll a, chlorophyll b, xanthophyll and carotenoids.

**08** Pigments are substances that have an ability to absorb light, at specific wavelengths.

**09** The wavelength at which there is maximum absorption of light is shown by chlorophyll-*a*, *i.e.*, in the blue and red regions, which also show higher rate of photosynthesis. This shows that chlorophyll-*a* is the chief pigment associated with photosynthesis.

**10** The other accessory pigments (thylakoid pigments) like chlorophyll-*b*, xanthophylls and carotenoids also absorb light and transfer it to chlorophyll-*a* and also protect it from photo oxidation.

**11** **Light reaction** or the **Photochemical** phase include light absorption, water splitting, oxygen release and the formation of high energy intermediates, ATP and NADPH.

**12** The pigments are associated with two discrete photochemical light harvesting complexes (LHC) within the Photosystem I (PS-I) and Photosystem II (PS-II).

**13** Each photosystem has all the pigments (except one molecule of chlorophyll-*a*) forming a light harvesting system also called antennae.

**14** The single chlorophyll-*a* molecule forms the reaction centre.

**15** In PS-I, the reaction centre chlorophyll-*a* has an absorption peak at 700 nm, hence is called P700, while in PS-II, it has absorption maxima at 680 nm and is called P680.

**16** In PS-II, the chlorophyll-*a* absorbs 680 nm wavelength of red light causing electrons to become excited and jump into an orbit.

**17** These electrons are picked up by an electron acceptor, which passes them to an electrons transport system consisting of cytochromes.

**18** These electrons are not used up but are passed on to the pigments of PS-I.

**19** The electrons in the reaction centre PS-I are also excited when they receive red light of wavelength 700 nm and are transferred to another acceptor molecule.

**20** These electrons moves downhill to a molecule of energy rich $NADP^+$. The addition of these electrons reduces $NADP^+$ to $NADPH + H^+$.

**21** This whole scheme of transfer of electrons, starting from PS-II, uphill to the acceptor and finally down hill to $NADP^+$ reducing it to $NADPH + H^+$ is called **Z-scheme**, due to its characteristic shape.

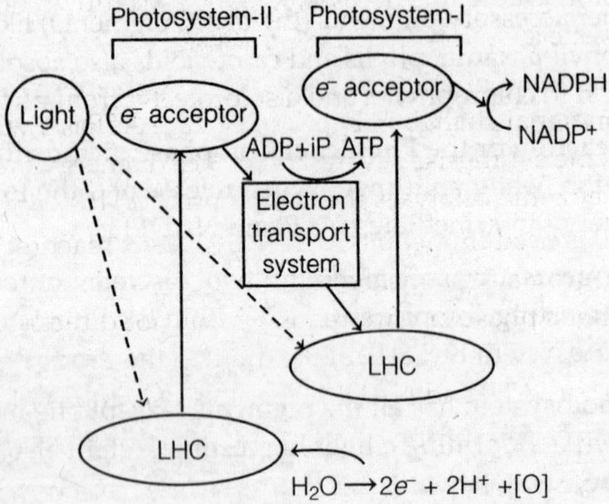


Non-Cyclic photophosphorylation

**22** PS-II supplies electrons continuously by splitting of water. Water is splited into $2H^+$, $[O_2]$ and electrons. This creates oxygen as the net product of photosynthesis.

$$2H_2O \longrightarrow 4H^+ + O_2 + 4e^-$$

**23** The process by which ATP is synthesised by cells (in mitochondria and chloroplasts) is called **phosphorylation**.

**24** Photophosphorylation is the synthesis of ATP from ADP and inorganic phosphate in the presence of light. It can be of two types:

(i) **Non-cyclic photophosphorylation** occurs when two photosystems work in a series, first PS-II and then PS-I.

(ii) **Cyclic photophosphorylation** occurs when only PS-I is functional, the electron is circulated within the photosystem and cyclic flow of electrons occur. It occurs in stroma lamelle and when wavelength of beyond 680 nm is available.

**25** The cyclic flow results only in synthesis of ATP, (not $NADPH + H^+$).

**26** Chemiosmotic hypothesis explains the mechanism of ATP synthesis in chloroplast. ATP synthesis is related to development of a proton gradient across a membrane.

**27** A proton gradient develops when within the chloroplast protons in the stroma decrease in number, while in the lumen there is accumulation of protons.

**28** The proton gradient is necessary as the breakdown of gradient releases energy.

**29** The breakdown of gradient provides enough energy to cause a conformational change in $F_1$ particle of the ATPase, which makes the enzyme synthesise several molecules of energy packed ATP. ATPase enzyme catalyses the formation of ATP.

**30** The ATP is used immediately in biosynthetic reaction taking place in stroma, responsible for fixing $CO_2$ and synthesis of sugar.

**31** Biosynthetic phase or dark reaction does not directly depend on the presence of light but is dependent on the products of light reaction, *i.e.*, ATP and NADPH, besides $CO_2$ and $H_2O$.

**32** $CO_2$ assimilation during photosynthesis follow two routes:

(i) $C_3$**-pathway**, in which first product of $CO_2$ fixation is a $C_3$ acid (PGA-3 phosphoglyceric acid).

(ii) $C_4$**-pathway**, in which the first product is a $C_4$ acid (Oxaloacetic acid-OAA).

**33** **Calvin cycle** occurs in all photosynthetic plants, whether they have $C_3$ or $C_4$-pathways.

**34** Three stages of Calvin cycle are (i) Carboxylation (ii) Reduction (iii) Regeneration.

(i) Carboxylation is the step in which $CO_2$ is utilised for the carboxylation of RuBP (Ribulose bisphosphate). Carboxylation is catalysed by RuBP carboxylose oxygenase enzyme (RuBisCO), which results in formation of 3-PGA.

(ii) **Reduction** involves two molecules of ATP for phosphorylation and two of NADPH for reduction per $CO_2$ molecule fixed.

(iii) **Regeneration** of $CO_2$ acceptor molecule RuBP require one ATP for phosphorylation to form RuBP.

**35** For every $CO_2$ molecule entering the Calvin cycle, 3 molecules of ATP and two molecules of NADPH are required. To make one molecule of glucose 6 turns of cycle are required.

**36** $C_4$-pathway is present in plants that are adapted to dry tropical regions. These plants ($C_4$-plants) have the $C_4$ oxaloacetic acid as the first $CO_2$ fixation product, they use the $C_3$-pathway or the Calvin cycle as the main biosynthetic pathway.

**37** $C_4$-plants have bundle sheath cells in their leaves called as 'Kranz anatomy'.

**38** $C_4$-plants follow Hatch and Slack pathway. In this, the primary $CO_2$ acceptor is a 3 carbon molecule phosphoenol pyruvate (PEP) and is present in mesophyll cells. The enzyme used is PEP carboxylase.

**39** The mesophyll cells lack RuBisCO enzyme. The $C_4$-acid OAA is formed in the mesophyll cells.

**40** It then forms other 4-carbon compounds like malic acid or aspartic acid.

**41** These $C_4$ acids *i.e.*, malic acid and aspartic acid are then transported to the bundle sheath cells.

**42** In bundle sheath cells these $C_4$ acids are broken down to yield pyruvic acid (3C) and $CO_2$.

**43** The 3-carbon molecule is transported back to mesophyll cells where it is converted to PEP again, thus completing the cycle.

**44** The $CO_2$ released in bundle sheath cells now enters the $C_3$ or the Calvin pathway (common to all plants). Calvin cycle occurs in mesophyll cells of $C_3$ plants and in $C_4$-plants occurs only in bundle sheath cells.

**45** Photorespiration is also a process, which creates an important difference between $C_3$ and $C_4$-plants.

**46** In $C_3$-plants, photorespiration occurs.

(i) $O_2$ bind to the RuBisCO, so $CO_2$ fixation is decreased.

(ii) Here, RuBP binds with $O_2$ to form one molecule of phosphoglycerate and phosphoglycolate in the pathway called **photorespiration**.

(ii) In this pathway, there is neither synthesis of sugars nor of ATP. Rather, it results in release of $CO_2$ with the utilisation of ATP. So, photorespiration is a wasteful process here.

**47** In $C_4$-plants, photorespiration does not occur, this is because they have the mechanism that increases the concentration of $CO_2$ at the enzyme site.

(i) This takes place when $C_4$-acid from mesophyll cells is broken down in the bundle sheath cells to release $CO_2$, this results in increasing the intracellular concentration of $CO_2$.

(ii) In turn, this ensures that the RuBisCO functions as a carboxylase minimising the oxygenase activity.

(iii) The $C_4$-plants lack photorespiration, that is why the productivity and yields are better in these plants.

**48** Photosynthesis is under the influence of both internal (plant) and external factors.

(i) Internal factors are the number, size, age and orientation of leaves, mesophyll cells and chloroplasts, internal $CO_2$ concentration and the amount of chlorophyll.

(ii) External factors are availability of sunlight, temperature, external $CO_2$ concentration and water.

**49** Blackman's law of limiting factors state that 'if a chemical process is affected by more than one factor then its rate will be determined by the factor (light, carbon dioxide or temperature) which is nearest to its minimal value, it is the factor, which directly affects the process, if its quantity is changed.

## Exercises

**Question 1** By looking at a plant externally can you tell whether a plant is $C_3$ or $C_4$? Why and how?

**Sol.** Usually plants growing in dry conditions use $C_4$-pathways. It cannot be said conclusively, if the plant is a $C_3$ or $C_4$ buy looking at external appearance.

**Question 2** By looking at which internal structure of a plant can you tell whether a plant is $C_3$ or $C_4$? Explain.

**Sol.** $C_4$ plants posses a particular large cells around the vascular bundles called bundle sheath cells and the leaves, which have such anatomy are said to have 'Kranz' anatomy. This makes them different from $C_3$ plants. 'Kranz' means 'wreath' and is a reflection of the arrangement of cells. The bundle sheath cells may form several layers around the vascular bundles; they are characterised by having a large number of chloroplasts, thick walls impervious to gaseous exchange and no intercellular spaces.

**Question 3** Even though a very few cells in a C4-plant carry out the biosynthetic-Calvin pathway, yet they are highly productive. Can you discuss why?

**Sol.** $C_4$-plants chemically fix carbon dioxide in the cells of the mesophyll by adding it to the three-carbon molecule phosphoenolpyruvate (PEP), a reaction catalysed by an enzyme called PEP carboxylase. It creates the four-carbon organic acid, oxaloacetic acid. Oxaloacetic acid or malate synthesised by this process is then translocated to specialised bundle sheath cells where the enzyme, RuBisCO and other Calvin cycle enzymes are located and where $CO_2$ released by decarboxylation of the four-carbon acid which is then fixed by RuBisCO activity to the three-carbon sugar 3-phosphoglyceric acid.

The physical separation of RuBisCO from the oxygen-generating light reactions reduces photorespiration and increases $CO_2$ fixation and thus photosynthetic capacity of the leaf.

**Question 4** RuBisCO is an enzyme that acts both as a carboxylase and oxygenase. Why do you think RuBisCO carries out more carboxylation in C4-plants?

**Sol.** RuBisCO has a much greater affinity for $CO_2$ than for $O_2$. It is the relative concentration of $O_2$ and $CO_2$ that determines which of the two will bind to the enzyme.

In $C_3$-plants some $O_2$ does bind to RuBisCO and hence, $CO_2$ fixation is decreased. Here the RuBP instead of being converted to two molecules of PGA binds with $O_2$ to form one molecule of phosphoglycerate and one molecule of phosphoglycolate in a pathway called photorespiration. In the photorespiratory pathway, there is neither synthesis of sugars, nor of ATP. Rather it results in the release of $CO_2$ with the utilisation of ATP. In the photorespiratory pathway, there is no synthesis of ATP or NADPH. Therefore, photorespiration is a wasteful process.

In $C_4$-plants, photorespiration does not occur. This is because they have a mechanism that increases the concentration of $CO_2$ at the enzyme site. This takes place when the $C_4$ acid from the mesophyll cell is broken down in the bundle cells to release $CO_2$-this results in increasing the intracellular concentration of $CO_2$. In turn, this ensures that the RuBisCO functions as a carboxylase minimising the oxygenase activity.

**Question 5** Suppose there were plants that had a high concentration of chlorophyll-*b*, but lacked chlorophyll-*a*, would it carry out photosynthesis? Then why do plants have chlorophyll-*b* and other accessory pigments?

**Sol.** Though chlorophyll-a is the major pigment responsible for trapping light, other thylakoid pigments like chlorophyll-*b*, xanthophylls and carotenoids, which are called accessory pigments, also absorb light and transfer the energy to chlorophyll-*a*.

Indeed, they not only enable a wider range of wavelength of incoming light to be utilised for photosynthesis but also protect chlorophyll-*a* from photo oxidation.

Hence, chlorophyll-a is essential for photosynthesis because only its special molecules function as reaction centres ($P_{700}$, $P_{680}$). Reaction centres convert light energy into chemical energy. Photosynthesis is therefore absent in plants lacking chlorophyll-a.

**Question 6** Why is the colour of a leaf kept in the dark frequently yellow or pale green? Which pigment do you think is more stable?

**Sol.** This is due to the interconversion of pigments, *i.e.*, change of green chlorophyll pigment into yellow coloured carotenoids. The carotene pigment is more stable.

**Question 7** Look at leaves of the same plant on the shady side and compare it with the leaves on the sunny side. Or, compare the potted plants kept in the sunlight with those in the shade. Which of them has leaves that are darker green? Why?

**Sol.** The leaves of the same plant on the shady side are dark green as compared to with the leaves on the sunny side. As the leaf surfaces in shade receive lesser sunshine, so they experience a lesser amount of photosynthesis than plants or leaves in direct sunlight. In leaves that get less sunlight, more chlorophyll is present to carry out photosynthesis efficiently.

**Question 8** The following figure shows the effect of light on the rate of photosynthesis. Based on the graph, Sol. the following questions

(i) At which point/s (*A*, *B* or *C*) in the curve is light a limiting factor?

(ii) What could be the limiting factor/s in region *A*?

(iii) What do *C* and *D* represent on the curve?

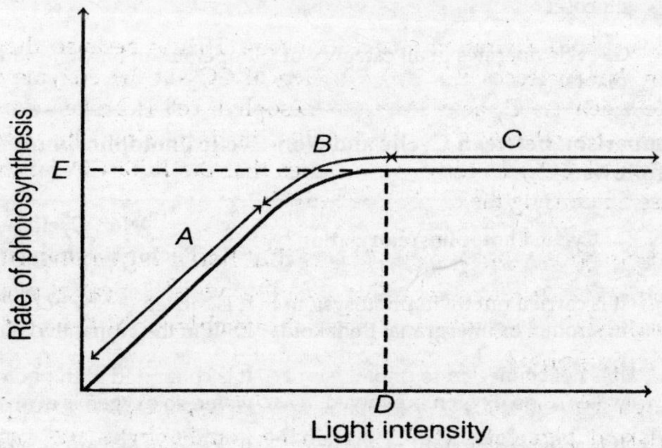


**Graph of light intensity on the rate of photosynthesis**

**Sol.**

(i) Light serves as a limiting factor where photosynthesis occurs to the lowest degree light is limiting at point *A*.

(ii) In *A* region, the rate of photosynthesis shows proportionate increase up to a certain $CO_2$ concentration, beyond, which the rate again becomes constant.

(iii) Point *C* indicates a stage beyond which light is not a limiting factor, and *D* is the line. beyond which the intensity of light does not affect the photosynthetic rate.

**Question 9** Give comparison between the following

(i) $C_3$ and $C_4$-pathways

(ii) Cyclic and non-cyclic photophosphorylation

(iii) Anatomy of leaf in $C_3$ and $C_4$-plants

**Sol.** (i) **Comparison between $C_3$ and $C_4$-Pathways are as follows:**

| S.N. | $C_3$-Pathway | $C_4$-Pathway |
|---|---|---|
| 1. | The primary acceptor of $CO_2$ is RuBP, a 5 carbon compound. | The primary acceptor of $CO_2$ is PEP, a 3 carbon compound. |
| 2. | It operates high under low concentration of $CO_2$ in mesophyll cells. | It can operate under very low d $CO_2$concentration in mesophyll cells. |
| 3. | $CO_2$ once fixed is not released back. | $CO_2$ once fixed is released back in bundle sheath cells. |
| 4. | Fixation of one molecule of $CO_2$ needs 3ATP and 2 $NADPH_2$ molecules. It requires 18 ATP for the synthesis of one molecule of glucose. | $C_4$-pathway requires 30 ATP for the synthesis of one molecules of glucose. |
| 5. | $C_3$-cycle operates in all category of plants. | It operates in only $C_4$-plants. |

(ii) **Comparison between Cyclic and Non-Cyclic Photophosphorylation are as follows:**

| S.N. | Cyclic Photophosphorylation | Non-Cyclic Photophosphorylation |
|---|---|---|
| 1. | It is carried out by in photosystem I in stromal or intergranal thylakoids | It is carried out by both PS-I and PS-II in the granal thylakoids. |
| 2. | It is not connected to photolysis of water so no oxygen is evolved. | It is connected with photolysis of water, so oxygen is evolved in it. |
| 3. | It is activated by light of 700 nm wavelength. | It occurs in 680 nm as well as 700 nm wavelength. |

| S.N. | Cyclic Photophosphorylation | Non-Cyclic Photophosphorylation |
|---|---|---|
| 4. | It generates ATP only there is no formation of $NADPH_2$. | It produces both ATP as well as $NADPH_2$. |
| 5. | Chlorophyll does not receive any electrons from donor. | The source of electrons is photolysis of water. |

**(iii) Comparison between Anatomy of Leaf in $C_3$ and $C_4$-Plants**

| S.N. | $C_3$ Leaf Anatomy | $C_4$ Leaf Anatomy |
|---|---|---|
| 1. | Only one type of chloroplast is present. | Kranz anatony, *i.e.*, two types of cell, mesophyll and bundle sheath cells each with its own type of chloroplast is present. |
| 2. | Less efficient in photosynthesis than $C_4$ leaves. | More efficient in photosynthesis than $C_3$ leaves. |
| 3. | Only mesophyll cells carryout photosynthesis. | Both mesophyll cells and bundle sheath cells carryout photosynthesis. |

# DIKSHA APP Questions

## ☐ Multiple Choice Questions

**Q.1** Bell jar experiments with mouse to show the role of green plants in purification of air were conducted by

(a) Joseph Priestley (b) Van Neil
(c) Hill and Bendall (d) Blackmann

**Sol.** (a) Bell jar experiments with mouse to show the role of green plants in purification of air was conducted by Joseph Priestley. Van Neil is famous for the experiment to prove that $O_2$ comes from water.

Blackmann proposed law of limiting factor.

**Q.2** Chloroplasts possess stacks of discs interspersed with lamellae. These stacks are called

(a) Thylakoids (b) Grana (c) Plastoglobules (d) Locules

**Sol.** (b) The chloroplasts possess stacks of discs (i.e. thylakoids) interspersed with lamallae. These stacks are called grana. There are about 10-100 thylakoids within a grana and 40-60 grana in a plant cell.

**Q.3** Chloroplasts are considered as semiautonomous duem to the presence of one of the following components

(a) Chlorophyll (b) RNA (c) DNA (d) Ribosomes

**Sol.** (c) Chloroplasts are considered as semiautomonous due to presence genetic material as DNA. RNA and ribosomes are also found in chloroplasts. The DNA found in these orgenelles is circular like in prokaryotes.

**Q.4** Which of the following is the correct point of difference between the structure of chlorophyll a and chlorophyll b

(a) Chlorophyll-a has $CH_3$ group whereas chlorophyll b has CHO group at C-3

(b) Chlorophyll-a has $CH_3$ group whereas chlorophyll has CHO group at C-5

(c) Chlorophyll-a ha s CHO group whereas chlorophyll b has $CH_3$ group at C-3

(d) Chlorophyll-a has CHO group whereas chlorophyll b has $CH_3$ group at C-5

**Sol.** (a) chlorophyll *a* and *b* are both photosynthetic pigment. The chlorophyll a has methyle group ($CH_3$) in the third carbon atom while chlorophyll-*b* has an aldehyde (CHO) group chlorophyll *a* is reaction centre while chlorophyll-b is accessory pigment in photosynthesis

**Q.5** Which one of the following is not produced as a result of light reaction during photosynthesis.

(a) NAD (b) ATP

(c) $O_2$ (d) $O_3$

**Sol.** (a) The light reaction of photosynthesis results in formation of ATP, $O_2$ and NADPH + $H^+$. $NAD^+$ is used during this process. This NADPH + $H^+$ releases energy by oxidation-reduction process. By light reaction sunlight (light energy) is converted to chemical energy.

**Q.6** PSI which consists of photocentre has more amount of

(a) chlorophyll b (b) Chlorophyll a

(c) Carotenoids (d) Xanthophyll

**Sol.** (b) Ps ( photosystem) is a reaction centre in light reaction of photosynthesis. The PSI comprises of chlorophylla, ll-*a*, chlorophyll-*b* and carotenoids. It is having more amount of chlorophyll-*a*

**Q.7** Photolysis requires one of the following elements for releasing Oxygen from water

(a) Mg (b) Mn

(c) Mo (d) K

**Sol.** (b) The light reaction of photosynthesis is characterised by photolysis of water. This leads to release of oxygen as by product. The mineral ion essential for photolysis of water are chlorine, manganese and calcium.

**Q.8** ATP synthesis in chloroplast according to Chemiosmotic hypothesis is based on–

(a) Osmotic pressure (b) Proton gradient
(c) Movement of $K^+$ ions (d) Potential difference in membranes

**Sol.** (b) The chemiosmatic hypothesis for ATP synthesis in chloroplast was explained by P. Mitchell. According to this hypothesis ATP synthesis is linked to development of proton gradient across the membrane of thylakoid and proton accumulation is towards the inside of membrane i.e lumen.

**Q.9** Enzymes catalysing dark reactions in photosynthesis are found in

(a) Thylakoids (b) Inner membrane of chloroplasts
(c) Stroma (d) Inside lamella

**Sol.** (c) The light reactions enzymens of photosynthesis is found thylakoids while the site of dark reaction of photosynthsis is stroma of chloroplast i.e the enzymes of dark reaction of photosyntheis are found in stroma.

**Q.10** First acceptor in $C_3$ plants is

(a) Phosphoenol pyruvate (b) Ribulose bis phosphate
(c) Glyceraldehyde (d) Phosphoglycerate

**Sol.** (b) In calvin cycle (dark reaction) of photosynthesis the $CO_2$ diffuses in chloroplast and fuses with ribulose 1,5-bis-phosphate to produce 3-phosphoglycerate i.e., the first stable product in $C_3$ plants 3.

**Q.11** In $C_4$ plants Kranz anatomy refers to arrangement of

(a) Bundle sheath cells around vascular bundles.
(b) Vascular bundles scattered in mesophyll
(c) Spongy parenchyma loosely held
(d) Sunken stomata in epidermis

**Sol.** (a) $C_4$ plants are characterised by presence of kranz anatomy. This anatomy refers to arrangment of budle sheath cells around vascular bundles. The mesophyll cells are clustered around the bundle sheath cells in a ring-like fashion.

**Q.12** Which one of the following processes is characteristic of $C_4$ plants

(a) Phototropism (b) Glycolysis
(c) Photorespiration (d) Parthenogenesis

**Sol.** (b) $C_4$ plants are characterised by presence of glycolysis. These plants (sugarcane, mairze, sorghum) do not have phototropism, photorespiration and parthenogensis. These are characteristic of $C_3$ plants while glycolysis is found in all the green plants.

**Q.13** First stable compound formed in Hatch Slack pathway is

(a) Pyruvate (b) Malic acid
(c) Aspartic acid (d) Oxaloacetic acid

**Sol.** (d) The first stable compound formed in Hatch and Slack pathway is oxaloacetic acid. In Hatch and Slack pathway ($C_4$ cycle) the $CO_2$ combines with phosphoenal pyruvate to produce oxaloacetic acid.

**Q.14** Which one of the following factors does not affect photosynthesis

(a) Temperature (b) Light
(c) Water (d) Pressure

**Sol.** (d) The main factors that affect the photosynthesis are light intensity, temperature, concentration of $CO_2$ as well as water and minerals. Pressure does not affect photosynthesis.

## □ Short Answer Type

**Q.1** RubisCO is a dual enzyme. Justify the statement and explain the nature of enzyme showing its characteristics under different condition.

**Sol.** RubisCO or Ribulose biphosphate carboxylase oxygenase acts as a $CO_2$ as well as $O_2$ acceptor.

It has more affinity for $CO_2$ as compared to Oxygen. So in $C_3$ plants it acts as a carboxylase ($CO_2$ acceptor).

At high temperature, concentration of dissolved $CO_2$ in equilibrium with air decreases more than the concentration of $O_2$. Then it favours oxygenation.

## □ Long Answer Type

**Q.1** State blackman's law of limiting factors. Explain taking any 3 factors that affect photosynthesis.

**Sol.** Blackman's law of limiting factors states that. "If a chemical process is affected by more than one factor, then its rate will be determined by the factor which is nearest to its minimal value: It is the factor which directly affects the process if its quantity is changed.

Three factors that affect photosynthesis are as follows:

1. Light as a limiting factor:

(i) At higher intensities, gradually the rate does not show further increase as other factors become limiting.

(ii) Light saturation occurs at 10% of the full sunlight.

(iii) Increase in incident light beyond a point causes the breakdown of chlorophyll and a decrease in photosynthesis.

2. Carbon dioxide as a limiting factor:

   (i) The $C_3$ and $C_4$-plants respond differently to $CO_2$ concentrations.

   (ii) At high light intensities, both $C_3$ and $C_4$-plants show increase in the rates of photosynthesis. $C_4$-plants show saturation at about 360μ/L$^{-1}$, while $C_3$ responds to increased $CO_2$ concentration and saturation only beyond 450 M/L$^{-1}$.

   (iii) This is the reason $C_3$plants like tomatoes and bell pepper are allowed to grow in $CO_2$ enriched atmosphere that leads to high yield.

3. Temperature as a limiting factor:

   (i) The $C_4$-plants respond to higher temperatures and show higher rate of photosynthesis, while $C_3$-plants have a much lower optimum temperature.

**Q.2** What do you understand by Absorption and action spectrum in light reaction of photosynthesis draw the two spectra and discuss the parallelism between the two.
Describe with the help of a flow diagram cyclic photophosphorylation.

Why is it so calles.

What is the purpose of proton gradient during the process thylakoids?

**Sol.**

(a) Curves showing absorption of energy and amount of oxygen liberated at various wavelengths of light. The amount of Oxygen liberated was found to be parallel to the absorption of light by chlorophyll a

(b) flow diagram It is a photophosphoryation in which an electron expelled by the excited photocenter is returned to it after passing through a series of electron carriers.
It is for synthesis of ATP from ADP.

# Respiration in Plants

CHAPTER 12

## Important Points

**01** **Cellular Respiration** is the mechanism of breakdown of food materials within the cell to release energy.

**02** Respiration is the oxidation of complex compounds in cells, releasing energy which is trapped in the form of ATP, the energy currency of the cell. The ATP powers cellular processes and the resulting carbon compounds are used for biosynthesis.

**03** **Types of Respiration Process** Two types of respiration process are present.

(i) Aerobic respiration ( It occurs in presence of oxygen).

(ii) Anaerobic Respiration (It occurs in absence of oxygen)

**04** **Glycolysis**

(i) It is first part of respiration and common to both anaerobic and aerobic respiration. Glycolysis takes place in the cytoplasm of cell and it is also known as EMP pathway.

(ii) This process complete in ten steps

(iii) Glycolysis involves breakdown of one glucose molecule (through partial oxidation) to yield two molecules of pyruvic acid.

**05 Fermentation**

It is incomplete oxidation of glucose under anaerobic conditions by sets of reactions where pyruvic acid is converted into lactic acid and ethyl alcohol.

**06 Aerobic Respiration**

(i) For aerobic respiration pyruvate produced in glycolysis is transported from cytoplasm into mitochondria. Pyruvate is fully oxidised, releasing hydrogen atoms and forming three molecules of $CO_2$ in the matrix of mitochondria.

(ii) The electrons from hydrogen are transferred to oxygen, producing ATP simultaneously in inner membrane of mitochondria.

(iii) Pyruvate undergoes oxidative decarboxylation forming acetyl CoA, $CO_2$ and NADH.

**07 Tricarboxylic Acid Cycle**

(i) Commonly called as Krebs' cycle after Hans Krebs scientist, who first elucidated it.

(ii) The kreb cycle, occuring in the mitochondrial matrix, oxidises acetyl- CoA to produce 3NADH, $1FADH_2$, 1ATP (or GTP) and $2CO_2$ per cycle. It also regenerate oxaloacetate and provides electron carriers for ATP production in the electron transport chain.

**08 Electron Transport System** (ETS) **and Oxidative Phosphorylation**

(i) In ETS, electrons from NADH and $FADH_2$ pass through protein complexes in the inner mitochondria membrane, creating a proton gradient.

(ii) Process occurs to release and utilise energy stored in NADH + $H^+$ and $FADH_2$.

(iii) During oxidative phosphoryation, this gradient drives ATP synthesis via ATP synthase, with oxygen as the final electron acceptor, forming water.

(iv) The metabolic pathway through which the electron passes from one carrier to another is called electron transport system (ETS).

**Steps**

(a) **Complex I** electrons from NADH produced in the mitochondrial matrix during citric acid cycle are oxidised by an NADH dehydrogenase, and electrons are then transferred to ubiquinone.

(b) **Complex II** $FADH_2$ generated during the citric acid cycle gets transferred to ubiquinone.

(c) **Complex III** The electrons from ubiquinone are received by cytochrome-$bc_1$ (complex III) and further transferred to cytochromo-c.

(d) **Complex IV** Cytochrome-*c* acts as a mobile carrier between complex III and cytochrome *c* oxidase complex (complex IV).

(e) **Complex V** During transfer of electrons from each complex, the process is accompanied by the production of ATP from ADP and inorganic phosphate by the action of ATP synthase (complex IV).

**09 Respiratory balance sheet :**

| Stage of respiration | Source | Number of ATP molecules produced |
|---|---|---|
| Glycolysis | Direct | 2 |
| | Indirect - through 2 molecules of NADH + $H^+$ (one NADH + $H^+$ = 3 ATP) | 6 |
| Link reaction | 2 molecules of NADH + $H^+$ | 6 |
| Citric acid or | 6 NADH + $H^+$ | 18 |
| Kreb's cycle | 2 $FADH_2$ [1 $FADH_2$ = 2 ATPs] | 4 |
| | Direct ATP | 2 |
| | Total | 38 ATPs |

**10 Amphibolic Pathway** Since, respiratory pathway is involved in both anabolism and catabolism, it is considered as **amphibolic pathway.**

**11 Respiratory Quotient** The ratio of volume of $CO_2$ evolved to the volume of $O_2$ consumed in respiration is called Respiratory Quotient (RQ)

$$RQ = \frac{\text{Volume of } CO_2 \text{ evolved}}{\text{Volume of } O_2 \text{ evolved}}$$

| Substrate | RQ |
|---|---|
| Carbohydrates | 1 (complete oxidation) |
| Fats | Less than 1 |
| Proteins | 0.9 |

# Exercises

**Question 1** Differentiate between

(a) Respiration and Combustion

(b) Glycolysis and Krebs' cycle

(c) Aerobic respiration and Fermentation

**Sol.** (a) **Differences between respiration and combustion are as follows:**

| S.N. | Respiration | Combustion |
|---|---|---|
| 1. | It is the breakdown of complex compounds through oxidation within the cells, leading to release of considerable amount of energy. | Combustion is the complete burning of glucose, which produces $CO_2$ and $H_2O$ and yield energy which is given out as heat. |
| 2. | It is a controlled biochemical process. | It is an uncontrolled physio chemical process. |
| 3. | Many chemical bonds break one after the other to release energy which is stored in the forms of ATPs | Chemical bonds break simultaneously and releases large amount of energy. |
| 4. | Enzymes are involved. | Enzymes are not involved. |

(b) **Differences between glycolysis and krebs' cycle are as follows**

| S.N. | Glycolysis | Krebs' cycle |
|---|---|---|
| 1. | It is also called as Embden Meyerhof-Parnas (EMP) pathway. | It is also known as citric acid cycle or tricarboxylic acid cycle. |
| 2. | It occurs in the cytosol of prokaryotes as well as eukaryotes. | In eukaryotes, it occurs in matrix of mitochondria. |
| 3. | It starts with the oxidation of glucose. | It starts with the oxidation of pyruvic acid. |
| 4. | It is an enzyme-controlled 10 steps process by which glucose, fructose or sucrose is reduced to form pyruvic acid with the production of ATP and NADH + $H^+$. | It involves 8 steps to oxidise two molecules of acetyl Co-A. |

(c) **Differences between aerobic respiration and fermentation are as follows**

| S.N. | Aerobic Respiration | Fermentation |
|---|---|---|
| 1. | The presence of $O_2$ is required for complete oxidation of organic substances. | Incomplete oxidation of glucose occurs in the absence of oxygen. |
| 2. | It releases $CO_2$ water and a large amount of energy present in the substrates. | Pyruvic acid is converted to $CO_2$ and ethanol and less amount of energy is released. |
| 3. | Many (38) molecules of ATPs are produced | There is net gain of only two molecules of ATPs. |
| 4. | NADH is oxidised to $NAD^+$ vigorously in case of aerobic respiration | NADH is oxidised to $NAD^+$ rather slowly in fermentation. |

**Question 2** What are respiratory substrates? Name the most common respiratory substrate.

**Sol.** The organic substances, which are catabolised in the living cells to release energy are called as respiratory substrates. Though any food stuff-carbohydrate, fat or protein may act as a respiratory substrate, the common respiratory substrate is glucose.

**Question 3** Give the schematic representation of glycolysis?

**Sol.** Glycolysis

(i) In this process, glucose undergoes partial oxidation to form two molecules of pyruvic acid.

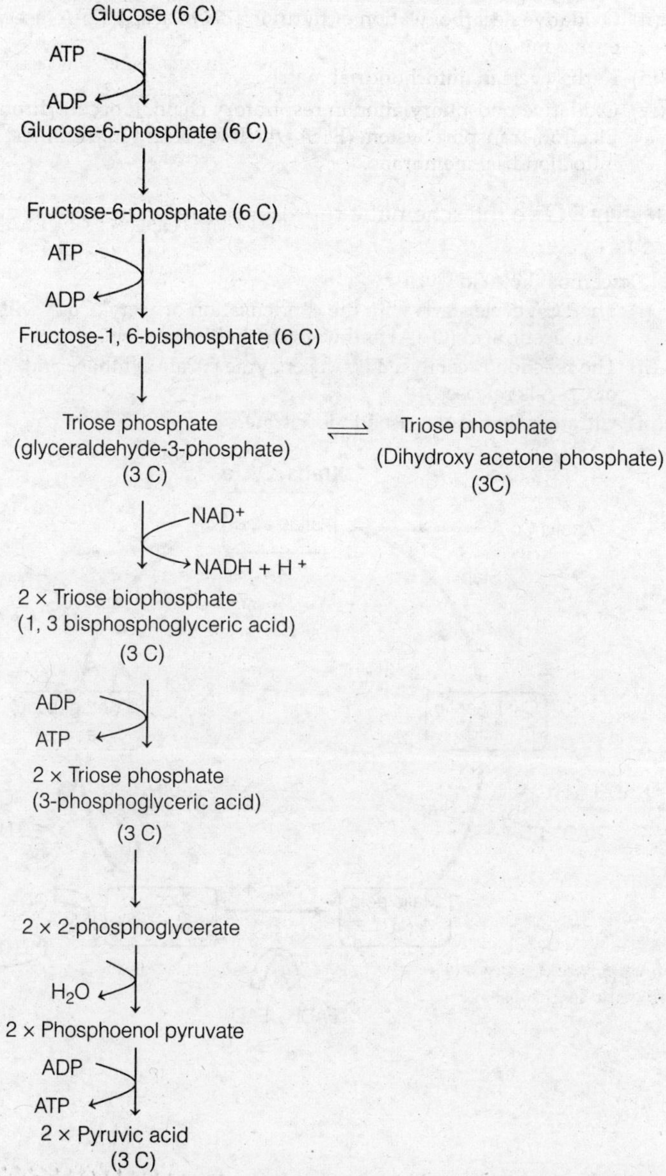

**Question 4** What are the main steps in aerobic respiration? Where does it take place?

**Sol.** The main steps in aerobic respiration are as follows

(i) Glycolytic breakdown of glucose in to pyruvic acid.

(ii) Oxidative decarboxylation of pyruvic acid to acetyl Co-A (acetyl coenzyme-A).

(iii) Kerbs' cycle in mitochondrial matrix..

(iv) Oxidative phosphorylation in respiratory chain. It occurs through Electron Transport System (ETS) which is present in the inner mitochondrial membrane.

**Question 5** Give the schematic representation of an overall view of Krebs' cycle.

**Sol.** Tricarboxylic Acid Cycle

(i) The TCA cycle starts with the condensation of acetyl Co-A with oxaloacetic acid (OAA) and water to yield citric acid.

(ii) The reaction is catalysed by the enzyme citrate synthase and a molecule of Co-A is released.

(iii) Citrate is then isomerised to isocitrate.

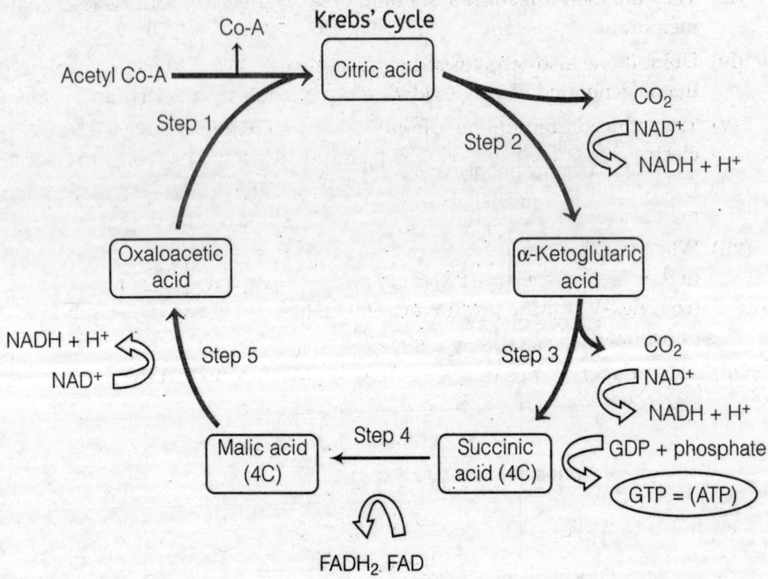

(iv) It is followed by two successive steps of decarboxylation, leading to the formation of → α-ketoglutaric acid and then succinyl Co-A.

(v) During the conversion of succinyl Co-A to succinic acid, a molecule of GTP is synthesised. This is a substrate level phosphorylation.

(vi) In a coupled reaction, GTP is converted to GDP with the simultaneous synthesis of ATP from ADP.

(vii) $NAD^+$ is reduced to $NADH+H^+$ + and $FAD^+$ is reduced to $FADH_2$.

The continued oxidation of acetye CoA acid *via* the TCA cycle requires the continued replenishment of oxaloacetic acid, the first member of the cycle. In addition, it also requires regeneration of $NAD^+$ and $FAD^+$ from $NADH_2$ and $FADH_2$ respectively.

**Question 6** Explain ETS.

**Sol. Electron Transport System** (ETS) The metabolic pathway through which the electron passes from one carrier to another, is called the Electron Transport System (ETS).

(i) It occurs in the inner mitochondrial membrane.

(ii) Electrons from NADH produced in the mitochondrial matrix during citric acid cycle are oxidised by an NADH dehydrogenase (complex-I).

(iii) They are then transferred to ubiquinone located within the inner membrane.

(iv) Ubiquinone also receives reducing equivalents *via* $FADH_2$ (complex-II) that is generated during oxidation of succinate in the citric acid cycle.

(v) The reduced ubiquinone (ubiquinol) is then oxidised with the transfer of electrons to cytochrome-*c* *via* cytochrome-$bc_1$ complex (complex-III).

(vi) Cytochrome-*c* is a small protein attached to the outer surface of the inner membrane.

(vii) When the electrons pass from one carrier to another via complex-I to IV in the electron transport chain, they are coupled to ATP synthase (complex-V) for the production of ATP from ADP and inorganic phosphate.

(viii) The number of ATP molecules synthesised depends on the nature of the electron donor.

(ix) Oxidation of one molecule of NADH gives rise to 3 molecules of ATP, while that of one molecule of $FADH_2$ produces 2 molecules of ATP.

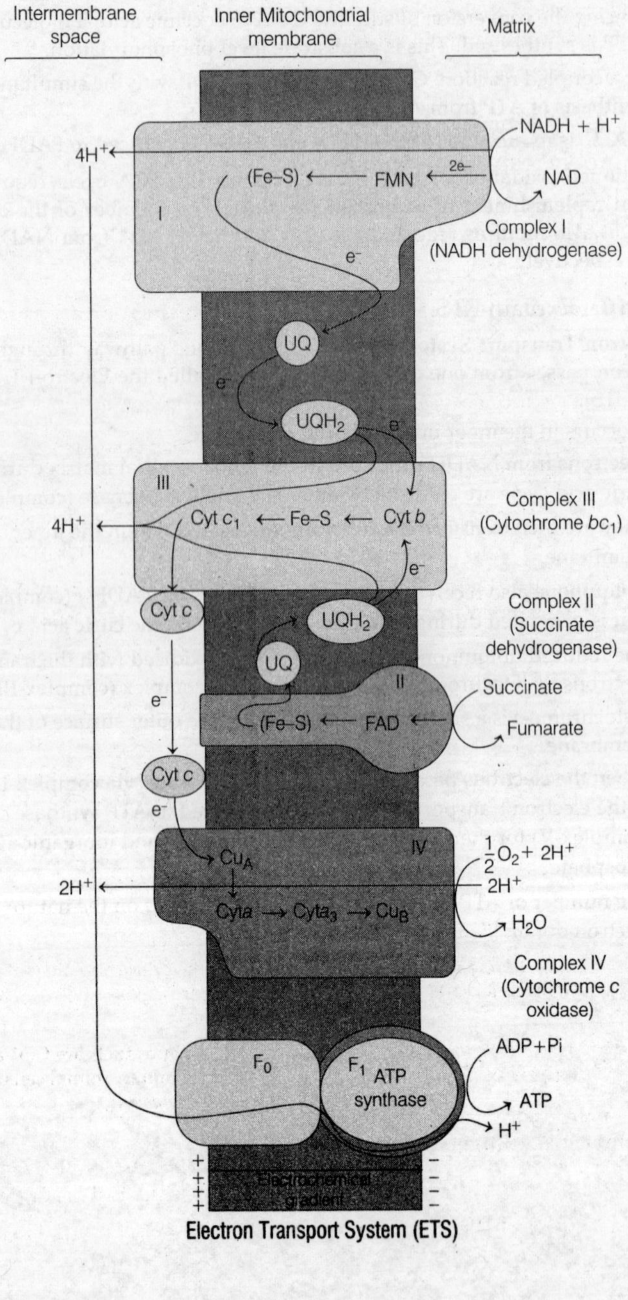


**Electron Transport System (ETS)**

(x) Although, the aerobic process of respiration takes place only in the presence of oxygen, the role of oxygen is limited to the terminal stage of the process. Yet, the presence of oxygen is vital, since, it drives the whole process by removing hydrogen from the system.

(xi) Oxygen acts as the final hydrogen acceptor.

**Question 7** Distinguish between the following

(a) Aerobic respiration and anaerobic respiration

(b) Glycolysis and fermentation

(c) Glycolysis and citric acid cycle

**Sol.**

(a) **Differences between aerobic and anaerobic respiration are as follows:**

| S.N. | Aerobic Respiration | Anaerobic Respiration |
|---|---|---|
| 1. | Presence of oxygen is essential. | Occurs without oxygen. |
| 2. | Complete oxidation of substrates occurs into $CO_2$ and $H_2O$. | Incomplete degradations of substrates. |
| 3. | End products are non-toxic. | End products are toxic when accumulated in large amount. |
| 4. | Involves glycolysis, krebs' cycle and terminal oxidation. | Involves only glycolysis followed by incomplete breakdown of pyruvic acid. |
| 5. | 38 ATP molecules are produced from each glucose molecule. | Only two molecules of ATP are produced from each glucose molecule. |

(b) **Differences between glycolysis and fermentation are as follows:**

| S.N. | Glycolysis | Fermentation |
|---|---|---|
| 1. | It occurs in cytoplasm of the cell and in all living things. | It occurs in yeast and muscle cells in animals when oxygen is not sufficient for cellular respiration. |
| 2. | Glucose undergoes partial oxidation to form two molecules of pyruvic acid. | The enzyme like pyruvic acid decarboxylase and alcohol dehydrogenase catalyse these reactions. |
| 3. | The end products are $CO_2$, $H_2O$ and energy. | The end products are $CO_2$ and ethanol and in animal cells lactic acid is released. |

(c) Refer to Sol. 1 (b) in this chapter.

**Question 8** What are the assumptions made during the calculation of net gain of ATP?

**Sol.** The calculations of net gain of ATP can be made only on certain assumptions

(i) There is a sequential, orderly pathway functioning, with one substrate forming the next and with glycolysis, TCA cycle and ETS pathway following one after another.

(ii) The NADH synthesised in glycolysis is transferred into the mitochondria and undergoes oxidative phosphorylation.

(iii) None of the intermediates in the pathways are utilised to synthesise any other compound.

(iv) Only glucose is being respired-no other alternative substrates are entering in the pathway at any of the intermediary stages.

But this kind of assumptions are not really valid in a living system. All pathways work simultaneously and do not take place one after another. Substrates enter the pathways and are withdrawn from it as and when necessary; ATP is utilised as and when needed; enzymatic rates are controlled by multiple meSol. In over all steps, there is a net gain of 38 ATP molecules during aerobic respiration of one molecule of glucose.

**Question 9** Discuss 'the respiratory pathway is an amphibolic pathway.'

**Sol.** Amphibolic Pathway Glucose is the favoured substrate for respiration. All carbohydrates are usually first converted into glucose before they are used for respiration. Other substrates can also be respired but they do not enter the respiratory pathway at the first step. Since, respiration involves breakdown of substrates, the respiratory process involves both catabolism and anabolism. That is why respiratory pathway is considered to be an amphibolic pathway rather than as a catabolic one.

**Question 10** Define RQ. What is its value for fats?

**Sol.** Respiratory Quotient The ratio of the volume of $CO_2$ evolved to the volume of $O_2$ consumed in respiration is called the respiratory quotient (RQ) or respiratory ratio.

$$RQ = \frac{\text{Volume of } CO_2 \text{ evolved}}{\text{Volume of } O_2 \text{ consumed}}$$

The respiratory quotient depends upon the type of respiratory substrate used during respiration. For fats, its value is less than 1. For example, RQ for a fatty acid, tripalmitin, if used as a substrate is shown as

$$\underset{\text{Tripalmitin}}{2(C_{51}H_{98}O_6)} + 145\,O_2 \longrightarrow 102CO_2 + 98\,H_2O + \text{energy}$$

$$RQ = \frac{102CO_2}{145O_2} = 0.7$$

$$RQ = 0.7$$

**Question 11** What is oxidative phosphorylation?

**Sol.** The final step of aerobic respiration is the oxidation of 10 molecules of NADH+ $H^+$ and 2 molecules of $FADH_2$ generated from a molecule of a glucose. These are oxidised in the presence of oxygen through electron transport chain. In this step, oxygen from the atmosphere is used for the oxidation of reduced co-enzymes and it is called **terminal oxidation**. This is also associated with ATP synthesis, so also called as oxidative phosphorylation.

Thus, the production of ATP with the help of energy liberated during oxidation of reduced co-enzymes and terminal oxidation is called oxidative phosphorylation. Oxidative phosphorylation is an endothermic process that occurs in the inner membrane including the cristae of mitochondria (eukaryotes).

**Question 12** What is the significance of step-wise release of energy in respiration?

**Sol.** During oxidation within a cell, all the energy contained in respiratory substrates is not released in a single step. It is released in a series of slow step wise reactions controlled by enzymes and it is trapped as chemical energy in the form of ATP. The significance of this step-wise release of energy is that some energy is used to synthesise ATP. This ATP is stored for the later utilisation wherever required. Hence, ATP acts as the energy currency of cell. The energy stored in ATP can be utilised for following purpose :

(i) In various energy requiring processes of organisms.

(ii) The carbon skeleton produced during respiration is used as precursors for the synthesis of other molecules.

# DIKSHA APP Questions

## ☐ Multiple Choice Questions

**Q.1** Which one of the following results in formation of water

(a) Clycolysis (b) Lactic acid fermintation

(c) Krebs cycle (d) Putrefaction

**Sol.** (a) Glycolysis is a common pathway of anaerobic and aerobic respirations. In glycolysis from one glucose molecule, we obtain 2 pyruvate molecules, 2 water molecules around so net loss of two water molecules.

**Q.2** Net ATP output as a result of breakdown of one molecule of glucose is

(a) 8 (b) 6 (c) 4 (d) 2

**Sol.** (d) Glycolysis is the process in which there in partial oxidation of the glucose molecule carried out. The glucose molecule is broken down to **give two molecules of pyruvate. There are 4ATPs produced but 2 are used** up, so the net yield of glycolysis is 2 ATP.

**Q.3** Glycolysis was discovered by

(a) Embden and krebs (b) Embden and Karl Lohmann

(c) Embden and Edward Buchner (d) Embden Meyerhof and Parnas

**Sol.** (d) Glycolysis also known as EMP pathway was discovered by G. Embden O Margh of J.K. Parmas. This is breakdown of glycose to pyuruvic acid.

**Q.4** As a result of fermentation Yeast produces

(a) $CO_2$ and Ethanol (b) $O_2$ and Ethanol

(c) $H_2O$ and Ethanol (d) $CO_2$ and pyruvic acid

**Sol.** (a) By the process of fermentation yeast produces ethanol and $CO_2$ . It is a well known natural process of making alcoholic beverages. During reduction of acetaldehyde to ethanol in presence enzyme alcohol dehydrogenase, these is regeneration of $NAD^+$ . Pyruvic acid is the end product of glycolysis.

**Q.5** Protons accumulate in mitochondria in

(a) inner membrane (b) intermediate space

(c) outer membrane (d) matrix

**Sol.** (b) During respiration proton accumulates in the space between outer and inner mitochondrical membrane. this accumulation of protons develop proton motive force, which facilitatis ATP formation by chemiosmosis.

**Q.6** During Krebs cycle Isocitrate is converted into Oxalosuccinate in the presence enzyme isocitrate dehydrogenase and one of the following ions

(a) $Fe^{++}$ (b) $Mg^{++}$ (c) $Mn^{++}$ (d) $Na^{++}$

**Sol.** (c) During krebs cylce isocitrate is converted into oxalosuccinate intwo step process in presence of enzyme isocitrate dehydrogenase. This enzyme is composed of 3-subunits and isoallosterically regulated and requires an integrateal $Mn^{2+}$ ion.

**Q.7** The reaction that is called link reaction between glycolysis and Krebs cycle

(a) conversion of pyruvate to Acetyl CoA

(b) conversion of Acetyi CoA to citric acid

(c) coversion of oxaloacetate to citrate

(d) oxidation of malate to oxaloacetate

**Sol.** (a) Conversion of pyruvate (product of glycolysis) to acetyl CoA is the link between glycolysis and Krebs cycle. In this step the enzyme involved is pyrurate dehydrogenese, during this process $NADH^+$ molecule is formed additionally.

**Q.8** Which one of the following statements is incorrect?

(a) ETS operates in the inner mitochondrial membrane

(b) NADPH yields 3ATP

(c) Glycolysis operates in he cytoplasm

(d) First product of Krebs cycle is succinate

**Sol.** Krebs cycle also called TCA cycle or citric acid cycle is found in mitochondiral matrix and in first step acetyl CoA complex condense with oxaloacetate and water to form 6 C compound, citric acid (citrate) in presence of enzyme citrate synthase.

**Q.9** The final electron acceptor in ETS is

(a) cytochrome-c (b) cytochrome-$a_3$
(c) cytochrome-b (d) cytochrome-a

**Sol.** (b) ETS (Electron Transport System) the final electron acceptor is oxygen. Oxygen received the electrons from cytochrome-$a_3$. Cytochrome-$bc_1$ is complex III while cytochrome-*a* and $a_3$ is complex IV.

**Q.10** Which one of the following substances is the starting point of various respiratory pathways?

(a) Acetyl CoA (b) Pyruvic acid
(c) Glucose (d) Glucose 6 phosphate

**Sol.** (c) Glucose is the starting point of various respiratory process. All the other forms of carbohydrate are first converted to glucose for oxidation.

**Q.11** Most commonly used respiratory substrate is

(a) ketones (b) glucose
(c) fructose (d) sucrose

**Sol.** (b) Most commonly used respiratory substrate is glucose. All the other monomer are converted to glucose for respiratory oxidation.

**Q.12** R.Q in case of protein being used as substrate is

(a) less than 1 (b) more than 1
(c) zero (d) sometimes less sometimes more than 1

**Sol.** R.Q. is the ratio of $CO_2$ produced to $O_2$ consumed in respiration R.Q. for proteins and fats will be less than one. This value will be one for carbohydrate and more than one for organic acids.

## ☐ Short Answer Type

**Q.1** Explain the structure of mitochondria describing the role of its each part in respiration.

**Sol.** Diagram with 3 labellings

Role

(a) ATP synthase located on oxysome

(b) Proton gradient in the inner space

(c) Matrix has DNA and enzymes for krebs cycle.

The structure of mitochondria describing the role of its each part is respiration are as follows:

(i) Outer membrane- It only allow small molecules to pass through it such as glucose needed for cellular respiration.

(ii) Inner membrane- This membrane is active site for the electron transport chain and ATP production.

(iii) Cristae - They provide a large surface area for the components of ETC and ATP synthase.

(iv) Matrix - It is site of the krebs cycle and also contain necessary enzymes for fatty acid oxidation and citric acid cycle.

(v) Intermembrane space - It play an important role in generating the proton gradient during oxidative phosphorylation.

**Q.2** "Krebs cycle is an amphibolic pathway". Justify the statement.

**Sol.** Amphibolic means-both catabolic and anabolic. Krebs cycle although mainly catabolic produces many intermediates that are raw materials for anabolic purposes *e.g.*, Acetyl CoA also used for building steroids and carotenoid.

Kreb's cycle is an amphibolic pathway because energy is both consumed and produced during this process. During the catabolic part, acetyl CoA is converted to produce $Co_2$ and energy, which are later used to produce FADH and NADH.

During the anabolic part, several intermediates of this pathway are converted to succinyl CoA to succinic acid using ATP

## □ Long Answer Type

**Q.1** (a) Discuss the relationship between glycolysis, krebs cycle and ETS.

(b) Form a table showing the total net gain of ATP as a result complete oxidation of one molecule of glucose.

**Sol.** NADH and $FADH_2$ molecules formed during glycolysis, krebs' cycle carry their electrons to the electron transport chain.

| Stage | Source | No, of ATP mol. Produced |
|---|---|---|
| Glycolysis | Direct<br>2-molecule of $NADH_2$ | 2<br>6 |
| Pyrvic acid to acetyl-CoA | 2-molecule of $NADH_2$ | 6 |
| Citric acid cycle | 6 $NADH_2$<br>2 $FADH_2$<br>Direct | 18<br>4<br>2 |
| Total = 38 | | |

# Plant Growth and Development

CHAPTER 13

## Important Points

**01** The most important fundamental and the conspicuous characteristic of living beings is **growth,** which is as an irreversible permanent increase in size of an organ or its parts or even an individual cell. Growth is accompanied by metabolic processes that require energy.

**02** Plants are capable of indeterminate growth and it could be measured by the variety of parameters like dry weight, fresh weight, length, area etc.

**03** Growth phase is divided into three phases

(i) Meristematic (ii) Elongation (iii) Maturation

**04** The growth rate shows an increase that may be arithmetic or geometrical.

(i) In arithmetic growth, following mitotic cell division , only one daughter cell continues to divide, while the others differentiate and matures. A linear curve is obtain on plotting the length of the organ against time.

(ii) **Geometrical growth** Usually sigmoid growth curve is seen.

In this, the initial growth is slow (lag phase) and it increases rapidly thereafter at an exponential rate (log or exponential phase). As the time progress, the growth become stationary.

**05** Growth rate is of two types, absolute growth rate and relative growth rate.

Essential elements of growth are water, oxygen and nutrients.

**06** Plant cells shows a very special property of differentiation, dedifferentiation and redifferentiation.

(i) Differentiation is the process through, which plant cell undergoes maturation.

(ii) Under certain conditions living differentiated cells which have lost the ability to divide regains ability of cell division. This process is called dedifferentiation.

(iii) The dedifferentiated cells divide to give rise to new cells, which differentiate to perform specific function and attains maturation and looses the capacity to divide further. Such process is known as **redifferentiation**.

**07** **Development** includes all the changes, which occurs during different stages of life cycle of an organism.

(i) Ability of plant to develop different types of plant structures in response to environment signals is known as plasticity, *e.g.*, in some plants, leaves at younger (juvenile phase) is different from the leaves at mature phase known as heterophylly, *e.g.*, heterophylly in cotton, larkspur and coriander.

**08** Physiological activities in plant are regulated by the action and interaction of some chemical substances known as plant growth regulators. Which are auxin cytokinin, gibberellin, ABA, ethylene.

**09** **Charles Darwin** and **Francis Darwin** first time observed that the coleoptile of canary grass bends towards unilateral illumination. Later FW Went isolated auxin from the tips of coleoptile of oat seedlings.

(i) **Auxins** were first isolated from human urine.

(ii) Auxin plays an important role in

(a) Growth of apical bud which inhibits the growth of axillary buds.

(b) Promotes flowering and induce parthenocarpy.

(c) It prevents leaf absicission and early fruit drop.

(d) Act as weedicides and controls xylem differentiation.

**10** E. Kurosawa identified the 'Bakane' (foolish seedling) disease of rice seedlings. Main role of gibberellic acids are

(i) They delays senescence and promote bolting.

(ii) $GA_3$ is used to speed up the malting process in brewing industry and break dormancy.

**11** Cytokinin is another naturally occurring growth hormone in plants. F. Skoog and his co-workers identified and crystallise the cytokinesis promoting substance called kinetin. Kinetin does not naturally occur in plants.

**Zeatin** is a natural **cytokinin** Role of cytokinin includes

(i) cell division in apical meristem.
(ii) they helps to produce new leaves, chloroplast in leaves.
(iii) they help to overcome apical dominance.
(iv) they promotes nutrient mobilisation, which helps in delay of leaf senescence (falling of leaves).

**12** The gaseous plant growth regulator ethylene was identified by Cousins. Role of ethylene

(i) it promotes senescence and abscission of plant organ.
(ii) promotes fruit ripening and flowing in pineapple and mango.
(iii) it breaks seed and bud dormancy.
(iv) it enhances respiratory climatic.

**13** ABA (abscisic acid) plays an important role in regulating abscission and dormancy. It usually acts as a plant growth inhibitor and also known as **stress hormone**.

# Exercises

**Question 1** Define growth, differentiation, development, dedifferentiation, redifferentiation, determinate growth, meristem and growth rate.

**Sol. Growth** It is an irreversible permanent increase in size of an organ or its parts or even of an individual cell.

**Development** It is the process of whole series of changes which an organism goes through during its life cycle.

**Meristems** The cells of which have the capacity to divide and self-perpetuate.

**Growth rates** The increased growth per unit time is termed as growth rate. Thus, rate of growth can be expressed mathematically. An organism, or a part of the organism can produce more cells in a variety of ways. The growth rate shows an increase that may be arithmetic or geometrical.

**Differentiation** The cells derived from root apical or shoot-apical meristems and cambium differentiate and mature to perform specific functions. This act leading to maturation is termed as differentiation.

**Dedifferentiation** The living differentiated cells, that by now have lost the capacity to divide can regain the capacity of division under certain conditions.

This phenomenon is termed as dedifferentiation. For example, formation of meristems; interfascicular cambium and cork cambium from fully differentiated parenchyma cells.

**Redifferentiation** While undergoing dedifferentiation plant cells once again lose their capacity to divide and become mature. This process is called redifferentiation.

**Question 2** Why is not any one parameter good enough to demonstrate growth throughout the life of a flowering plant?

**Sol.** Any one parameter is not good enough to demonstrate growth throughout the life of a flowering plant because the plants exhibit different types of growths during different stages of their life cycle.

In the seedling stage, they are in state of active cell division (*i.e.,* mitotic divisions), then they undergo active cell enlargement stage during growing stage. In the reproductive or flowering stage of their life cycle, they exhibit reductional divisions. Finally, after the formation of various organs, they undergo cell differentiation or get matured.

**Question 3** Describe briefly

(a) Arithmetic growth (b) Geometric growth

(c) Sigmoid growth curve (d) Absolute and relative growth rates

**Sol.**

(a) **Arithmetic growth** In arithmetic growth, following mitotic cell division, only one daughter cell continues to divide while the other differentiates and matures. Example is a root elongation at a constant rate.

(b) **Geometric growth** In geometrical growth, in most systems, the initial growth is slow (lag phase), and it increases rapidly thereafter at an exponential rate (log or exponential phase). Here, both the progeny cells following mitotic cell division retain the ability to divide and continue to do so. However, with limited nutrient supply, the growth slows down, leading to a stationary phase.

(c) **Sigmoid growth curve** If we plot the parameter of growth against time, we get a typical sigmoid or S-curve. A sigmoid curve is a characteristic of living organism growing in a natural environment. It is typical for all cells, tissues and organs of a plant.

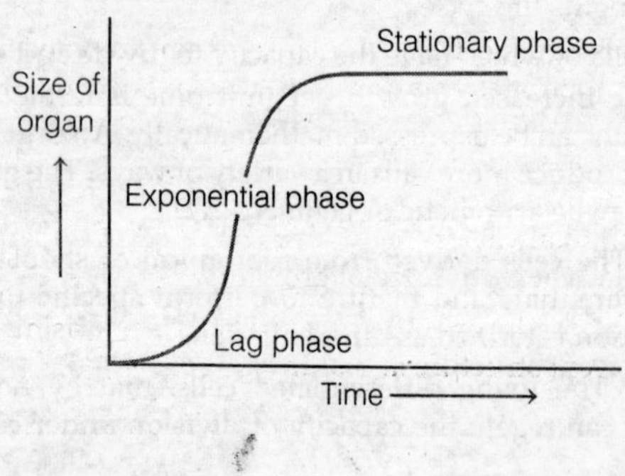

(d) **Absolute and relative growth rates** The measurement and the comparison of total growth per unit time is called the absolute growth rate and the growth of the given system per unit time expressed on a common basis, *e.g.*, per unit initial parameter is called the relative growth rate.

**Question 4** List five main groups of natural plant growth regulators. Write a note on discovery, physiological functions and agricultural/horticultural applications of any one of them.

**Sol.** Five main groups of natural plant growth regulators are auxins, gibberellins, ethylene, cytokinins and ABA.

**Auxins**

(i) **Discovery** Auxin was first isolated from human urine. They are generally produced by the growing apices of the stems and roots. Auxins like IAA and indole butyric acid (IBA) have been isolated from plants. NAA (naphthalene acetic acid) and 2, 4-D (2, 4-dichlorophenoxyacetic acid) are synthetic auxins.

(ii) **Physiological function** They help to initiate rooting in stem cuttings, an application widely used for plant propagation. Auxins promote flowering, *i.e.*, in pineapples. They help to prevent fruit and leaf drop at early stages but promote the abscission of older mature leaves and fruits.

(iii) **Agricultural Horticultural applications** Auxins also induce parthenocarpy, *e.g.*, in tomatoes. They are widely used as herbicides 2, 4-D, widely used to kill dicotyledonous weeds, does not affect mature monocotyledonous plants. It is used to prepare weed-free lawns by gardeners. Auxin also controls xylem differentiation and helps in cell division.

**Question 5** Why is abscisic acid also known as stress hormone?

**Sol.** Abscisic acid acts as a general plant growth inhibitor and an inhibitor of plant metabolism. ABA inhibits seed germination. ABA stimulates the closure of stomata in the epidermis and increases the tolerance of plants to various kinds of stresses. Therefore, it is also called the stress hormone.

**Question 6** 'Both growth and differentiation in higher plants are open'. Comment.

**Sol.** Plant growth is unique because plants retain the capacity for unlimited growth throughout their life. This ability of the plants are due to the presence of meristems at certain locations in their body. The cells of such meristems have the capacity to divide and self-perpetuate. The product, however, soon loses the capacity to divide and such cells make up the plant body. This form of growth where in new cells are always being added to the plant body by the activity of the meristem is called the open form of growth.

Differentiation in plants in open because cells/tissues arising out of the same meristem have different structure at maturity.

**Question 7** 'Both a short day plant and a long day plant can produce, can flower simultaneously in a given place'. Explain.

**Sol.** A short day plant flowers only when it receive a long dark period and short photoperiod. On the other hand a long day plant will flower only when it receives a long photoperiod and short dark period. Thus, critical photoperiod is that continuous duration of light which must not be exceeded in short day plant and should always be exceeded in long day plant in order to bring them to flower.

**Question 8** Which one of the plant growth regulators would you use if you are asked to

(a) induce rooting in a twig
(b) quickly ripen a fruit
(c) delay leaf senescence
(d) induce growth in axillary buds
(e) 'bolt' a rosette plant
(f) induce immediate stomatal closure in leaves.

**Sol.** (a) Auxins (b) Ethylene
(c) Cytokinins (d) Cytokinins
(e) Gibberellins (f) Abscisic acid.

**Question 9** Would a defoliated plant respond to photoperiodic cycle? Why?

**Sol.** No, a defoliated plant do not respond to photoperiodic cycle because leaves of a plant are the sites of light perception for the induction of flowering.

**Question 10** What would be expected to happen if

(a) $GA_3$ is applied to rice seedlings
(b) dividing cells stop differentiating
(c) a rotten fruit gets mixed with unripe fruits
(d) you forget to add cytokinin to the culture medium.

**Sol.**

(a) If $GA_3$ is applied to rice seedlings then the rice seedlings will exhibit internode elongation and increase in height.
(b) If dividing cells stops differentiating then the plant organs such as leaves and stem are not going to be formed.
(c) If a rotten fruit gets mixed with unripe fruits then the ethylene produced from the rotten fruits will hasten the ripening of unripe fruits.
(d) If one forget to add cytokinin to the culture medium then cell division, growth and differentiation will not be observed.

# DIKSHA APP *Questions*

## ☐ Multiple Choice Questions

**Q.1** Type of growth in which only one daughter cell divides while the other differentiates is called

(a) Geometric growth (b) Logarithmic growth
(c) Arithmetic growth (d) Relative growth

**Sol.** (c) Arithmetic growth only one daughter cell divides while the other differentiates and matures.

**Q.2** Instrument used to measure growth in plant length

(a) Anemometer (b) Auxanometer
(c) Ammeter (d) Sphigmometer

**Sol.** (b) Auxanometer is a device that measures the rate of growth of a plant.

**Q.3** Why water is required for plant growth ?

(a) Provides th medium for enzymatic activities
(b) Releasing metabolic energy
(c) For the sysnthesis of protoplasm
(d) Act as sources of energy

**Sol.** (a) Water is required for plant growth to provide the medium for enzymatic activity i.e., involved in chemical reaction water is essential for photosynthesis, nutrient transport, seed germination cell reponsion etc.

**Q.4** What is incorrect for meristematic tissues ?

(a) Rich in protoplasm
(b) Cell walls are primary in nature
(c) Increased vacuolation
(d) Large conspicuous nuclei

**Sol.** (c) Meristematic tissue is undifferentiated tissue. The cells of this tissue are rich in cytoplasm having thin cell wall and prominent nucleus.

**Q.5** Name the act in which the living differentiated cells, that by now have lost the capacity to divide can regain the capacity of division under certain conditions.

(a) Differentiation (b) Dedifferentiation
(c) Redifferentiation (d) Plasticity

**Sol.** (b) Dedifferentiation is the act in which the living differentiatied cells that lost the capacity to divide can region the capacity of division under certain condition.

**Q.6** Name the act in which root apical and shoot apical meristems and cambium differentiate and mature to perform specific functions and leading to maturation

(a) Differentiation (b) Dedifferentiation
(c) Redifferentiation (d) Plasticity

**Sol.** (a) Differentiation is the act in which meristematic tissue (root or shoot apex) or cambium differentiate and mature to perform specific functions and leading to maturation.

**Q.7** Plant that shows plasticity due to environmental changes

(a) Cotton (b) Coriander
(c) Buttercup (d) Larkspur

**Sol.** (c) The butter cup plant shows plasticity due to environmental changes. These plants are known for exhibiting different shape of leaves known as heterophylly. Which is a adaptation in response to environmental changes.

**Q.8** Intrinsic factor responsible for controlling development is

(a) Nutrition (b) Plant growth regulators
(c) Light (d) Oxygen

**Sol.** (b) Plant growth regulators or intrinsis factors responsible for controlling growth and development. Nutrition, light and oxygen are extrinsic factors.

**Q.9** Auxin was isolated by

(a) F.W. Went from coleoptile of canary grass
(b) Charles Darwin from coleoptile of canary grass
(c) F.W. Went from coleoptile of oats seedings
(d) Charles Darwin from coleoptile of oats seedlings

**Sol.** (c) F.W. Went isolated auxin from the tip of oat coleoptiles. After that IAA (Indole 3-Acetic Acid) was then isolated from human urine also.

**Q.10** Early fruit drop can be prevented by

(a) Cytokinin (b) Gibberellin
(c) Phytochrome (d) Auxin

**Sol.** (d) Auxin prevents early fruit drop

**Q.11** The phenomenon of elongation of stem of rosette plants is called

(a) perrenation (b) bolting
(c) necrosis (d) lodging

**Sol.** (b) Bolting is the phenomenon of elongation of stem of rosette plants.

**Q.12** The ability of plants to follow different pathways in response to environment to form different type of structures is called

(a) totipotency (b) phyllotaxy
(c) plasticity (d) cytokinesis

**Sol.** (c) Plasticity is the ability of plants to follow different pathways in response to environment to form different type of structures.

**Q.13** Which one of the following is employed for eradication of broad leaved weeds?

(a) 2 : 4 D (b) Gibberellin
(c) Abscissic acid (d) Ethylene

**Sol.** (a) 2, 4-D is used to kill dicot weeds.

**Q.14** Which PGR is responsible for increasing length of sugarcane stem and increasing yield ?

(a) Auxin (b) Cytokinin
(c) Abscisic Acid (d) Gibberellins

**Sol.** (d) Plant Growth Regulators (PGR) are chemical compound which affect growth and development of plants. Gibberelin is responsible for increasing the length of sugarcane stem and increasing yield also.

**Q.15** Which one of the following is not performed by a differentiated cell?

(a) Cell division (b) Photosynthesis
(c) Conduction of sap (d) Mechanical strength

**Sol.** (a) Cell division is not performed by differentiated cell.

**Q.16** A hormone that promotes seed germination by mobilising its stored food is

(a) gibberellin (b) ethylene
(c) cytokinin (d) auxin

**Sol.** (a) Gibberellin promotes seed germination by mobilising its store food.

**Q.17** A hormone that is antagonistic to Gibberellin is

(a) auxin (b) ethylene
(c) cytokinin (d) abscissic acid

**Sol.** (d) ABA acts as an antagonistic to Gibberellin.

**Q.18** Hormone responsible for seed dormancy

(a) abscissic acid (b) IAA
(c) 2, 4 (d) ethylene

**Sol.** (a) ABA responsible for seed dormancy.

**Q.19** Photoperiodic response in plants is mediated by

(a) phytochrome (b) cytochrome
(c) quinones (d) zeatin

**Sol.** (a) Phytochrome mediate photoperiodic response in plants.

**Q.20** Which is the site of perception of light/dark duration ?

(a) Leaves (b) Perianth
(c) Internodes (d) Stem

**Sol.** (a) Leaves are the site of perception of light/dark duration becasue photosynthesis is found only in green parts of the plants.

**Q.21** Why plants need a periodic exposure to light ?

(a) For the root elongation (b) For fruit formation
(c) To induce flowering (d) For seed germination

**Sol.** (c) The plants need periodic reposure to light to induce flowering short day plants require short duration while long day plants need long duration of light.

**Q.22** Which plant doesn't have both spring and winter varieties ?

(a) Mango (b) Wheat
(c) Rye (d) Barley

**Sol.** (a) Spring and winter varietes are found in wheat, rye barley but not in mango.

**Q.23** Which of the following is nota biennial plant?

(a) Mango (b) Sugar beet
(c) Cabbage (d) Carrot

**Sol.** (a) Mango (*Mangifera indica*) is a perrenial plant. It is a tree. It is also known as king of fruits in India.

## ☐ Short Answer Type

**Q.1** "Abscisic acid is known as a stress hormone" Justify the statement.

**Sol.** Abscisic acid is known as stress hormone because

(a) Causes closure of stomata during drought.
(b) Induces leaf fall during harsh coditions.
(c) Promotes seed dormancy to tide over adverse conditions.

**Q.2** A hormone was discovered from rice plants suffering from a fungal disease called Bakane. Name the fungus. What was the nature of disease? Name the hormone discovered. Give its characteristic features.

**Sol.** Gibberella fujikuroi was a hormone discovered from rice plants suffering from fungal disease, bakane. Nature of disease are as follows

Thin, pale green, longer by 50% than healthy plants Gibberellin was discoverd and its characteristic features are as follows:

(a) Overcomes dormancy of seeds (b) Causes elongation of reduced stem.

**Q.3** What is apical dominance? Which phytohormone regulates this phenomenon in plants?

**Sol.** The growing apical bud inhibits the growth of the lateral (axillary) buds. In most of the higher plants it is called apical dominance. Auxin is the phytohormone involved in the phenomenon of apical dominance.

**Q.4** What are the conditions required for plant growth?

**Sol.** The conditions required for plant growth are as follows

(a) **Water** For turgidity of cells which helps in extension growth and provides medium for enzymatic activities.

(b) **Oxygen** Release metabolic energy.

(c) **Nutrients** For synthesis of protoplasm and acts as source of energy.

## ☐ Long Answer Type

**Q.1** Given the role of plant hormone under following conditions. Identify the plant hormone

(a) You want to induce maleness in certain cucubit plants.

(b) You observe a whole basket of fruits rotting only because a few bad pieces.

(c) You want a proper differentiation of callus in your tissue culture.

(d) You want to promote seed dormancy of your preserved seeds.

(e) You want a bushy growth in your hedge plants.

**Sol.** (a) Gibberellin (b) Ethylene (c) Cytokinin and auxin (d) Abscissic acid (e) Removal of apical dominance. Explanation of all these hormones.

(a) **Gibberellic acid** induce maleness in cucurbit plants by promoting the formation of male flower.

(b) **Ethylene** is a gas that diffuses easily and will have the same effect on a whole basket of fruits due to few acid pieces.

(c) Specific **auxin** to **cytokinin** ratios give to proper differentiation of a callus in tissue culture.

(d) **Abscissic acid** promotes seed dormancy, helps seeds to withstand desiccation and other factors unfavourable for growth.

(e) Removal of shoot tip (decapitation) results in growth of lateral buds by **auxins** led to the formation of bushy growth in hedge plants.

# Breathing and Exchange of Gases

CHAPTER 14

## Important Points

**01** Respiration is the process of exchange of $O_2$ with $CO_2$ along with its transport. It includes mainly two processess *i.e.*, breathing and gaseous exchange along with its transport.

**02** Breathing is the process of moving of air in and out of the lungs-including inspiration and expiration.

**03** Mechanism of breathing vary among different group of animals depending upon habitat and level of organisation, *e.g.*, like in sponges, coelenterates, flatworms, etc. $O_2$ is exchanged with $CO_2$ by a simple diffusion over the entire body surface.

**04** Human respiratory system is well-developed and formed by nostrils, nasal passage, pharynx, larynx, trachea, bronchi and lungs.

(i) Nostrils are the openings above the upper lips. It leads to nasal chamber through the nasal passage.

(ii) Nasal chamber opens into pharynx, which act as common passage for food and air.

(iii) Pharynx extends/opens through the glottis of larynx region into trachea.

The trachea divides into primary bronchi, which further branch into secondary and tertiary bronchi, ending in terminal bronchioles that leads to alveoli, where gas exchange occurs.

(v) This whole network of bronchi, bronchioles and alveoli comprises the lungs. The lungs are situated in a thoracic chamber. The thoracic chamber is formed by vertebral column at dorsal side, ventrally by sternum, ribs at the lateral side and at the lower side, a dome-shaped diaphragm

**05** Breathing (pulmonary ventilation) involves two steps i.e. inspiration and expiration.

(i) Inspiration occurs when the contraction of the diaphragm and external intercostal muscles increases thoracic and pulmonary volume, reducing intra-pulmonary pressure and drawing air into the lungs.

(ii) Expiration occurs as the diaphragm and intercostal muscle relax, reducing lung volume and pulmonary volume and increasing intra-pulmonary pressure. This cause exhalation of air.

**06** Respiratory volumes and capacities are expressed in different ways

(i) **Tidal Volume** (TV) It is the amount of air exchanged during normal respiration, about 500ml per breath or 6000-8000 mL of air per min.

(ii) **Inspiratory Reserve Volume** (IRV) It is the extra volume (2500-3000 mL) of air, a person inhaled through forible inspiration.

(iii) **Expiratory Reserve Volume** (ERV) It is the additional amount of air, which could be expelled out of lungs by forcible expiration. It is 1000 to 1100 mL.

(iv) **Residual Volume** (RV) It is measured as the volume of air remaining in the lungs after forced expiration.

(v) **Vital Capacity** (VC) It is the maximum volume of air, which can be moved in after a forced expiration.

$$VC = \text{Tidal volume} + IRV + ERV$$

(vi) **Inspiratory Capacity** (IC) Total volume of air a person can inspire after normal expiration. It is IRV+ TV.

(vii) **Expiratory Capacity** (EC) Volume of air a person can expire after normal inspiration. It is TV+ ERV.

(viii) **Functional Residual Capacity** (FRC) It is the volume of air that will remain in lungs after a normal expiration. It includes ERV+ RV.

(ix) **Total lung capacity** It is the volume of air accomodated in lungs at the end of forced inspiration. It is vital capacity + residual volume.

**07** Gases like $O_2$ and $CO_2$ are exchanged in the alveoli and tissues by simple diffusion.

(i) This process is driven by partial pressure gradents, with $PO_2$ higher in alveoli than in the blood and tissues and $PCO_2$ higher in the tissues than in the blood (oxygenated) and alveoli.

(ii) As solubility of $CO_2$ is 20-25 times higher than $O_2$, so the amount of $CO_2$ that can diffuse through diffusion membrane is higher than $O_2$.

(iii) Diffusion membrane of alveoli is made up of three major layers namely thin squamous epithelium, endothelium and basement membrane.

**08** Blood is the main medium for the transport of $O_2$ and $CO_2$

(i) $O_2$ is mainly (97%) transported by RBC in the blood where as the remaining 3% of $O_2$ is carried in dissolved state through the plasma.

(ii) Nearly 20-25 percent of $CO_2$ is transported by RBCs whereas 70% percent of it is carried as bicarbonate and about 7% of $CO_2$ is carried in a dissolved state through plasma.

**09** Oxygen is transported in bound form with haemoglobin, which is a red coloured iron containing pigment. $O_2$ binds with Hb to form oxyhaemoglobin.

(i) Each molecule of haemoglobin can binds with four $O_2$ molecule,

Binding of haemoglobin with $O_2$ depends upon partial pressure of $O_2$. Partial pressure of $CO_2$, hydrogen ion concentration and temperature are the other factors, which can interfere with this binding.

(ii) When the percentage saturation of haemoglobin is plotted against the $pO_2$ than curve is called **oxygen dissociation curve.**

(iii) Factors like low temperature, high $pO_2$, low $pCO_2$ and less $H^+$ ion concentration (acidic pH) shifts the curve toward left indicating formation of oxyhaemoglobin, whereas in low $pO_2$, high $pCO_2$, basic pH, high temperature shifts the curve towards right which indicates the dissociation of $O_2$ from the oxyhaemoglobin.

**10** $CO_2$ transport is carried out in form of carbamino-haemoglobin (*i.e.*, about 20-25%).

(i) Binding of $CO_2$ in tissues occurs due to high $pCO_2$ and low $pO_2$.

(ii) From high concentration (high $pCO_2$) at tissue site, $CO_2$ diffuses into blood and forms $HCO_3^-$ and $H^+$ ions under the action of enzyme carbonic anhydrase.

This reaction can proceeded in opposite direction, where $pCO_2$ is low at alveolar site leading to the formation of $CO_2$ and $H_2O$.

**11** Respiration is under the control of our neural system

(i) Respiratory rhythm centre present in the medulla region of the brain is responsible for regulation of respiration.

(ii) **Pneumotaxic centre** is also present in the pons region of the brain. It can moderate the function of respiratory rhythm centre.

(iii) A chemosensitive area present adjacent to the rhythmic centre is highly sensitive to $CO_2$ and $H^+$ ion concentration.

**12** Various disorder is associated with respiratory system

(i) **Asthma** Inflammation of bronchi and bronchioles occur, which causes difficulty in breathing and cause wheezing.

(ii) **Emphysema** It is a chronic disorder in which respiratory surface is decreased due to damage in alveolar walls.

(iii) **Fibrosis** It is occupational respiratory disorder. Long term exposure to dust causes inflammation in lungs. It is usually seen in workers involved in grinding or stone breaking.

## Exercises

**Question 1** Define vital capacity. What is its significance?

**Sol.** The maximum volume of air a person can breathe in after a forced expiration is called vital capacity. Vital capacity is higher in atheletes and singers. Vital capacity includes ERV, TV and IRV.

**Question 2** State the volume of air remaining in the lungs after a normal breathing.

**Sol.** The volume of air remaining in the lungs even after a forcible expiration averages 1100 mL to 1200 mL.

**Question 3** Diffusion of gases occurs in the alveolar region only and not in the other parts of respiratory system. Why?

**Sol.** Gas diffusion primarily occurs in the alveolar region of the respiratory system due to its specialized structure. This can be explained by the following points

(i) **Thin walls** Alveoli have very thin walls (one cell thick), allowing efficient gas diffusion.

(ii) **Large surface area** Alveoli provide a large surface area for gas exchange due to their numerous, small, sac-like structure.

(iii) **Capillary network** Each alveolus is surrounded by capillaries, facilitating easy diffusion of gases between the alveolar air and blood.

**Question 4** What are the major transport mechanisms for $CO_2$? Explain.

**Sol.** The major transport mechanisms for $CO_2$ in the blood are as follows

(i) **Dissolved in Plasma (7-10%)** A small portion of $CO_2$ is dissolved directly in the plasma of the blood. This is the most immediate form of transport but is not significant in terms of total $CO_2$ carried.

(ii) **Bicarbonate ion (70-75%)** The majority of $CO_2$ is converted into bicarbonate ($CHO_3^-$) in red blood cells. This reactionis catalyzed by the enzyme carbonic anhydrase. $CO_2$ reacts with water to form carbonic acid ($H_2CO_3$), which quickly dissociates into bicarbonate and hydrogen ions ($H^+$). The bicarbonate is then transported into the plasma.

(iii) **Carbamino** haemoglobin (20-25%) $CO_2$ is transported with the help of RBCs as carbamino-haemoglobin. $CO_2$ will bind to the amino groups on the polypeptide chains of haemoglobin and form a compound known as carbamino-haemoglobin.

**Question 5** What will be the $pO_2$ and $pCO_2$ in the atmospheric air compared to those in the alveolar air?

(i) $pO_2$ lesser and $pCO_2$ higher
(ii) $pO_2$ higher and $pCO_2$ lesser
(iii) $pO_2$ higher and $pCO_2$ higher
(iv) $pO_2$ lesser and $pCO_2$ lesser

**Sol.** (ii) $pO_2$ higher and $pCO_2$ lesser.

Atmospheric air has more oxygen ($pO_2$) and less carbon dioxide ($pCO_2$) than alveolar air because, in the alveoli, oxygen diffuses into the blood, lowering $pO_2$, while carbon dioxide diffuses from the blood into the alveoli, raising $pCO_2$.

**Question 6** Explain the process of inspiration under normal conditions.

**Sol.** Inspiration is the process during which atmospheric air is drawn in. Inspiration is initiated by the contraction of diaphragm, which increases the volume of thoracic chamber in the antero-posterior axis. The contraction of external inter costal muscles lifts up the ribs and the sternum causing an increase in the volume of the thoracic chamber in the dorso-ventral axis.

The overall increase in the thoracic volume causes a similar increase in pulmonary volume. An increase in pulmonary volume decreases the intra pulmonary pressure to less than the atmospheric pressure, which forces the air from outside to move into the lungs, *i.e.,* inspiration. On an average, a healthy human breathes 12-16 times/minute.

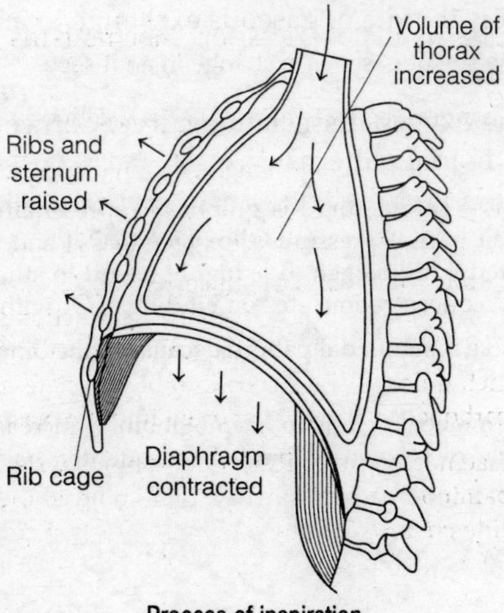


**Process of inspiration**

**Question 7** How is respiration regulated?

**Sol.** A specialised centre present in the medulla region of the brain called respiratory rhythm centre is primarily responsible for the regulation of respiration.

Another centre present in the pons region of the brain called pneumotaxic centre can moderate the functions of the respiratory rhythm centre. Neural signal from this centre can reduce the duration of inspiration and thereby alter the respiratory rate.

**Question 8** What is the effect of $pCO_2$ on oxygen transport?

**Sol.** Partial pressure of $CO_2$ ($pCO_2$) can interfere with the binding of oxygen and haemoglobin, to form carbamino-haemoglobin.

(i) In the alveoli, where there is high $pO_2$ and low $pCO_2$, lesser $H^+$ concentration and lower temperature, more formation of oxyhaemoglobin occur.

(ii) In the tissues, where low $pO_2$, high $pCO_2$, high $H^+$ concentration and high temperature exist, the conditions are responsible for dissociation of oxygen from the oxyhaemoglobin and formation of carbamino-haemoglobin.

**Question 9** What happens to the respiratory process in a man going up a hill?

**Sol.** At hills, the pressure of air falls and the person does not get enough oxygen with each breath. This cause the amount of oxygen in the blood to decline. The respiratory rate increases in response to decrease in the oxygen content of blood and due to this the person feels breathlessness, headache, dizziness, nausea, mental fatigue and a bluish colour on the skin, nails and lips.

**Question 10** What is the site of gaseous exchange in an insect?

**Sol.** Trachea are the site of gaseous exchange in an insect.

**Question 11** Define oxygen dissociation curve. Can you suggest any reason for its sigmoidal pattern?

**Sol.** The oxygen dissociation curve is graphical representation that show the relationship between partial pressure of oxygen ($pO_2$) and the percentage of hemoglobin saturated with oxygen. It is highly useful in studying the effect of factors like $pCO_2$, $H^+$ concentration, etc., on binding of $O_2$ with haemoglobin.

The dissociation curve is sigmoidal pattern because of the bindning of oxygen to haemoglobin.

As the first oxygen molecule binds to haemoglobin, it increases the affinity for the second molecule of oxygen to bind. Subsequently, haemoglobin attracts more oxygen.

The sigmoidal pattern of oxygen hemoglobin dissociation curve is the result of two properties.

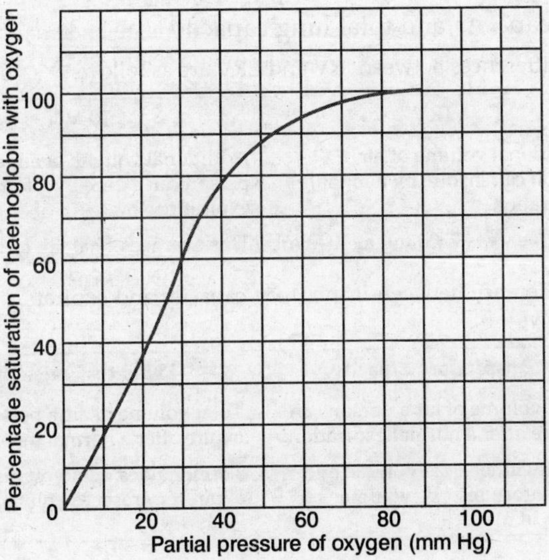


Oxygen dissociation curve

**Question 12** Have you heard about hypoxia? Try to gather information about it, and discuss with your friends.

**Sol.** Hypoxia is low levels of oxygen in the blood tissues. It causes symptoms like confusion, restlessness, difficulty in breathing, rapid heart rate and bluish skin.

**Question 13** What are the values of $pO_2$ and $pCO_2$ of the following:

(i) Alveolar air (ii) Systemic arteries

(iii) Systemic veins

**Sol.** (i) Alveolar air $pO_2 = 104$ mmHg

$pCO_2 = 40$ mmHg

(ii) Systemic arteries

$pO_2 = 95$ mmHg

$pCO_2 = 40$ mmHg

(iii) Systemic veins

$pO_2 = 40$ mmHg

$pCO_2 = 45$ mmHg

**Question 14** Distinguish between

(a) IRV and ERV

(b) Inspiratory capacity and Expiratory capacity

(c) Vital capacity and total lung capacity

**Sol.** (a) The differences between IRV and ERV are as follows

| IRV | REV |
|---|---|
| Additional volume of air, a person can inspire by a forcible inspiration. | Additional volume of air, a person can expire by a forcible expiration. |
| This averages 2500 mL to 3000 mL | This avergaes 1000 mL to 1100 mL |

(b) The difference between inspiratory capacity and expiratory capacity are as follows

| Inspiratory capacity | Expiratory capacity |
|---|---|
| Total volume of air a person can inspire after a normal expiration. | Total volume of air a person can expire after a normal inspiration. |
| This includes tidal volume and inspiratory reserve volume (TV + IRV) | This includes tidal volume and expiratory reserve volume (TV + ERV) |

(c) The differences between vital capacity and total lung capacity are as follows

| Vital capacity | Total lung capacity |
|---|---|
| The maximum volume of air a person can breathe in after a forced expiration. | Total volume of air accommodated in the lungs at the end of a forced inspiration. |
| This includes ERV, TV and IRV or the maximum volume of air a person can breathe out after a forced inspiration | This includes RV, ERV, TV and IRV or vital capacity + residual volume |

**Question 14.** What is Tidal volume? Find out the Tidal volume (approximate value) for a healthy human in an hour.

**Sol.** Volume of air inspired or expired during a normal respiration is called tidal volume. It is about 500 mL., *i.e.*, a healthy man can inspire or expire approximately 6000 to 8000 mL of air per minute.

## DIKSHA APP *Questions*

### ☐ Multiple Choice Questions

**Q.1** What isn't the role of conducting part of human respiratory system?

(a) Clears air from foreign particles
(b) Humidifier air
(c) Allows diffusion of oxygen and carbon dioxide
(d) Brings air to body temperature

**Sol.** (c) Diffusion of $O_2$ and $CO_2$ is not the role of conducting part of human respiratory system. This conducting part transports the air to alveoli, clears, filters and humidifies this air.

**Q.2** Vital capacity is the sum of

(a) ERV + TV + RV (b) EVR +TV
(c) ERV + TV + IRV (d) ERV + IRV

**Sol.** (c) Vital capacity is the sum of Tidal volume (TV), Inspiratory Reserve volume (IRV) and expiratory Reserve volume (ERV), It is total volume of air inhaled and Exhalted by lungs.

**Q.3** What is the capacity of IRV in mL?

(a) 1000-1100 (b) 2500-3000
(c) 1100-1200 (d) 1200-1300

**Sol.** (b) IRV (Inspiratory Reserve Volume) for a normal adult is 2500-3200 ml. It is the amount of air that can be inhaled after a normal breath.

Expiratory Reserve Volume (ERV) is 1100 ml.

**Q.4** Epithelium of alveoli is made up of ?

(a) Squamous epithelium (b) Cuboidal epithelium
(c) Columnar epithelium (d) Ciliated epithelium

**Sol.** (a) Alveoli are tiny baloon shaped, air sacs. Their wall is lined with simple squamous epithelium. The cells of this epithelium are flat and thin which allow passage of small molecules across the epithelium easily.

**Q.5** The thickness of diffusion membrane in human respiratory system is less than a

(a) mm (b) nm
(c) pm (d) cm

**Sol.** (a) The diffusion membrane of lungs is designed for efficient gas exchange. The thickness of this membranes is much less than a mm (around 0.5 to 1 μm).

**Q.6** How much mL of oxygen is delivered by 100 mL of oxygenated blood ?

(a) 3 (b) 4

(c) 5 (d) 6

**Sol.** (c) Under normal conditions 5 ml of oxygen is delivered by 100 mL of oxygenated blood while 4 ml of $CO_2$ is delivered by 100 mL of deoxygenated blood.

**Q.7** How much percentage of carbon dioxide is transported by RBC ?

(a) 97 (b) 70 (c) 20-25 (d) 7

**Sol.** 20-25% of $CO_2$ is transported by RBCs (Red blood cells). RBCs transport $CO_2$ in form of carbamino-haemoglobin, while 70% $CO_2$ is carried as bicarbonate in blood plasma.

**Q.8** Pneumotaxic centre is present in?

(a) Medulla (b) Pons

(c) Cerebrum (d) Cerebellum

**Sol.** (b) Respiratory rhythm centre is located in medulla region of brain while pneumotaxic centre is located in upper part of pons. This centre is responsible for regulating the rate and pattern of breathing.

**Q.9** Respiratory rhythm is present in

(a) Medulla (b) Pons

(c) Cerebrum (d) Cerebellum

**Sol.** (a) The respiratory rhythm centre is present in the medulla oblongata region of the brain.

**Q.10** What is false in case of emphysema?

(a) Is a chronic disorder

(b) Respiratory surface is increased

(c) Alveolar walls are damaged

(d) Caused due to cigarette smoking

**Sol.** (b) A lower respiratory tract disorder named emphyema is characterised by decreased respiratory surface and damage of a alveolar wall. This is a chronic disorder majorty caused by cigarette smoking.

**Q.11** Occupational respiratory disorders can be avoided by

(a) Wearing gloves (b) Wearing full hand shirt

(c) Wearing protective mask (d) maintaining personal hygiene

**Sol.** (c) Occupational Respiratory Disorders is a group of work related problems that affect the lungs respiratory organs and blood vessels. These can be avaided by wearing protective mask.

## ☐ Short Answer Type

**Q.1** Write the steps involved in pulmonary respiration in humans.

**Sol.** Steps in pulmonary respiration in humans are as follows.

(i) Breathing or pulmonary ventilation by which atmospheric air is drawn in and $CO_2$ rich alveolar air is released out.

(ii) Diffusion of gases ($O_2$ and $CO_2$) across alveolar membrane.

(iii) Transport of gases by the blood.

(iv) Diffusion of $O_2$ and $CO_2$ between blood and tissues.

(v) Utilisation of $O_2$ by the cells for catabolic reactions and resultant release of $CO_2$.

**Q.2** What is meant by the following terms and given their approximate values in human adult:

(i) Inspiratory Reaserve Volume

(ii) Residual Volume

(iii) Expiratory Reserve Volume

**Sol.** (i) **Inspiratory Reaserve Volume** It refers to additional volume of air, a person can inspire by a forcible inspiration. This averages 2500ml-3000ml.

(ii) **Residual Volume** It refers to the volume of air remaining in the lungs even after forcible expiration. This averages 1100ml to 1200ml.

(iii) **Expiratory Reserve Volume** It refers to additional volume of air a person can expire by a forcible expiration. This averages 1000ml-1100ml.

# Body Fluids and Circulation

CHAPTER 15

## Important Points

**01** In order to provide nutrients, $O_2$ and other essential substances to each and every part of our body, different organism have evolved different mechanism of transport.

**02** Blood is the most commonly used body fluid by most of the higher organism including human.

It is a special connective tissue made up of plasma fluid matrix and formed elements. Plasma, which constitutes about 55% of blood, is a straw-colored, viscous fluid composed mainly of water (90-92%) and proteins (6-8%), including fibrinogen, globulins, and albumins. Plasma also containes minerals, glucose, amino acids, lipids, and inactive clotting factors. Without clotting factors, plasma is called serum.

Formed elements, making up 45% of blood, include:

**Erythrocytes (RBCs)** These are biconcave, nucleus-free cells that transport oxygen and carbon dioxide.

**Leucocytes (WBCs)** These cells are involved in immune defense, categorized into granulocytes (neutrophils, eosinophils, basophils) and agranulocytes (lymphocytes, monocytes).

**Platelets** Thrombocytes these cell fragments are essential for blood clotting and their deficiency can cause excessive bleeding.

**03** On the basis of surface antigens present on the surface of blood cells, these are grouped in two grouping system ABO and Rh grouping system.

ABO blood grouping system

(i) It depends on the presence or absence of antigens A and B and natural antibodies in plasma.

(ii) Based on the presence or absence of antigens and antibodies, blood groups are classified as A, B, AB, and O.

(iii) Blood group AB is the universal recipient, while blood group O is the universal donor.

(iv) Careful matching is essential during blood transfusions to avoid complications.

Rh blood grouping system

(i) The Rh antigen, present on most people's RBCs classifies individuals as Rh-positive or Rh-negative.

(ii) If an Rh-negative mother carries an Rh-positive fetus, it can lead to *erythroblastosis foetalis,* a condition where the mother's antibodies destroy the foetal RBCs, which can be prevented by administering anti-Rh antibodies to the mother.

**04** Blood clotting refers to the coagulation of blood in order to prevent excessive loss of blood from the body.

(i) Damage or rupture of a blood vessel due to an injury activates platelets, which release clotting factors the that can initiate a cascade of reactions.

(ii) This cascade converts prothrombin into thrombin, which then transforms fibrinogen into fibrin, forming a mesh that traps blood cells and creates a clot to prevent further bleeding.

**05** Lymph is an interstitial connective tissue composed of blood plasma and white blood corpuscles (mostly lymphocytes). It has same mineral distribution as that in plasma. It contain B and T-lymphocytes, which plays an important role in cell defense system.

**06** The system which plays a key role in the circulation of body fluids, constitutes a circulatory system, which consist of heart arteries, veins and capillaries

**07** Circulatory system is of two types open or closed.

(i) In open type of blood circulation, blood is pumped by heart passes through lar ge vessels into open spaces called sinuses like in arthropods and molluscs.

(ii) Annelids and chordates show closed circulatory system in which blood is pumped by heart and is circulated through a closed network of blood vessels.

**8** The human circulatory system constitute of blood vessels and heart and blood.

(i) Blood vessels are the tubular structure in which blood flows. They are of three types arteries, capillaries and veins.

(ii) Heart is a hollow muscular and mesodermally derived organ, which acts as a pumping machine.

(iii) Human, birds and mammals have a four-chambered heart, fishes have two chambered heart, while reptiles and amphibians have three-chambered heart.

(iv) The human heart has two atria and two ventricles, spearated by septa. The right atrium and right ventricle is guarded by the tricuspid valve, while the left atrium and left ventricle is guarded by the bicuspid (mitral) valve. The semilunar valves control blood flow right and left from the ventricles in to the pulmonary artery and aorta respectively. These valves ensure unidirectional blood flow, preventing backflow.

(v) The heart is composed of cardiac muscles, with thicker ventricular walls compared to the atria. It also contains specialized nodal tissue, including the sino-atrial node (SAN) in the right atrium, which acts as the pacemaker by generating the highest number of action potentials (70-75 per minute). The atrio-ventricular node (AVN), atrio-ventricular bundle, and Purkinje fibers form a conduction system that ensures coordinated hearbeats. The SAN initiates the heart's rhythmic contractions, controlling the normal heart rate of about 70-75 beats per minute.

**9** The cardiac cycle refers to the sequence of events that occurs during one complete heartbeat, consisting of the contraction and relaxation of both the atria and ventricles.

(i) The cycle begins with diastole, where blood flows from the atria into the ventricles.

(ii) The sino-atrial node (SAN) generates an action potential, causing atrial contraction (atrial systole), which increases blood flow into the ventricles.

(iii) The action potential travels to the atrioventricular node (AVN), triggering ventricular contraction (ventricular systole).

(iv) The ventricles relax (ventricular diastole), closing the semilunar valves to prevent backflow.

(v) Each ventricle pumps approximately 70mL of blood per beat, leading to a cardiac output of 5 liters per minute.

(vi) The heart produces two sounds: "lub" (closure of atrioventricular valves) and "dub" (closure of semilunar valves)

**10** Electrical activity of heart during a cardiac cycle is graphically represented by ECG (Electrocardiogram).

(i) Each peak of ECG is identified with a letter from P to T. The p-wave represents the electrical excitation or depolarisation of the artria.

(ii) Depolarisation of ventricles is represented by QRS complex.

(iii) T represents repolarisation, i.e. the return of ventricles from excited to normal state.

**11** The two types of circulation occurs in humans i.e. systemic circulation and pulmonary circulation.
**Hepatic portal** system includes vascular connection between the digestive tract and liver. Before delivering to systemic circulation hepatic portal vein carries blood from intestine to liver.

**12** **Cardiac Activity** is regulated by specialised muscles (nodal tissues), hence the heart is called myogenic. Cardiac function is also controlled by autonomic nervous system (ANS), a special neural centre present in medulla oblongata. Neural signals through the sympathetic nerves part of (ANS) can, increases the rate of heart beat and there by cardiac output. Parasympathetic nerves decreases the rate of heart beat and the speed of conduction of action potential and there by cardiac output.

**13** Various disorders are associated with circulatory system

(i) **High blood pressure (hypertension)**. It is the state of body in which blood pressure is higher than normal (120/80). In this, 120 mm Hg is systolic, while 80 mm Hg is diastolic pressure. In high pertension blood pressure is 140/90 and above.

(ii) **Coronary Heart Diseases (CAD)** These are referred to as antherosclerosis, which is caused by deposits of calcium, fat cholesterol and fibrous tissues. Making the lumen of arteries narrower.

(iii) **Angina** It is also known as 'angina pectoris'. In this, sufficient $O_2$ is not reached to the heart muscle characterized by acute chest pain.

(iv) **Heart failure** It is the state of heart when it is not pumping blood effectively to meet the needs of the body. In heart attack muscles of heart is suddenly damaged by an inadequate blood supply.

# Exercises

**Question 1** Name the components of the formed elements in the blood and mention one major function of each of them.

**Sol.** The formed elements of the blood are erythrocytes, leucocytes and platelets and they constitute nearly 45% of the blood.

Major functions of formed elements are as follows:

(i) Erythrocytes The erythrocytes or red blood cells play a significant role in transport of respiratory gases ($O_2$ and $CO_2$).

(ii) **Leucocytes** The leucocytes or white blood cells play an important role to fight against infections.

(iii) **Platelets** Platelets or thrombocytes, are involved in the coagulation or clotting of blood. A reduction in their number can lead to clotting disorders, which will lead to excessive loss of blood from the body.

**Question 2** What is the importance of plasma proteins?

**Sol.** Fibrinogen, globulins and albumins are the major plasma proteins. Fibrinogens are needed for clotting or coagulation of blood. Globulins primarily are involved in defense mechanisms of the body and the albumins help in osmotic balance.

**Question 3** Match column I with column II.

| Column I | Column II |
|---|---|
| (a) Eosinophils | (i) Coagulation |
| (b) RBCs | (ii) Universal recipient |
| (c) AB group | (iii) Resist infection |
| (d) Platelets | (iv) Contraction of Heart |
| (e) Systole | (v) Gas transport |

**Sol.** (a)-(iii), (b)-(v), (c)-(ii), (d)-(i), (e)-(iv)

| Column I | Column II |
|---|---|
| a. Eosinophils | (i) Coagulation |
| b. RBC | (ii) Universal recipient |
| c. AB Group | (iii) Resist infections |
| d. Platelets | (iv) Contraction of heart |
| e. Systole | (v) Gas transport |

**Question 4** Why do we consider blood as a connective tissue?

**Sol.** Blood is a mobile connective tissue derived from mesoderm which consists of fibre free fluid matrix, plasma and other cells. It regularly circulates in the body, takes part in transport of materials.

**Question 5** What is the differences between blood and lymph?

**Sol.** **Differences between blood and lymph are as follows:**

| S.N. | Blood | Lymph |
|---|---|---|
| 1. | It is reddish in colour. | It is colourless. |
| 2. | Blood is opaque. | It is almost transparent. |
| 3. | Water content is nearly 55%. | Water content is nearly 94%. |
| 4. | It contains erythrocytes. | It contains lymphocytes. |
| 5. | Blood possess a lot of platelets. | It has no platelets. |
| 6. | Calcium and phosphate conent is high. | Calcium and phosphate conent is low. |
| 7. | Blood flow is rapid. | Lymph flow is very slow. |
| 8. | Blood circulates throughout the body. | It passes from tissues to Lymph vessels. |

**Question 6** What is meant by double circulation? What is its significance?

**Sol.** In double circulation, the blood passes twice through the heart during one complete cycle. Double circulation is carried out by two ways

(i) Pulmonary circulation

(ii) Systemic circulation

Significance

There is a complete seperation of oxygenated and deoxygenated blood in double circulation which allows a more efficient supply of oxygen to the body cells.

**Question 7** Write the differences between

(a) Blood and lymph

(b) Open and closed system of circulation

(c) Systole and diastole

(d) P-wave and T-wave

**Sol.** (a) Differences between Blood and Lymph. Refer to Sol. 5 of this chapter.

(b) **Differences between open and closed circulatory system are as follows**

| S.N. | Open Circulatory System | Closed Circulatory System |
|---|---|---|
| 1. | It is present in arthropods and molluscs. | It is present in annelids and chordates. |
| 2. | Blood pumped by heart passes through large vessels into open spaces or body cavities called sinuses. | Blood pumped by the heart is circulated through a network of blood vessels. |
| 3. | Flow of blood is not regulated precisely. | It is more advantageous as the blood flow is more precisely regulated. |

(c) **Differences between systole and diastole are as follows:**

| S.N. | Systole | Diastole |
|---|---|---|
| 1. | During systole, blood pressure is increased inside the heart | During diastole, blood pressure is decreased inside the heart. |
| 2. | Ventricles are contracted and they push the blood in this phase. | Ventricles are relaxed and filed with blood in this phase |

(d) **Difference between P-wave and T-wave is as follows:**

| P-wave | T-wave |
|---|---|
| The P-wave represents the electrical excitation (or depolarisation) of the atria, which leads to the contraction of both the atria. | The T-wave represents the return of the ventricles from excited to normal state (repolarisation). The end of the T-wave marks the end of systole. |

**Question 8** Describe the evolutionary change in the pattern of heart among the vertebrates.

**Sol.** (b) The heart among the vertebrates show different patterns of evolution. Different groups of animals have evolved different methods for blood transport.

All vertebrates possess a muscular chambered heart.

(i) Fishes have a 2-chambered heart with an atrium and a ventricle and the heart pumps out deoxygenated blood which is oxygenatec by the gills and supplied to the body parts from where deoxygenated blood is returned to the heart.

(ii) Amphibians and the reptiles (except crocodiles) have a 3-chambered heart with two atria and a single ventricle and the left atrium receives oxygenated blood from the gills/lungs/skin and the right atrium gets the deoxygenated blood from other body parts. However, they get mixed up in the single ventricle which pumps out mixed blood.

(iii) In crocodiles, birds and mammals possess a 4-chambered heart with two atria and two ventricles. and oxygenated and deoxygenated blood received by the left and right atria respectively passes on to the ventricles of the same sides.

The ventricles pump it out without any mixing up, i.e., two separate circulatory pathways are present in these organisms, hence, these animals have double circulation.

**Question 9.** Why do we call our heart myogenic?

**Sol.** The normal activities of the heart are regulated intrinsically. It means the heart is autoregulated by specialised muscles (nodal tissue), hence, it is called myogenic.

**Question 10.** Sino-atrial node is called the pacemaker of our heart. Why?

**Sol.** Sino-atrial node of heart is responsible for initiating and maintaining its rhythmic activity, therefore it is known as pacemaker of the heart.

**Question 11.** What is the significance of atrio-ventricular node and atrio-ventricular bundle in the functioning of heart?

**Sol.** **Atrioventricular Node (AVN)** is the mass of tissue present in the lower left corner of the right atrium close to the atrioventricular septum. It is stimulated by the impulses that sweep over the atrial myocardium. It is too capable of initiating impulses that cause contraction but at slower rate than SA node.

**Atrioventricular bundle (AV bundle)** is a bundle of nodal fibres, which continues from AVN and passes through the atrioventricular septa to emerge on the top of interventricular septum. The AV bundle, bundle branches and Purkinje fibres convey impulses of contraction from the AV node to the apex of the myocardium. Here the wave of ventricular contraction begins, then sweeps upwards and outwards, pumping blood into the pulmonary artery and the aorta.

This nodal musculature has the ability to generate action potentials without any external stimuli.

**Question 12.** Define a cardiac cycle and the cardiac output.

**Sol.** The sequential event in the heart which is cyclically repeated is called the cardiac cycle and it consists of systole and diastole of both the atria and ventricles.

**Cardiac output** is the volume of blood pumped out by each ventricle per minute and averages 5000 mL or 5 L in a healthy individual.

**Question 13.** Explain heart sounds.

**Sol.** During each cardiac cycle, two prominent sounds are produced which can be easily heard through a stethoscope. The first heart sound (lub) is associated with the closure of the tricuspid and bicuspid valves, whereas the second heart sound (dup) is associated with the closure of the semilunar valves. These sounds are of clinical diagnostic significance.

**Question 14.** Draw a standard ECG and explain the different segments in it.

**Sol.** ECG is a graphical representation of the electrical activity of the heart during a cardiac cycle. A patient is connected to the machine (electro-cardiograph) with three electrical leads (one to each wrist and to the left ankle) that continuously monitor the heart activity. For a detailed evaluation of the heart's function, multiple leads are attached to the chest region.

Each peak in the ECG is identified with a letter from P to T that corresponds to a specific electrical activity of the heart. The **P-wave** represents the electrical excitation (or depolarisation) of the atria, which leads to the contraction of both the atria. The **QRS complex** represents the depolarisation of the ventricles, which initiates the ventricular contraction. The contraction starts shortly after Q and marks the beginning of the systole.

The **T-wave** represents the return of the ventricles from excited to normal state (repolarisation). The end of the T-wave marks the end of systole. Obviously, by counting the number of QRS complexes that occur in a given time period, one can determine the heart beat rate of an individual. Since the ECGs obtained from different individuals have roughly the same shape for a given lead configuration, any deviation from this shape indicates a possible abnormality or disease. Hence, it is of a great clinical significance.

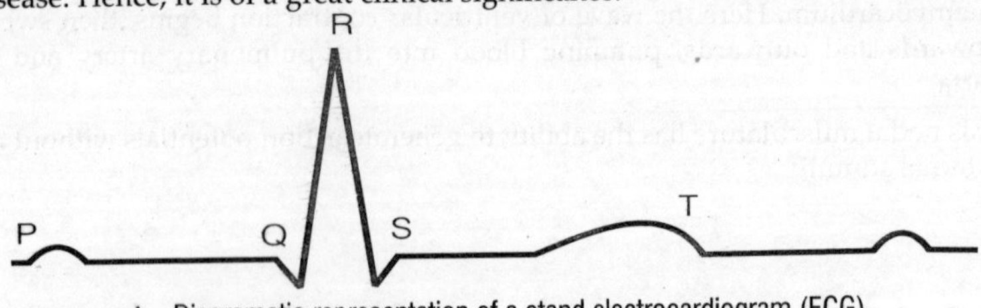


▲ Diagramatic representation of a stand electrocardiogram (ECG)

# DIKSHA APP Questions

## ☐ Multiple Choice Questions

**Q.1** Which formed elements secretes histamine, serotonin and heparin?

(a) Basophil (b) Eosinophil
(c) Neutrophil (d) Monocyte

**Sol.** (a) Basophils are a type of white Blood cells (WBCs). These cells secrete histamine, serotonin and heparin. There number increases during allergy and inflammatory conditions. Histamine is a vasodilator (lowering blood pressure) serotonin is a vasoconstrictor (increasing blood pressure) and heparin is an anticoagulent.

**Q.2** Lymphocyte is responsible is

(a) secreting heparin (b) immune response
(c) inflammatory reaction (d) secreting histamine

**Sol.** (b) Lymphocytes are WBCs (white Blood cells). These are responsible for immune responses like antibody production, killing infected cells etc. Low level of lymphocytes increase the risk of infection. Heparin is secreted by basophils (histamine also).

**Q.3** How much percentage of Rh antigen is present in humans ?

(a) Nearly 80% (b) Nearly 70%
(c) Nearly 90% (d) Nearly 60%

**Sol.** (a) Antigens are present on red blood cells. About 80% of world population have Rh antigen. This antigen is similar to an antigen formed in Rhesus monkey.

**Q.4** What are absorbed through lymph in lacteals present in the intestinall villi?

(a) Proteins (b) Fats
(c) Lipids (d) Carbohydrates

**Sol.** (b) Lacteals are milky, lymphatic capillaries present in villi of small intestine. They absorb fats and fat soluble vitamins. The proteins are absorbed in stomach.

**Q.5** Deoxygenated blood is not carried by

(a) venules (b) veins
(c) vena cava (d) capillaries

**Sol.** (d) All veins carry deoxygenated blood back to heart except pulmonary vein which carry oxygenated blood. Deoxygenated blood from the peripheral veins transported back to heart through venules and veins.

**Q.6** Double circulation is absent in

(a) aves (b) mammals
(c) reptiles (d) crocodiles

**Sol.** (c) A circulatory system where blood passes through the heart twice and has two separate circulatory is known as double circulatory system. It is found in crocodiles, birds and mammals and is absent in amphibians and reptiles.

**Q.7** Hapatic portal system carries blood from

(a) pancreas to intestine (b) intestine to liver
(c) intestine to kidney (d) stomach to pancreas

**Sol.** (b) Hepatic poartal system is the network is of vein in body which carries blood from intestine to liver. Here the raw nutrients in blood are processed before the blood return to heart.

**Q.8** QRS complex in electroacardiograph represents

(a) excitation of atria (b) depolarisation of atria
(c) depolarisation of ventricle (d) repolarisation of ventricle

**Sol.** (c) QRS complex in ECG (electro cardiograph) represents the depolarization of ventricles. This shows the starting of system and contraction of ventricle.

**Q.9** What is myogenic?

(a) Specialised muscles in the gut
(b) Specialised muscles in the heart
(c) Specialised muscles inthe pancreas
(d) Specialised muscles in the kidney

**Sol.** (b) Myogenic is a character of cardiac muscles in heart . Here muscle can initiate its own contraction without the need of nervous stimulation.

**Q.10** Which is not the property of autonomic nervous system?

(a) Increase the rate of heart beat
(b) Decrease the speed of conduction of action potential
(c) Increase the strength of ventricular contraction
(d) Increase the cardiac output

**Sol.** (b) ANS (Autonomic Nervous System) is a part of peripheral Nervous system. It regulates invaluntary physiological process such as, blood pressure, heart, rate, digestion and respiration. Dreasing the speed of conduction of action potential, is not the property of autonomic nervous system.

**Q.11** What is not the property of high blood pressure?

(a) 140 mm Hg is systolic pressure
(b) 80 mm Hg is diastolic pressure
(c) Leads to heart disease
(d) Affect vital organ like brain and kidney

**Sol.** (b) High Blood Pressure (or hypertension ) is a condition of blood flow in arteries. In high BP the top number (sytolic pressure) is 130 mm Hg or high, while bottom number (diastolic pressure) is 90 mm Hg or higher. It leads to heart attack and heart failure and affect vital organ like brain and kidney.

**Q.12** What is not the property of angina?

(a) Cause acute chest pain
(b) More common in middle-aged people
(c) The lumen of arteries are narrow
(d) Occur in both men and women

**Sol.** (c) Angina is a type of chest pain in which the heart muscles not getting enough oxygen. It is common in middle-aged and elderly people, both male and fomale.

## ☐ Short Answer Type

**Q.1** How many types of ABO blood group? What is the basis for ABO blood grouping?

**Sol.** Blood groups are four types-
A, B, AB and O are the blood groups. ABO blood grouping is based on the presence or absence of two surface antigens on the RBCs namely antigen A and antigen B.

**Q.2** Mention the function of each of

(i) Neutrophils (ii) Basophils (iii) T-lymphocytes

**Sol.** (i) Functions of neutrophils is as follows.

Phagocytic and destroy the foreign organisms entering the body.

(ii) Functions of basophils is as follows

Secrete histamine, serotonin, heparin, etc.

Involved in inflammatory reactions.

(iii) Functions of T-lymphocytes is as follows

Responsible for immune responses of the body.

## ☐ Long Answer Type

**Q.1** With reference to human heart, answer the following:

1. What are SA and AV nodes? Where they located?
2. How heart sounds are produced ? Name the two heart sounds?

**Sol.** 1. **SA node (Sino-atrial node)**

A specialised cardiac musculature called nodal tissue, distributed in the heart.

A patch of this tissue is called SA node, which is located in the right upper corner of the right atrium.

**AV node (Atrio-ventricular node)**

Another mass of nodal-tissue located in the lower left corner of the right atrium close to the atria-ventricular septum called AV node (Atrio-ventricular node).

2. **Heart sounds:**

First heart sound (lub) is associated with the closure of the tricuspid and bicuspid valves whereas the second heart sound (dub) is associated with the closure of semilunar valves.

The two heart sounds are lub and dup.

# Excretory Products and Their Elimination

CHAPTER 16

## Important Points

**01** **Excretion** is the removal or elimination of waste products from the body either in solid, liquid or in gaseous state.

**02** The organs involved in the process of excretion are called excretory organs, which show a great variety in different organisms.

**03** Human excretory system consists of kidneys (one pair), ureters (one pair), urinary bladder (single) and urethra (single)

**04** Kidneys are reddish brown, bean-shaped structures situated between the levels of last thoracic and third lumbar vertebra, with a tough outer capsule. Inside the kidney, there are two zones, an outer cortex and inner medulla and a hilum through which vessels and nerves enter. Inside the kidney, the renal pelvis connects to projections called calyces and the medulla is divided into a few conical masses known as medullary pyramids.

**05** Basic functional unit of kidney is nephron which is complex tubular structure consisting of two parts, *i.e.*, glomerulus and renal tubule.

**06** **Glomerulus** is the network of capillaries formed by the afferent arteriole.

**07** **Renal tubules** begins with a double walled cup-like structure called Bowman's capsule which encloses glomerulus. Glomerulus and Bowman's capsule together known as malpighian body or renal corpuscle.

**08** The tubule continues further to form Proximal Convoluted Tubule (PCT) and Distal Convoluted Tubule (DCT), in between them a hair pin-shaped Henle's loop is present which has a anascending and a descending limb. Ascending limb continues to form DCT.

**09** The DCTs of many nephrons open into collecting duct, many of which converge and open into renal pelvis through medullary pyramids in calyces.

**10** **Loop of Henle** is present in medulla, while malpighian corpuscle, PCT and DCT of the nephron are present in the cortical region.

**11** A minute vessel run parallel to the Henle's loop and forms U-shaped **vasa recta**.

**12** Three main processes occur in different parts of the nephron during urine formation namely glomerular filtration/ultrafiltration, reabsorption and tubular secretion

(i) **Glomerular filtration** Blood is filtered by the glomerulus, where almost all plasma components, except proteins, pass into the Bowman's capsule, forming the filtrate. The glomerular Filtration Rate (GER) is about 125 ml/min in healthy individuals.

(ii) **Reabsorption** Nearly 99% of the filtrate is reabsorbed by the renal tubule, with substances like glucose and amino acids reabsorbed actively, while water and nitrogenous waste are absorbed passively.

(iii) **Tubular Secretion** In urine formation, tubular cells secreate substances like $H^+$, $K^+$ and ammonia into filtrate and also helps in maintenance of ionic and acidic balance of body fluids.

**13** Reabsorption, secretion and the regulation of water, electrolytes and pH occur in renal tubules, including PCT, henle's loop, DCT and collecting duct.

(i) PCT all the essential nutrients, 70-80% of electrolytes and water are reabsorbed.

(ii) Henle's loop- descending limb absorb water, while ascending limb reabsorb electrolyte.

(iii) DCT- conditional reabsorption of $Na^+$ and water. It maintains pH and sodium-potassium balance.

(iv) Collecting duct large amount of water is reabsorbed to produce concentrated urine.

**14** The counter-current mechanism involves the opposite flow of filtrate in the Henle's loop and blood in the vasa recta. As the filtrate flows down the descending limb of the loop, water is reabsorbed and in the ascending limb, NaCl is actively transported out, creating an osmotic gradient in the kidney. The vasa-recta, running in the opposite direction, helps maintain this gradient by exchanging NaCl and urea, which allows water to be reabsorbed from the collecting duct ultimately concentrating the urine.

**15** Kidney function is regulated by two feed back mechanism which are

(i) control by Juxta glomerular apparatus (JGA).

(ii) control by antidiuretic hormone.

(a) A fall in glomerular blood flow/glomerular blood pressure/GFR can activate Juxtaglomerular cells release renin which converts angiotensinogen in blood to angiotensin I and further to angiotensin II.

(b) Angiotensin II, being a powerful vasoconstrictor, increases the glomerular blood pressure. It also activates the adrenal cortex to release aldosterone. It causes selective reabsorption from distal parts of tubule. This leads to the increase in blood pressure and GFR. This complex mechanism is known as Renin-Angiotensin **mechanism**.

(c) Increase in blood flow to atria of the heart causes the release of ANF (Atrial Natriuretic Factor), which causes vasodilation (*i.e.*, dilation of blood vessels) and thereby decrease the blood pressure. It also acts as a check on renin angiotensin mechanism.

**16** Micturition is the act of releasing the urine, which occurs by contraction of smooth muscle of urinary bladder wall and relaxation of urethral sphincter. Voluntary signals for urination are given by **central nervous system**.

**17** Apart from kidney, lungs, liver and skin help in the elimination of excretory wastes.

**18** Various disorders associated with excretory system are

(i) **Uremia** Accumulation of urea in blood due to malfunctioning of kidneys. Patients suffering from uremia undergoes haemodialysis.

(ii) **Renal failure** Inability of kidney to carry out excretory and salt water regulatory functions called renal or kidney failure.

(iii) **Renal calculi/Renal stones** It is the insoluble mass of crystallised salts. (oxalates, etc) formed within the kidney.

(iv) **Glomerulonephritis** Inflammation of glomeruli of kidney

## Exercises

**Question 1** Define Glomerular Filtration Rate (GFR).

**Sol.** The amount of the filtrate formed by the kidneys per minute is called Glomerular Filtration Rate (GFR). GFR in a healthy individual is approximately 125 mL/minute, *i.e.*, 180 L per day.

**Question 2** Explain the autoregulatory mechanism of GFR.

**Sol.** The kidneys have built in mechanisms for the regulation of glomerular filtration rate. One such efficient mechanism is carried out by juxtaglomerular apparatus (JGA). JGA is a special sensitive region formed by cellular modifications in the distal convoluted tubule and the afferent arteriole at the location of their contact. A fall in GFR can activate the JG cells to release renin which can stimulate the glomerular blood flow and thereby increasing GFR back to normal.

**Question 3** Indicate whether the following statements are true or false

(a) Micturition is carried out by a reflex.

(b) ADH helps in water elimination, making the urine hypotonic.

(c) Protein-free fluid is filtered from blood plasma into the Bowman's capsule.

(d) Henle's loop plays an important role in concentrating the urine.

(e) Glucose is actively reabsorbed in the proximal convoluted tubule.

**Sol.** (a) True (b) False (c) True

(d) True (e) True

**Question 4** Give a brief account of the counter current mechanism.

**Sol.**

(i) The counter current mechanism takes place in Henle's loop and vasa recta.

(ii) The flow of filtrate in the two limbs of Henle's loop is in opposite directions and thus, forms a counter-current.

(iii) The flow of blood through the two limbs of vasa recta is also in a counter current pattern.

(iv) NaCl is transported by the ascending limb of Henle's loop which is exchanged with the descending limb of vasa recta.

(v) NaCl is returned to the interstitium by the ascending portion of vasa recta.

(vi) Similarly, small amount of urea enter the thin segment of the ascending limb of Henle's loop, which is transported back to the interstitium by the collecting tubule.

(vii) This transport of substances facilitated by the special arrangement of Henle's loop and vasa recta is called the counter current mechanism.

(viii) It helps to maintain a concentration gradient in the medullary interstitium which facilitates an easy passage of water from the collecting tubule thereby concentrating the filtrate (urine).

**Question 5** Describe the role of liver, lungs and skin in excretion.

**Sol. Lungs** It remove large amount of $CO_2$ (200 ml/min) and also significant quantities of water everyday.

**Liver** It secretes bile containing substances like bilirubin, biliverdin, cholesterol, degraded steroid hormones, vitamins and drugs. Most of these substances ultimately pass out along with digestive wastes.

**Skin** The sweat and sebaceous glands in the skin can eliminate certain substances through their secretions. Sweat produced by the sweat glands is a watery fluid containing NaCl, small amount of urea, lactic acid, etc. Sebaceous glands eliminate certain substances like sterols, hydrocarbons and waxes through sebum. This secretion provides a protective oily covering to the skin.

**Question 6** Explain micturition.

**Sol.** The process of release of urine is called micturition and the neural mechanisms causing it is called the micturition reflex. An adult human excretes, on an average, 1 to 1.5 L of urine per day. The urine formed is a light yellow coloured watery fluid which is slightly acidic (pH-6.0) and has a characteristic odour.

**Question 7** Match the items of column I with those of column II

| S.N. | Column I | Column II |
|---|---|---|
| A. | Ammonotelism | 1. Birds |
| B. | Bowman's capsule | 2. Water reabsorption |
| C. | Micturition | 3. Bony fish |
| D. | Uricotelism | 4. Urinary bladder |
| E. | ADH | 5. Renal tubule |

**Sol.**

| S.N. | Column I | Column II |
|---|---|---|
| A. | Ammonotelism | 3. Bony fish |
| B. | Bowman's capsule | 5. Renal tubule |
| C. | Micturition | 4. Urinary bladder |
| D. | Uricotelism | 1. Birds |
| E. | ADH | 2. Water reabsorption |

Hence, A-3, B-5, C-4, D-1 and E-2

**Question 8** What is meant by the term osmoregulation?

**Sol.** It is the regulation of change in the concentration of body fluids according to the concentration of external environment.

**Question 9** Terrestrial animals are generally either ureotelic or uricotelic, not ammonotelic, why?

**Sol.** Terrestrial adaptation requires the production of lesser toxic nitrogenous wastes like urea and uric acid for the conservation of water. Mammals, many terrestrial amphibians and marine fishes mainly excrete urea and are called ureotelic animals. Ammonia produced by metabolism is converted into urea in the liver of these animals and released into the blood which is filtrated and excreted out by the kidneys.

Some amount of urea may be retained in the kidney matrix of some of these animals to maintain a desired osmolarity. Reptiles, birds, land snails and insects excrete nitrogenous wastes as uric acid in the form of pellet or paste with a minimum loss of water and are called uricotelic animals.

**Question 10** What is the significance of juxtaglomerular apparatus (JGA) in kidney function?

**Sol.** The juxta glomerular apparatus regulates kidney function through the renin-angiotensin mechanism.

A decrease in glomerular blood flow, pressure, or GFR activates JG cells to release renin.

Renin convert angiotensinogen into angiotensin I, which is further converted into angiotensin II.

Angiotensin II, a potent vasoconstrictor, increases glomerular blood pressure and there by GFR.

Angiotensin II activates the adrenal cortex to release aldosterone, which enhances reabsorption of $Na^+$ and water, raising blood pressure and GFR.

**Question 11** Name the following

(a) A chordate animal having flame cells as excretory structures.

(b) Cortical portions projecting between the medullary pyramids in the human kidney.

(c) A loop of capillary running parallel to the Henle's loop.

**Sol.** (a) Amphioxus (b) Columns of Bertini (c) Vasa recta

**Question 12** Fill in the gaps

(a) Ascending limb of Henle's loop is ...... to water, whereas the descending limb is ...... to it.

(b) Reabsorption of water from distal parts of the tubules is facilitated by hormone ...... .

(c) Dialysis fluid contain all the constituents as in plasma except ...... .

(d) A healthy adult human excretes (on an average) ...... gm of urea/day.

**Sol.**

(a) impermeable, permeable

(b) antidiuretic hormone (ADH)

(c) nitrogenous wastes

(d) 25-30.

# Locomotion and Movement

CHAPTER 17

## Important Points

**01** Change in the body position or a part of body is known as movement. Some of the movements result in change of position or location. Such voluntary movement is known as locomotion. All **locomotions** are movements but all movements are not locomotions.

**02** Various type of movements exhibited by cells of human body are amoeboid movement, ciliary movement and muscular movement.

**03** Muscle is a specialised tissue of mesodermal origin. It have special properties like excitability, contractility extensibility and elasticity. It constitute about 40-50% of the total body weight. On the basis of location these are identified as

(i) Sketetal muscles : These are striated, voluntary muscles that facilitate movement and posture control.

(ii) Visceral muscles : These are smooth, involuntary muscles, found in hollow organs,aiding functions like food and gamete transportation.

(iii) Cardiac muscles : These are striated, involuntary muscles of heart, forming a branching network for continuous functioning

**04** **Skeletal muscles** are organised into strong compact bundles called **muscle bundles** or fascicles. These are held together by collagenous connective tissue layer called fascia.

(i) Each muscle bundle consists of muscle fibers, which contain cylindrical structures, myofibriles, responsible for contraction.

(ii) These myofibrils have alternating dark (A-band)and light (I-band) bands formed by actin (thin) and myosin (thick) filaments.

(iii) The functional unit of contraction, the sarcomere, lies between two successive Z-lines, with thin filament anchored to the Z-line and thick filament anchored at M-line.

(iv) In resting state, thin filament partially overlap on either side of thick filaments, leaving central H-zone where no overlap occurs.

**05** Thin filament is composed of actin tropomyosin and troposin. Actin filaments are made up of two helical strands of *F*-actin, with tropomyosin running along their length and troponin marks the myosin binding sites in resting state.

**06** Thick filaments (myosin) are made up of meromyosins, consisting of globular heads (HMM), with ATPase activity and binding sites for ATP and active site for actin, as well as tails (LMM)

**07** Muscle contraction occurs in accordance with sliding filament theory which states that contraction of a muscle fibre takes place by the sliding of the thin filaments over the thick filaments.

(i) Muscle contraction is initiated by the signal sent from a motor neuron, generating an action potential in the muscle fiber.

(ii) The action potential triggers the release of $Ca^{++}$ from the sarcoplasmic reticulum.

(iii) $Ca^{2+}$ activates actin, allowing it to bind to the myosin head, forming a cross-bridge.

(iv) The cross-bridges pull actin filaments, causing them to side over the myosin filaments and leading to contraction.

(v) $Ca^{2+}$ is returned to the sarcoplasmic reticulum, inactivating actin.

(vi) The cross-bridges break, and the muscle relaxes.

**08** Hard supportive or protective element of animal body form skeletal system or skeleton. It consists of frame work of bones and few cartilages

**09** The skeletal system is divisible into axial and appendicular skeleton. The axial skeleton consists of 80 bones, which includes the skull, vertebral column, sternum, and ribs. The skull has 22 bones, including 8 cranial bones, 14 facial bones and the hyoid, with three ear ossicles in each middle ear.
The vertebral column consists of 26 vertebrae and protects the spinal cord. It is divided into cervical (7), thoracic (12), lumbar (5), sacral (1-fused), and coccygeal regions (1-fused). The rib cage, formed by thoracic vertebrae, ribs, and sternum, includes true ribs, false ribs, and floating ribs.

**10** The appendicular skeleton includes the bones of the limbs and their girdles.
**Limbs** Each limb consists of 30 bones, including the humerus (1), radius (1), ulna (1), carpals (8), metacarpals (5), and phalanges (14) in the forelimb, and femur (1), tibia (1), fibula (1), tarsals (7), metatarsals (5), and phalanages (14) in the hind limb.
**Girdles** The pectoral girdle consists of the clavicle (2) and scapula (2), and the pelvic girdle consists of the coxal bones (2), which are formed by the fusion of the ilium, ischium, and pubis.

**11** Joints are the structural arrangement of tissues by which bones are joined together. These are classified into three major structural forms

(a) **Fibrous joints** These do not allow any movement, *e.g.*, in flat skull bones which fuses end to end to form cranium .

(b) **Cartilaginous joints** It permits limited movement. *e.g.*, in joints between adjacent vertebrae in the vertebrae column.

(c) **Synovial joints** are characterised by presence of synovial fluid between the articulating surfaces of the two bones. Such type of joints are ball and socket joint (between humerus and pectoral girdle), hinge joint (knee joint), pivot joint (between atlas and axis) gliding joint (between the carpals) and saddle joint (between carpal and matacarpal of thumb).

**12** Disorders associated with muscular and skeletal system

(i) **Myasthenia gravis** An autoimmune disease affecting neuro-muscular junction causing fatigue, weakening and paralysis of skeletal muscle.

(ii) **Muscular dystrophy** Progressive degeneration of skeletal muscle occurs mostly due to genetic disorder.

(iii) **Tetany** Due to low $Ca^{2+}$ ion content in the body fluid wild contractions/rapid spasms occur in muscles.

(iv) **Arthritis** inflammation of joints.

(v) **Osteoporosis** It is reduction in bone tissue causing weakening of skeletal strength.

(vi) **Gout :** Excess amount of uric acid and crystals of uric acid are deposited in the syovial joints leads to severe arthritis.

# Exercises

**Question 1** Draw the diagram of a sarcomere of skeletal muscle showing different regions.

**Sol.**

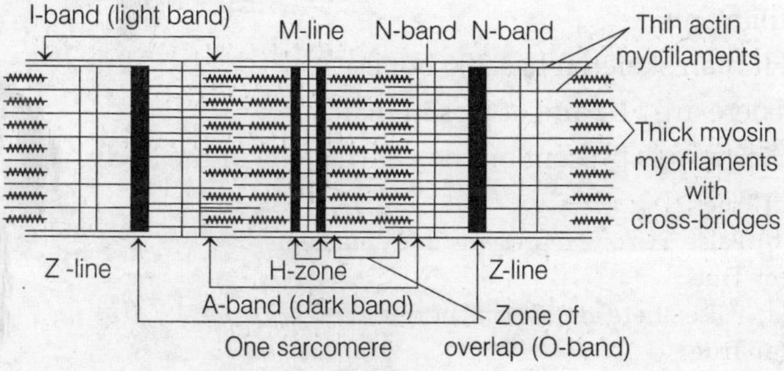


A Sarcomere

**Question 2** Define sliding-filament theory of muscle contraction.

**Sol.** The sliding-filament theory states that the contraction of a muscle fibre takes place by the sliding of the thin filaments over the thick filaments.

**Question 3** Describe the important steps in muscle contraction.

**Sol.**

(i) A neural signal reaching the neuromuscular junction releases a neurotransmitter (acetyl choline) which generates an action potential in the sarcolemma.

(ii) This action potential spreads through the muscle fibre and causes the release of calcium ions into the sarcoplasm.

(iii) Increase in $Ca^{2+}$ level leads to the binding of calcium with a sub-unit of troponin on actin filaments and thereby remove the masking of active sites for myosin.

(iv) Utilising the energy from ATP hydrolysis, the myosin head now binds to the exposed active sites on actin to form a cross bridge.

(v) This pulls the attached actin filaments towards the centre of A-band.

(vi) The Z-line attached to these actins are also pulled inwards thereby causing a shortening of the sarcomere, *i.e.*, contraction.

(vii) During shortening of the muscle, *i.e.*, contraction, the I-bands get reduced, whereas, the A-bands retain the length.

(viii) The myosin, releasing the ADP and Pi goes back to its relaxed state. A new ATP binds and the cross-bridge is broken.

(ix) The ATP is again hydrolysed by the myosin head and the cycle of cross bridge formation and breakage is repeated causing further sliding.

(x) The process continues till the $Ca^{2+}$ ions are pumped back to the sarcoplasmic cisternae resulting in the masking of actin filaments. This causes the return of Z-lines back to their original position, *i.e.*, relaxation.

**Question 4** Write true or false. If false change the statement so that it is true.

(a) Actin is present in thin filament.

(b) H-zone of striated muscle fibre represents both thick and thin filaments.

(c) Human skeleton has 206 bones.

(d) There are 11 pairs of ribs in man.

(e) Sternum is present on the ventral side of the body.

**Sol.** (a) True

(b) False, H-zone represents thick filaments.

(c) True

(d) False, there are 12 pairs of ribs in man.

(e) True

**Question 5** Write the differences between

(a) Actin and myosin

(b) Red and white muscles

(c) Pectoral and pelvic girdle

**Sol.**

(a) **Differences between actin and myosin are as follows.**

| S.N. | Actin | Myosin |
|---|---|---|
| 1. | These are thin filaments. | These are thick filaments. |
| 2. | G-Actins (Globular Actin) polymerise to form F-Actin (Filamentous actin). | It is a globular protein. |
| 3. | The thin filament also contain the contractile protein called tropomyosin. | Each myosin molecule also has two components, a tail and a head meromysin. |
| 4. | Found in I-band of the sarcomere | Found in A-bond of the sarcomere |

(b) **Differences between red and white muscles are as follows**

| S.N. | Red Muscles | White Muscles |
|---|---|---|
| 1. | In some muscles, myoglobin content is high, which gives a reddish colour to them, such muscles are called red muscles. | Some muscles possess very less quantity of myoglobin, so they appear whitish called as white muscles. |
| 2. | These contain plenty of mitochondria. | These have less number of mitochondria but amount of sarcoplasmic reticulum is high. |
| 3. | These are called aerobic muscles. | They depend on anaerobic process of energy. |

(c) **Differences between pectoral and pelvic girdle are as follows :**

| S.N. | Pectoral Girdle | Pelvic Girdle |
|---|---|---|
| 1. | It helps in the articulation of upper limbs. | It helps in the articulation of lower limbs. |
| 2. | Each half of pectoral girdle is formed of a clavicle and a scapula. | Pelvic girdle consists of two coxal bones. |
| 3. | Scapula is a large triangular, flat bone and clavicle is a long slender bone. | Each coxal bone is formed of three bones, ilium, ischium and pubis. |
| 4. | An expanded process, acromion, from scapula forms a depression called glenoid cavity, which articulates with the head of humerus to form shoulder joint. | Ilium, ischium and pubis fuse at a point to form a cavity called acetabulum to which the thigh bone articulates. |

**Question 6** Match the column I with column II.

| S.N. | Column I | | Column II |
|---|---|---|---|
| A. | Smooth muscle | 1. | Myoglobin |
| B. | Tropomyosin | 2. | Thin filament |
| C. | Red muscle | 3. | Sutures |
| D. | Skull | 4. | Involuntary |

**Sol.**

| S.N. | Column I | | Column II |
|---|---|---|---|
| A. | Smooth muscle | 4. | Involuntary |
| B. | Tropomyosin | 2. | Thin filament |
| C. | Red muscle | 1. | Myoglobin |
| D. | Skull | 3. | Sutures |

**Question 7.** What are the different types of movements exhibited by the cells of human body?

**Sol.** Cells of the human body exhibit three main types of movements which are amoeboid, ciliary and muscular.

**Amoeboid movement** Some specialised cells in human body like macrophages and leucocytes in blood exhibit amoeboid movement. It is effected by pseudopodia formed by the streaming of protoplasm (as in *Amoeba*). Cytoskeletal elements like microfilaments are also involved in amoeboid movement.

**Ciliary movement** Ciliary movement occurs in most of our internal tubular organs which are lined by ciliated epithelium. The coordinated movements of cilia in the trachea help in removing dust particles and some of the foreign substances inhaled along with the atmospheric air. Passage of ova through the female reproductive tract is also facilitated by the ciliary movement.

**Muscular movement** Movement of limbs, jaws, tongue, etc., require muscular movement.

**Question 8.** How do you distinguish between a skeletal muscle and a cardiac muscle?

**Sol. Differences between a skeletal muscles and cardiac muscles are as follows :**

| S.N. | Skeletal Muscle | Cardiac Muscle |
|---|---|---|
| 1. | These are associated with skeletal parts of the body. | These are present only in heart. |
| 2. | They are voluntary in nature. | They are involuntary in nature. |
| 3. | They are involved in locomotory actions and changes in body postures. | They are related to heart activities |

**Question 9** Name the type of joint between the following

(a) Atlas/axis
(b) Carpal/metacarpal of thumb
(c) Between phalanges
(d) Femur/acetabulum
(e) Between cranial bones
(f) Between pubic bones in the pelvic girdle

**Sol.** (a) Pivot joint (b) Saddle joint
(c) Hinge joint (d) Ball and socket joint
(e) Fibrous joint (f) Cartilagenous joint

**Question 10** Fill in the blank spaces.

(a) All mammals (except a few) have ...... cervical vertebra.
(b) The number of phalanges in each limb of human is ......
(c) Thin filament of myofibril contains 2 'F' actins and two other proteins namely ...... and ...... .
(d) In a muscle fibre $Ca^{2+}$ is stored in ......
(e) ...... and ...... pairs of ribs are called floating ribs.
(f) The human cranium is made of ...... bones.

**Sol.**
(a) seven (b) fourteen
(c) troponin and tropomyosin (d) sarcoplasmic reticum
(e) 11 th; 12th (f) eight

## DIKSHA APP Questions

### ☐ Multiple Choice Questions

**Q.1** Which of the following is an age related disorder?
(a) Arthritis (b) Gout
(c) Tetany (d) Osteoporosis

**Sol.** (d) Osteoporosis is a disease which causes bones to become brittle and weak. It is mainly a diseae of old age but also affected by gender family

**Q.2** Which of the following is an auto immun disorder?
(a) Muscular dystrophy (b) Myasthenia gravis
(c) Tetany (d) Osteoporosis

**Sol.** (b) Myasthenia Gravis (MG) is an autoimmune disorder. This affects the muscular tissues cause weakness in muscles which control mouth, eye, limb.

**Q.3** Where is saddle joint present?

(a) Between carpal and metacarpal of thumb
(b) Between atlas and axis
(c) Between humerus and pectoral girdle
(d) Between the carpals

**Sol.** (a) Saddle joint is a type of synovial joint which allows for wide range of movement including backward and forward, up and down. This is found between carpal and metacarpal of thumb upper part of breast bone and inner ear.

**Q.4** Where is pivot joint present?

(a) Between Carpal and metacarpal of thumb
(b) Between between atlas and axis
(c) Between humerus and pectoral girdle
(d) Between the carpals

**Sol.** (b) A pivot joint allows bones to rotate around a single axis. It is found between atlas and axis bones.

**Q.5** How many cranial bones are present ?

(a) 6 (b) 7
(c) 8 (d) 0

**Sol.** (c) Cranium *i.e.* human skull consists of 22 bones including 8 cranial bones and 14 facial skeletal bones. The cranial bones are ethmoid (1), frontal bone (1), occipetal bone (1), parietal bones, (2) sphenoid bone (1) temporal bones (2).

**Q.6** How many bones are human beings made up of?

(a) 204 (b) 205
(c) 206 (d) 207

**Sol.** (c) The skeleton of adult human is composed of 206 bones. Bones are actually connective tissue. There are 270 bones at the time of birth which fuse with time to become 206.

**Q.7** What isn't the property of smooth muscles?

(a) It is present in alimentary canal
(b) Doesn't show striation
(c) It shows striation
(d) They are involuntary muscles

**Sol.** (c) Smooth muscles are involuntary non-striated muscle. These muscles are found in walls of hollow organs such as digestive tract, blood vessels and urinary bladder.

**Q.8** About how many percent of body weight of a human adult is contributed by muscles?

(a) 40-50 (b) 50-60

(c) 45-55 (d) 55-65

**Sol.** (a) On an average 40–50% of human body weight is contributed by muscles. Skeletal muscle makes up around 40% of body weight and contains 50%-75% of all body proteins.

## ☐ Short Answer Type

**Q.1** Explain striated and non striated muscles which is identified on the basis of location?

**Sol.** On the basis of location striated and non-stare describe below

| | Striated Muscle | Unstriated Muscle |
|---|---|---|
| 1. | The cells of this tissue are long, cylindrical, unbranched and multi-nucleate. | These cells are long with pointed ends and uninucleate. |
| 2. | These muscles show alternate light and dark bands or striations. | No striations are present. |
| 3. | These are present in our limbs. | These are present in the iris of eye, ureters and in bronchi. |

## ☐ Long Answer Type

**Q.1** List the different types of synovial Joints along with examples.

**Sol.** Different types fo synovial joints along with examples areas follows :

(i) Ball and socket joint

between humerus and pectoral girdle.

between femur and pelvic girdle.

(ii) Hinge joint-knee joint, elbow joint

(iii) Pivot joint-between atlas and axis.

(iv) Saddle joint-between Carpal and metacarpal of thumb.

(v) Gliding joint-between the carpals.

# Neural Control and Coordination

CHAPTER 18

## Important Points

**01** Coordination is the process through which two or more organs interact and complement the functions of one other. For quick coordination, our neural system provides an organised network of point to point connections.

**02** Nervous system provides the fastest means of communication within the body.

**03** Basic unit of neural system is neuron which can detect, receive and transmit different kinds of stimuli.

**04** Human neural system is composed of

(i) Central Nervous System (CNS), which includes brain and spinal cord.

(ii) Peripheral Nervous System (PNS) which, includes nerves of body associated with CNS (brain and spinal cord).

The nerve fibre of PNS are of two types.

(a) Afferent fibres transmit impulses from tissue organ to the CNS.

(b) Efferent fibres transmit impulse from CNS to the target organ tissue.

(iii) The peripheral nervous system is divided into somatic nervous system (transmit impulse from CNS to skeletal muscles) and autonomic nervous system (transmit impulse from CNS to involuntary organs).

(iv) Autonomic Nervous System (ANS) is further divided into sympathetic and parasympathetic nervous system.

**05** The basic structural and functional unit of nervous system is neuron which consist of mainly three major parts namely cells body, dendrites and axon.

(i) **Cell Body** contains cytoplasm, which contains certain granular bodies called **Nissl's granules.**

(ii) **Dendrites** are the short fibre which branch repeatedly and projects out of the cell body.
They transmit impulse towards the cell body.

(iii) Axon is a long fibre, its distal end is branched and each branch terminates as **synaptic knob,** which possess synaptic vesicles.

(iv) **Neurons** are divided into three types on the basis of number of axon and dendrites. These are multipolar, bipolar and unipolar.

(v) Axons are mainly of two types, *i.e.*, **myelinated** and **non-myelinated nerve fibres**.

(vi) The gaps between the two adjacent myelin sheath are called **nodes of Ranvier**.

(vii) Unmyelinated nerve fibres are present in autonomous and somatic neural system and myelinated nerve fibres are present in spinal and cranial nerves.

**06** Neurons are excitable cells because their membranes are polorised, with a negative charge inside and a positive charge outside, maintained by the sodium-potossium pump. When a stimulus occurs, $Na^+$ channels open, causing depolarization and generating an action potential, which spreads along the axon, $K^+$ then flows out to restore the resting potential, enabling the neuron to transmit impulses.

**07** Synapse is a junction in which nerve impulse are transmitted from one neuron to another which is formed by the membranes of a pre synaptic neuron and a post synaptic neuron.

(i) Synapses is of two types

(a) Chemical synapses (b) Electrical synapses

(ii) At electrical synapse the membranes of pre and post synaptic neurons are in close proximity. Electric current can flow directly from one neuron into another. It is faster than the chemical synapse.

(iii) At a chemical synapse, the membranes of pre and post synaptic neuron is separated by fluid filled space called **synaptic cleft**.

Neurotransmitters released from the pre-synaptic neuron bind to receptors on post-synaptic neuron, opening ion channels and generating a new excitatory or inhibitory potential.

**08** Central nervous system controls various voluntary and involuntary movement.

(i) Human brain is well protected by skull which is covered by membrane called cranial meninges consisting of duramater (outer layer), arachnoid (middle layer) and piamater (inner layer).

(ii) Brain is divided into three major parts which are

(i) **Forebrain** Consists of the cerebrum, thalamus and hypthalamus. The cerebrum is divided into two hemispheres connected by the corpus collosum. It controls complex functions like sensory processing, motor control, memory, emotions and regulates body temperature, hunger and sexual behavious through limbic system and hypothalamus.

(ii) **Midbrain** is located between thalamus/hypothalamus of forebrain and pons of hindbrain.

- Cerebral aqueduct passes through midbrain.
- Dorsal portion consists of four lobes called corpora quadrigemia.

(iii) **Hindbrain** consists of

- **Pons** has fibre tracts
- **Cerebellum** has convoluted surface to provide additional space for many more neurons.
- **Medulla oblongata** is connected to the spinal cord which controls, respiration, cardiovascular reflexes and gastric secretions.

# Exercises

**Question 1** Briefly describe the structure of the Brain.

**Sol.**

(a) **Structure of Brain** The human brain is well protected by the skull. The brain can be divided into three major parts forebrain, midbrain and hindbrain.

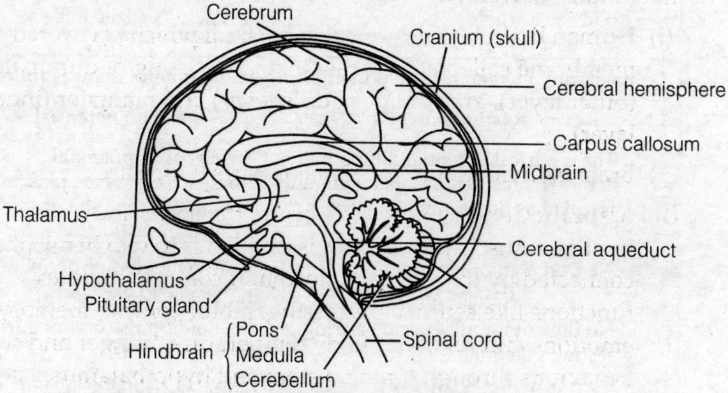


**Sagital section of human brain**

(i) **Forebrain** The various parts of forebrain are cerebrum, thalamus and hypothalamus. Cerebrum is responsible for complex functions like intersensory associations, memory and communication.

(ii) **Midbrain** The midbrain is located between the thalamus/hypothalamus of the forebrain and pons of the hindbrain. Cerebrael aqueduct passes through mid brain and mid brain at its dorsal side has four round lobes called corpora quadrigemina.

(iii) **Hindbrain** The hindbrain comprises pons, cerebellum and medulla (also called the medulla oblongata). Pons consists of fibre tracts that interconnect different regions of the brain. Cerebellum has very convoluted surface in order to provide the additional space for many neurons. The medulla contains centres, which control respiration cardiovascular reflexes and gastric secretions.

**Question 2** Compare the following

(a) Central neural system (CNS) and Peripheral neural system (PNS)

(b) Resting potential and action potential

**Sol.** Comparison between central neural system and peripheral neural system are as follows:

| S.N. | Central neural system | Peripheral neural system |
|---|---|---|
| 1. | It consists of brain and spinal cord | It consists of nerves that arise from brain and spinal cord. |
| 2. | Both brain and spinal cord receive information that controls all the activities of the body | The cranial nerves carry information from sense organs to the brain |
| 3. | A problem with the CNS effect the body as a whole | Damage to the PNS tends to produce localized effects. |

**Comparison between resting potential and action potential are as follows :**

| S.N. | Resting potential | Action potential |
|---|---|---|
| 1. | The electrical potential difference across the resting plasma membrane is called as the resting potential | The electrical potential difference across the plasma membrane at the site of stimulus is called the action potential |
| 2. | Neuron membrane is permeable to $K^+$ ions and impermeable to $Na^+$ | Neuron membrane becomes permeable to $Na^+$ ions. |
| 3. | No flow of impulse occurs during resting potential | Flow of impulse occurs during action potential |
| 4. | Resting axon membrane is in polarised state. | Action potential results in depolarisation |

**Question 3** Explain the following processes

(a) Polarisation of the membrane of a nerve fibre

(b) Depolarisation of the membrane of a nerve fibre

(c) Transmission of a nerve impulse across a chemical synapse

**Sol.**

(a) **Polarisation of the membrane of a nerve fibre** In resting state, the neuron membrane is polarized with outer surface being positively charged and inner surface being negatively charged. At resting state or polarised state the axonal membrane is comparitively more permeable to $K^+$ ions and nearly impermeable to $Na^+$ ions.

Axoplasm has high concentration of $K^+$ and negatively charged proteins and the fluid outside the axon has a low concentration of $K^+$ and high concentration of $Na^+$ and thus forms a concentration gradient which is maintained by active transport of ions by sodium-potassium pumps which transport of 3 $Na^+$ outwards for $2K^+$ into the neuron.

(b) **Depolarisation of the membrane of a nerve fibre** In a depolarised membrane, a stimulus causes the opening of voltage gated $Na^+$ channels resulting in a rapid inflow of $Na^+$ ions which wipes out the local electrical potential difference.

Thus, the polarity of axonal membrane is reversed, positive charge inside and negative charge outside the neuron (axon).

(c) **Transmission of a nerve impulse across a chemical synapse** A nerve impulse is transmitted from one neuron to another through junctions called synapses. A synapse is formed by the membranes of a pre-synaptic neuron and a post-synaptic neuron, which may or may not be separated by a gap called synaptic cleft. At a chemical synapse, the membranes of the pre- and post-synaptic neurons are separated by a fluid-filled space called synaptic cleft.

Chemicals called neurotransmitters are involved in the transmission of impulses at these synapses. The axon terminals contain vesicles filled with these neurotransmitters.

When an impulse (action potential) arrives at the axon terminal, it stimulates the movement of the synaptic vesicles towards the membrane where they fuse with the plasma membrane and release their neurotransmitters in the synaptic cleft.

The released neurotransmitters bind to their specific receptors, present on the post-synaptic membrane. This binding opens ion channels allowing the entry of ions which can generate a new potential in the post-synaptic neuron. The new potential developed may be either excitatory or inhibitory.

**Question 4.** Draw labelled diagrams of the following

(a) Neuron (b) Brain

**Sol.** (a) **Diagram of Neuron**

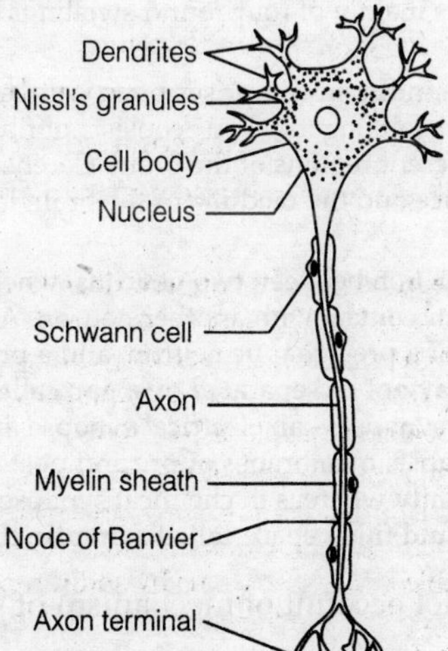


Structure of neuron

(b) **Diagram of Brain** Refer to Sol. 1 (a) of this chapter (Exercises).

**Question 5.** Write short notes on the following

(a) Neural coordination (b) Forebrain (c) Midbrain
(d) Hindbrain (e) Synapse

**Sol.**

(a) **Neural Coordination** The organised network of point-to-point connection for quick coordination provided by neural system is called neural coordination. The mechanism of neural coordination involves transmission of nerve impulse, across a synapse and the physiology of reflex action.

(b) **Forebrain** The various parts of forebrain are cerebrum, thalamus and hypothalamus cerebrum form the major part of human brain. It consists of two cerebral hemispheres connected by a tract of nerve fibres called corpus callosum. The layer of cells which covers the cerebral hemisphere is called cerebral cortex which contains motor areas and sensory areas and large regions that are neither sensory nor motor in function. These regions are responsible for complex functions like intersensory associations, memory and communication.

The cerebrum wraps around a structure called thalamus, which is a major coordinating centre for sensory and motor signaling. The **hypothalamus** lies at the base of the thalamus. It controls body temperature, urge for eating and drinking

(c) **Midbrain** The midbrain is located between the thalamus/hypothalamus of the forebrain and pons of the hindbrain. A canal called the cerebral aqueduct passess through the midbrain. The dorsal portion of the midbrain consists mainly of four round swellings (lobes) called corpora quadrigemina.

(d) **Hindbrain** The hindbrain comprises pons, cerebellum and medulla (also called the medulla oblongata). Pons consists of fibre tracts that interconnect different regions of the brain. Cerebellum has very convoluted surface and the medulla of the brain is connected to the spinal cord.

(e) **Synapse** It is junction between two neurons, where one neuron expands and comes in near contact with another neuron. A synapse is formed by the membranes of a pre-synaptic neuron, and a post-synaptic neuron, which may or may not be separated by a gap called synaptic cleft. There are two types of synapses– an electrical synapse and a chemical synapse. At electrical synapse, membranes of pre and post-synaptic neurons are in very close proximity whereas in chemical synapse, the membranes are separated by a fluid filled space called **synaptic cleft**.

**Question 6** Give a brief account of mechanism of synaptic transmission.

**Sol.** Synaptic transmission is the process by which a nerve impulse is transmitted from one neuron to another across a synapse. This involves the following steps :

1. Action potential arrival : When an action potential reaches the axon terminal of the pre-synaptic neuron, it triggers the next steps in the transmission process.
2. Neurotransmitter release : The action potential causes synaptic vesicles containing neurotransmitters to move towards and fuse with the pre-synaptic membrane, releasing neurotransmitters into the synaptic cleft.
3. Binding to receptors : The released neurotransmitters bind to specific receptors on the post-synaptic membrane of the receiving neuron.
4. Ion channel opening : This binding opens ion channels in the post-synaptic membrane, leading to either an excitatory or inhibitory potential depending on the type of neurotransmitter.

**Question 7** Explain the role of $Na^+$ in the generation of action potential.

**Sol.** When a stimulus is applied to a nerve, the membrane of the nerve becomes freely permeable to $Na^+$. This leads to a rapid influx of $Na^+$ followed by the reversal of the polarity at that site, *i.e.*, the outer surface of the membrane becomes negatively charged and the inner side becomes positively charged. The electrical potential difference across the plasma membrane is called the action potential, which is in fact termed as a nerve impulse. Thus, this shows that $Na^+$ ions play an important role in the conduction of nerve impulse.

**Question 8** Differentiate between

(a) Myelinated and non-myelinated axons
(b) Dendrites and axons
(c) Thalamus and hypothalamus
(d) Cerebrum and cerebellum

**Sol.**

(a) **Differences between myelinated and non-myelinated axons** are as follows :

| S.N. | Myelinated Axon | Non-myelinated Axon |
|---|---|---|
| 1. | The myelinated nerve fibres are enveloped with Schwann cells, which form a myelin sheath around the axon. | Unmyelinated nerve fibre is enclosed by a Schwann cell that does not form a myelin sheath around the axon. |
| 2. | Myelinated nerve fibres are found in spinal and cranial nerves. | There are commonly found in autonomous and the somatic nervous systems. |

(b) **Differences between dendrites and axons** are as follows :

| S.N. | Dendrite | Axon |
|---|---|---|
| 1. | Short fibres which branch repeatedly and project out of the cell body also contain Nissl's granules are called dendrite | The axon is a long branched fibre and each branch terminates, as a bulb-like structure called synaptic knob which possess synaptic vesicles containing chemicals called neurotransmitters. |
| 2. | These fibres transmit impulses towards the cell body. | The axons transmit nerve impulses away from the cell body to a synapse. |

(c) **Differences between thalamus and hypothalamus are as follows :**

| S.N. | Thalamus | Hypothalamus |
|---|---|---|
| 1. | The cerebrum wraps around a structure called thalamus. | It lies at the base of the thalamus. |
| 2. | All types of sensory input passes synapses in the thalamus. | It contains neurosecretory cells that secrete hypothalamus hormones. |
| 3. | It is the co-ordinating centre for sensory and motor signaling. | It regulates, sexual behaviour expresion of emotional reactions and motivation. |

(d) **Differences between cerebrum and cerebellum are as follows :**

| S.N. | Cerebrum | Cerebellum |
|---|---|---|
| 1. | It is the most developed part in brain. It is a part of fore brain. | It is the second developed part of brain also called as little cerebrum. It is the part of hind brain. |
| 2. | A deep cleft divides cerebrum into two cerebral hemispheres. | It has very convoluted surface in order to provide the additional space for many neurons. |
| 3. | Its functions are intelligence, learning, memory, speech, etc. | It contains centres for coordination and balance of body. |

**Question 9** Sol. the following

(a) Which part of the human brain is the most developed?

(b) Which part of our central neural system acts as a master clock?

**Sol.** (a) Cerebrum (b) Brain

**Question 10** Distinguish between

(a) afferent neurons and efferent neurons

(b) impulse conduction in a myelinated nerve fibre and unmyelinated nerve fibre

(c) Cranial nerve and spinal nerve

**Sol.**

(a) **Differences between afferent and efferent neurons is as follows :**

| S.N. | Afferent Neurons | Efferent Neurons |
|---|---|---|
| 1. | The afferent nerve fibres transmit impulses from tissues/organs to the CNS. | The efferent fibres transmit regulatory impulses from the CNS to the concerned peripheral tissues/organs. |

(b) **Differences between the impulse conduction in a myelinated and unmyelinated nerve fibre** are as follows :

| S.N. | Impulse conduction in a myelinated nerve fibre | Impulse conduction in a unmyelinated nerve fibre |
|---|---|---|
| 1. | In a myelinated nerve fibre, the action potential is conducted from one node to another. | In an unmyelinated nerve fibre, the action potential is not conducted from node to node. It is carried along the whole length of the nerve fibre. |
| 2. | The conduction of impulses is faster. | The conduction of impulses is slower. |

(c) **Differences between Cranial and Spinal Nerves**

| S.N. | Cranial Nerve | Spinal Nerve |
|---|---|---|
| 1. | The cranial nerves originate in the brain and terminate mostly in sense organs, head and upper body. | The spinal nerves originate in the spinal cord and extend to parts of the body below the head. |
| 2. | There are 12 pairs of cranial nerves. | There are 31 pair of spinal nerves. |
| 3. | Most of the cranial nerves contain axon and both sensory and motor neurons. | All of the spinal nerves contain axons of both sensory and motor neurons. |

# DIKSHA APP Questions

## ☐ Multiple Choice Questions

**Q.1** Chemicals which are released at the synaptic junction are called

(a) hormones (b) neurotransmitters
(c) cerebrospinal fluid (d) lymph

**Sol.** (b) Neurotransmitters are chemicals which are released at the synaptic junction from the neuron in response to stimulus. These chemicals travel across the synapse, *e.g.*, dopamine, acetylcholine, nor-epinephrine-etc.

**Q.2** Which is not the property of autonomic nervous system?

(a) Increase the rate of heart beat.
(b) Decrease the speed of conduction of action potential.
(c) Increase the strength of ventricular contraction.
(d) Increase the cardiac output.

**Sol.** (b) ANS increases the speed of conduction of action potential.

## ☐ Very Short Answer Type

**Q.1** Compete the statement by choosing appropriate match among the following :

| | | | |
|---|---|---|---|
| a. | Resting potential | i. | chemicals involved in the transmission of impulses at synapses. |
| b. | Nerve impulse | ii. | the gap between the presynaptic and postsynaptic neurons |
| c. | Synaptic cleft | iii. | the electrical potential difference across the resting neural membrane |
| d. | Neurotransmitters | iv. | an electrical wave-like the response of a neuron to a stimulation. |

**Sol.** The correct match is as follows

a-iii b-iv
c-ii d-i

# Chemical Coordination and Integration

CHAPTER 19

## Important Points

01 Chemical coordination and integration in our body depends on two system.

(i) **Nervous** coordination (ii) **Chemical** coordination

Nervous system is very fast but short lived. Nerve fibres do not innervate all cells of the body and cellular functions need to be continuously regulated, which is carried out by hormones.

02 **Hormones** are released by endocrine glands and these gland lack ducts , hence known as ductless gland.

03 **Hypothalamus**, a part of the forebrain, produces releasing (GnRH) and inhibiting (somatostatin) hormones that regulate the secretions of pituitary hormones. These hormones reach the pituitary gland via a portal circulatory system, while the posterior pituitary is directly controlled by neural signals from the hypothalamus.

04 **Pituitary Gland** It is located in the sella turcica and is divided into an adenohypophysis (anterior) and neurohypophysis (posterior).

Adenohypophysis (anterior pituitary) : The anterior pituitary can further be divided into pars distalis and pars intermedia.

- **Pars Distalis** Secretes key hormones like GH (growth hormone), which regulates growth; PRL (prolactin) for milk production; TSH (Thyroid Stimulating Hormone) for thyroid hormone production; ACTH (Adrenocorticotrophic Hormone) for cortisol production; and LH and FSH (gonadotropins) that regulate reproduction.

- **Pars intermedia** Secretes MSH (Melanocyte Stimulating Hormone), which controls skin pigmentation.

Neurohypophysis (Posterior Pituitary) : Stores and releases hormones produced by the hypothalamus *i.e.*, oxytocin, which stimulates uterine contractions and milk ejection, and Vasopressin (ADH), which regulates water balance. Its deficiency causes diabetes insipidus, leading to excessive water loss.

**05** Pineal gland is located on the dorsal side of forebrain. It secretes melatonin. It plays a very important role in the regulation of a 24 hour rhythm or circardian rhythm of our body.

**06** Thyroid gland, located on either side of the trachea, produces the hormones thyroxine ($T_4$) and triiodothyronine ($T_3$).

(i) The thyroid homones maintain basal metabolic rate, control metabolism of macromolecules and support the process of RBC formation.

(ii) The thyroid also secretes thyrocalcitonin (TCT), which helps regulate blood calcium levels.

(iii) Iodine deficiency can lead to hypothyroidism, causing goitre and developmental issues like cretinism, while excessive hormone production leads to hyperthyrodism as seen in conditions like Graves disease.

**07** Parathyroid gland is present as four small pouches. It is present on the back side of thyroid gland, two each embedded in the posterior surface of each lobe of thyroid gland.
It increase blood calcium levels by stimulating bone resorption, reabsorption of calcium in kidneys and enhancing calcium absorption from food, working alongside thyrocalcitonin (TCT) to maintain calcium balance.

**08** **Thymus gland** is a lobular structure present on ventral side of heart and aorta, located between lungs. This gland secretes the peptide hormones called thymosin and plays an important role in development of immune system.

**09** There are two **adrenal glands** situated on the anterial part of each kidney which is composed of two type of tissues, *i.e.*, adrenal medulla and adrenal cortex.
The adrenal glands, located above each kidney, consists of :

**Aderenal Medulla** Produces adrenaline and noradrenaline, the "fight or flight" hormones, which increase heart rate, alertness, blood glucose levels, and support stress responses.

**Adrenal Cortex** Produces cortisol, which regulates metabolism and reduces inflammation, aldosterone, which maintains water and electrolyte balance, and androgens, which influence hair growth during puberty.

The deficiency of Adrenal hormone causes Addison's disease, leading to weakness and fatigue.

**10** **Pancreas** is a composite gland, which acts as both exocrine and endocrine gland.

(i) The endocrine pancreas consists of Islets of Langerhans with $\alpha$-cells producing glucagon (a hyperglycemic hormone) and $\beta$-cells producing insulin (a hypoglycemic hormone).

(ii) Glucagon increases blood glucose by stimulating glycogen breakdown glycogenolysis and gluconeogensis while insulin lowers blood glucose by enhancing its uptake and storage.

(iii) Imbalances in these hormones can lead to diabetes mellitus, which is treated with insulin therapy.

**11** In male individuals a pair of **testis** is present in the scrotal sac. It is primary sex organ and also functions as endocrine gland also.

(i) It secrete androgens mainly testosterone which plays an important role in the process of spermatogenesis (*i.e.*, formation of spermatozoa.

(ii) It regulates the development, maturation and functions of male accessory sex organs and also stimulates development of secondary sex characteristics.

**12** **Ovary** is the primary female sex organ located in the abdomen and also produce two groups of steroid hormone, called oestrogen and progesterone.

(i) Estrogen stimulate the growth of female secondary sex organs, mammary gland development as well as regulate female sexual behaviors.

(ii) Progesterone supports pregnancy. It acts on the mammary gland and stimulates the formation of alveoli and milk secretion.

**13** (i) The atrial wall of heart secretes **atrial natriuretic factor (ANF),** which lowers blood pressure by dilating blood vessels.

(ii) The kidney produces **erythropoietin,** stimulating the production of red blood cells.

(iii) The gastrointestinal tract secretes hormones like **gastrin** (stimulates acid secretion), **secretin** (stimulates bicarbonate secretion), **CCK** (stimulates enzyme and bile secretion), and **GIP** (inhibits gastric function).

(iv) **Growth factors** secreted by non-endocrine tissues, promote tissue growth, repair, and regeneration.

**15** **Mechanism of hormone action** Hormones are transported through the blood stream and produce their effects on the target tissues.

(i) They exert their effects by binding to specific receptors on target tissues and forming a hormone-receptor complex.

(ii) The receptors can be membrane-bound (protein receptors on the cell surface) or intracellular (steroid receptors inside the cell).

(iii) Membrane-bound receptors activate second messengers like cyclic AMP to regulate cellular metabolism, while intracellular receptors mainly affect gene expression.

(iv) On the basis of chemical nature, hormones are divided into groups

(a) peptide, polypeptide, protein hormone (insulin, glucagon, etc).

(b) steroids (testosterone, cortisol, etc).

(c) iodothyronines (thyroid hormone).

(d) amino acid derivatives (*e.g.*, epinephrine).

# Exercises

**Question 1** Define the following

(a) Exocrine gland (b) Endocrine gland

(c) Hormone

**Sol.**

(a) **Exocrine Gland** It is a gland that pours its secretion on the surface or into a particular region by means of ducts for performing metabolic activity, *e.g.*, sebaceous glands, sweat glands, salivary glands, etc.

(b) **Endocrine Gland** It is a gland that pours its secretion into blood or lymph for reaching the target organ because the gland is not connected with the target organ by any duct. It is also known as ductless gland.

(c) **Hormone** Hormones are non-nutrient chemicals which act as intercellular messengers and are produced in trace amount.

**Question 2.** Diagrammatically indicate the location of the various endocrine glands in our body.

**Sol.**

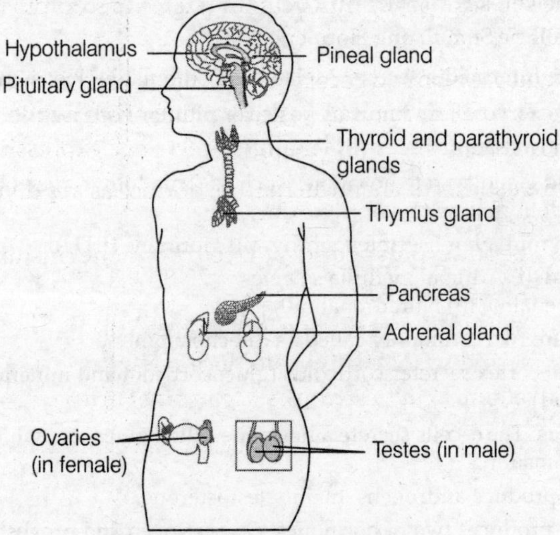


Endocrine glands in human body

**Question 3.** List the hormones secreted by the following

(a) Hypothalamus (b) Pituitary (c) Thyroid
(d) Parathyroid (e) Adrenal (f) Pancreas
(g) Testis (h) Ovary (i) Thymus
(j) Atrium (k) Kidney (l) GI Tract

**Sol.**

(a) Two types of hormones are secreted by **Hypothalamus**

(i) Releasing hormones such as GnRH (Gonadotropin releasing hormone)

(ii) Inhibiting hormones such as Somatostatin or Growth hormone inhibiting hormone

(b) (i) **Pars distalis part of pituitary (anterior pituitary) produces**

- Growth Hormone (GH)
- Prolactin (PRL)
- Thyroid Stimulating Hormone (TSH)
- Adrenocorticotrophic Hormone (ACTH)
- Luteinizing Hormone (LH)
- Follicle Stimulating Hormone (FSH)

(ii) **Pars intermedia** secrete Melanocyte Stimulating Hormone (MSH)

(iii) Pars nervosa also know as posterior pituitary release

(a) Oxytocin (b) Vasopressin

(c) **Thyroid** gland secrete hormones such as, Triiodothyronine ($T_3$) and tetraiodothyronine ($T_4$) or thyroxine.

(d) **Parathyroid** gland secrete Parathyroid Hormone (PTH).

(e) **Adrenal** (i) Adrenal medulla secretes
(a) Adrenaline (b) Noradrenaline

These are two commonly called as catecholamines.

(ii) Adrenal cortex secretes corticoids (glucocorticoid and mineralo corticoid).

(f) **Pancreas** The $\alpha$-cells secrete a hormone called glucagon, while the $\beta$-cells secrete insulin.

(g) **Testis** produce androgens, mainly testosterone.

(h) **Ovary** produces two of hormones, *i.e.*, oestrogen and progesterone.

(i) **Thymus** gland secrete Thymosins.

(j) **Atrium** secretes Atrial Natriuretic Factor (ANF).

(k) **Kidney** produces Erythropoietin

(l) **GI Tract** secretes Gastrin, secretin, cholecystokinin (CCK) and gastric inhibitory peptide (GIP).

**Question 4.** Fill in the blanks

| **Hormones** | **Target gland** |
|---|---|
| (a) Hypothalamic hormones | ........................... |
| (b) Thyrotrophin (TSH) | ........................... |
| (c) Corticotrophin (ACTH) | ........................... |
| (d) Gonadotrophins (LH, FSH) | ........................... |
| (e) Melanotrophin (MSH) | ........................... |

**Sol.**

| **Hormones** | | **Target gland** |
|---|---|---|
| (a) Hypothalamic hormones | – | Pituitary gland |
| (b) Thyrotrophin (TSH) | – | Thyroid gland |
| (c) Corticotrophin (ACTH) | – | Adrenal glands |
| (d) Gonadotrophins (LH, FSH) | – | Testis and ovary |
| (e) Melanotrophin (MSH) | – | melanocytes in the skin. |

**Question 5.** Write short notes on the functions of the following hormones

(a) Parathyroid hormone (PTH) (b) Thyroid hormones
(c) Thymosins (d) Androgens
(e) Estrogen (f) Insulin and Glucagon

**Sol.** Functions of the following hormones are as follows

(a) **Parathyroid Hormone** (PTH) The parathyroid glands secrete a peptide hormone called parathyroid hormone (PTH). PTH acts on bones and stimulates the process of bone resorption (dissolution/ demineralisation). PTH also stimulates reabsorption of $Ca^{2+}$ by the renal tubules and increases $Ca^{2+}$ absorption from the digested food. It plays a significant role in calcium balance in the body.

(b) **Thyroid Hormones** Thyroid hormones play an important role in the regulation of the basal metabolic rate. These hormones also support the process of red blood cell formation. Thyroid hormones control the metabolism of carbohydrates, proteins and fats. The maintenance of water and electrolyte balance is also influenced by thyroid hormones. Thyroid gland also secretes a protein hormone called thyrocalcitonin (TCT), which regulates the blood calcium levels (lowers the $Ca^{++}$ level in blood).

(c) **Thymosins** The thymus gland secretes the peptide hormones called thymosins. Thymosins play a major role in the differentiation of T-lymphocytes, which provide cell-mediated immunity. In addition, thymosins also promote production of antibodies to provide humoral immunity.

(d) **Androgens** Androgens regulate the development, maturation and functions of the male accessory sex organs like epididymis, vas deferens, seminal vesicles, prostate gland, urethra, etc. These hormones stimulate muscular growth, growth of facial and axillary hair, aggressiveness, low pitch of voice, etc. Androgens play a major stimulatory role in the process of spermatogenesis (formation of spermatozoa), influence the male sexual behaviour (libido).

(e) **Estrogens** Oestrogens produce wide ranging actions such as stimulation of growth and activities of female secondary sex organs, development of growing ovarian follicles, appearance of female secondary sex characters (*e.g.*, high pitch of voice, etc.), mammary gland development, Estrogens also regulate female sexual behaviour.

(f) **Insulin and Glucagon** Glucagon acts mainly on the liver cells (hepatocytes) and stimulates glycogenolysis resulting in an increased blood sugar (hyperglycemia). In addition, this hormone stimulates the process of gluconeogenesis, which also contributes to hyperglycemia. Glucagon reduces the cellular glucose uptake and utilisation.

Insulin is a peptide hormone, which plays a major role in the regulation of glucose homeostasis. Insulin acts mainly on hepatocytes and adipocytes and enhances cellular glucose uptake and utilisation. Insulin also stimulates conversion of glucose to glycogen (glycogenesis) in the target cells. The glucose homeostasis in blood is thus maintained jointly by these two hormones – insulin and glucagons.

**Question 6** Give example(s) of

(a) Hyperglycemic hormone and hypoglycemic hormone
(b) Hypercalcemic hormone
(c) Gonadotrophic hormones
(d) Progestational hormone
(e) Blood pressure lowering hormone
(f) Androgens and Estrogens

**Sol.**

(a) Glucagon and insulin respectively
(b) Parathyroid hormone (PTH)
(c) Follicle stimulating hormone and luteinising hormones
(d) Progesterone
(e) Atrial Natriuretic Factor (ANF)
(f) Androgens are mainly testosterone and estrogens include estradiol

**Question 7.** Which hormonal deficiency is responsible for the following

(a) Diabetes mellitus (b) Goitre (c) Cretinism

**Sol.** (a) Diabetes mellitus is due to deficiency of insulin.

(b) Goitre is due to deficiency of thyroxine ($T_4$) and triiodothyronine ($T_3$).

(c) Cretinism is due to deficiency of thyroid hormone.

**Question 8** Briefly mention the mechanism of action of FSH.

**Sol.** Action of FSH (Follicle Stimulating Hormone) produces its effect by binding to its specific receptors present in the ovarian cell membrane. Binding of FSH hormone to its receptor leads to the formation of hormone receptor complex. The ovarian follicle rupture and releases a mature ovum in the Fallopian tube for fertilisation.

**Question 9** Match the following columns.

| Column I | Column II |
|---|---|
| A. $T_4$ | 1. Hypothalamus |
| B. PTH | 2. Thyroid |
| C. GnRH | 3. Pituitary |
| D. LH | 4. Parathyroid |

**Sol.**

| Column I | Column II |
|---|---|
| A. $T_4$ | 2. Thyroid |
| B. PTH | 4. Parathyroid |
| C. GnRH | 1. Hypothalamus |
| D. LH | 3. Pituitary |

## DIKSHA APP Questions

### ☐ Multiple Choice Questions

**Q.1** Which of the following hormones is not secreted by the anterior pituitary?

(a) Growth hormone
(b) Follicle stimulating hormone
(c) Oxytocin
(d) Adrenocorticotrophic hormone

**Sol.** (c) Oxytocin is secreted by posterior lobe of pituitary gland. Anterior lobe of pituitary gland secreted hormones namely-Adrenocorticotropic. Hormone (ACTH), Follicle Stimulating Hormone (FSH), Growth Hormone (GH), Luteinising Hormone (LH), Prolactin (PRL) and Thyroid Stimulating Hormone (TSH).

**Q.2** Mary is about to face an interview. But during the first five minutes before the interview, she experiences sweating, increased rate of heart, respiration, etc. Which of the following hormones are responsible for her restlessness?

(a) Estrogen and progesterone
(b) Oxytocin and vasopressin
(c) Adrenaline and noradrenaline
(d) Insulin and glucagon

**Sol.** (c) Adrenaline (epinephirne), and noradrenaline (norepinephrine) hormones are responsible for sweating, increased heart beat rate, respiration, etc. Adrenal medulla secretes these hormone and receives neural secreted form axons. Estrogen and progesterone are female hormones secreted by ovaries. Oxytocin and vasopressin are secreted by posterior lobe of pituitary gland.

## ☐ Very Short Answer Type

**Q.1** What is the function of Leydig's cells?

**Sol.** Leydig cells or interstitial cells of the testes secretes testosterone hormone. It stimulates the development of external male sex characters such as beards, moustaches and low pitch voice is man and stimulates the formation of sperms in testis.

**Q.2** Which of the two adrenocortical layers, zona glomerulosa and zona reticularis lies outside enveloping the other?

**Sol.** Zone glomerulosa is the outermost layer which envelops the other layers. The middle layer is zona fasciculate and innermost layer is zona recticularis

## ☐ Short Answer Type

**Q.1** Name the gland that functions as a bilogical clock in our body where it is located? Name its one secretion.

**Sol.** Pineal gland functions as biological clock in our body.
Location-It is located on the dorsal side of the forebrain.
Secretion-It secretes melatonin.

**Q.2** On an educational trip to Uttaranchal, Ketki and her friends observe that many local people were having swollen necks. Please help Ketki and her friends to find out the solutions to the following questions.

(a) Which probable disease are these people suffering from?

(b) How is caused ?

(c) What effect does this condition have on pregnancy?

**Sol.** (a) These people are suffering from Goitre. This is due to the overstimulation of thyroid gland which causes an enlargement in the gland.

(b) It is caused due to the defiency of iodine in the diet that results in the enlargement of the thyroid gland.

(c) In pregnant ladies it may lead to defective develpment and maturation of the growing baby leads to stunted growth (cretinism), mental retardation etc.

## □ Long Answer Type

**Q.1** Explain the mechanism of Hormone action

**Sol.** Upon the target cells, two main kinds of hormone action have been observed

(i) Action at membrane level

(ii) Induction of protein synthesis at gene leel.

1. Hormone acts as first messenger : It is attached to some integral protein at specific receptor site on the surface of cell membrance (of target cell). It stimulates Adenylyl cyclase (enzyme). It catalyzes conversion of ATP to cyclic AMP which acts as second messengers. It affects cell metabolism.

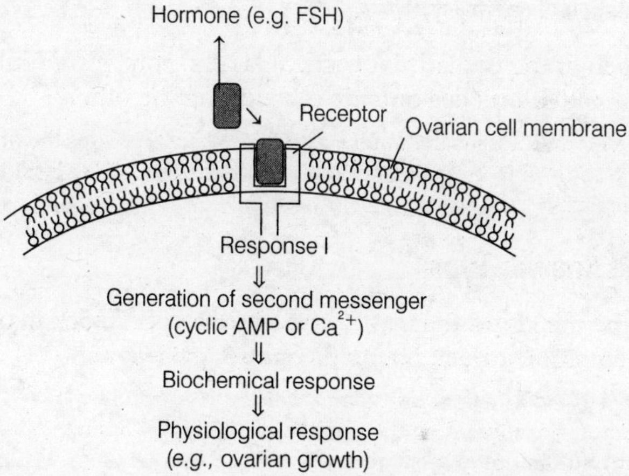


2. Gene activation : The steroid hormone enters into the cytoplasm through cell membrane and binds to protein receptors of the target cells. This hormone receptors complex stimulate the gene to synthesize a particular enzyme.